3ESSAYS

ON IMAGEREALITY

First Montag Press E-Book and Paperback Original Edition February 2018

Montag Press
ISBN: 978-1-940233-47-5
Cover design © 2018 Rick Febré
Author photo © 2018 Joyce Sampson

Montag Press Team:
Project Editor – Charlie Franco
Managing Director – Charlie Franco

A Montag Press Book
www.montagpress.com
Montag Press
1066 47th Ave. Unit #9
Oakland CA 94601 USA

Montag Press, the burning book with the hatchet cover, the skewed word mark and the portrayal of the long-suffering fireman mascot are trademarks of Montag Press.

Printed & Digitally Originated in the United States of America
10 9 8 7 6 5 4 3 2 1

This book is a work of fiction. Names, characters, places, and incidents are either products of the author's vivid and sometimes disturbing imagination or are used fictiously without any regards with possible parallel realities. Any resemblance to actual persons, living or dead, events, or locales is entirely coincidental.

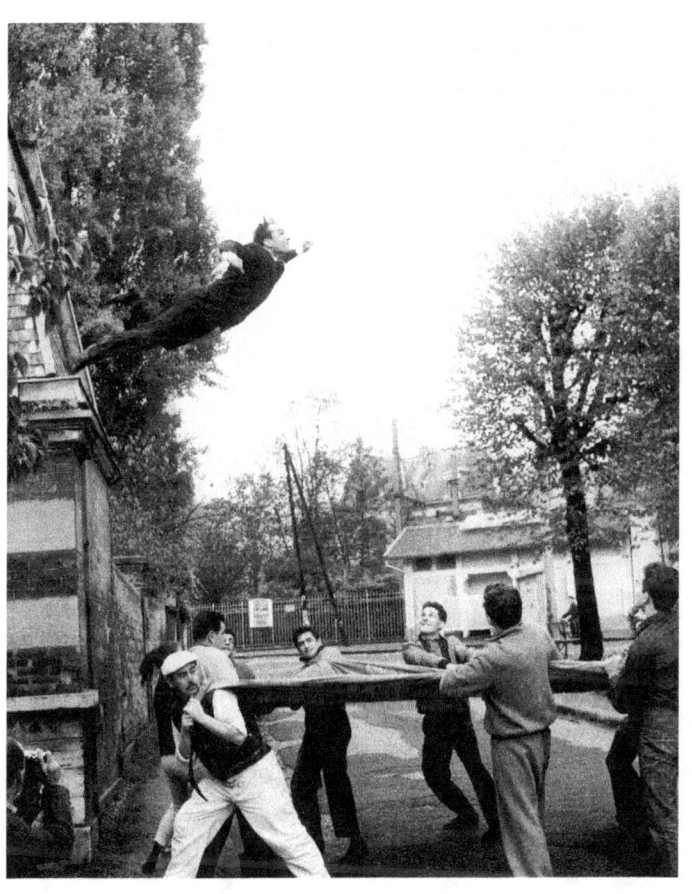

3ESSAYS

ON IMAGEREALITY

by

SCOTT NAVICKY

TABLE OF CONTENTS

Essay I
f/01

An Introduction to Photosloganeering

Alternative Title:
C'mon, Paul Auster, that's your fucking author photo?
I mean, *seriously?*

Essay II
f/54

Roland Barthes ♥ Annie Leibovitz? Y or N (Circle One)

Alternative Title:
"Honey, I put the B on eautiful, don't switch it to itch,"
said the drag queen.

Essay III
f/100

ClockHead

Alternative Title:
Reflections on watching thirty-two hours of
Christian Marclay's The Clock.

LIST OF ILLUSTRATIONS

For I have sworn thee fair, and thought thee bright,
Who art as black as hell, as dark as night.

- Shakespeare Sonnet 14

Nietzsche uses very precise new terms for
very precise new concepts.

- Gilles Deleuze *Nietzsche & Philosophy*

To the *endlessnessnessness* of my own desire:
my rugbyloving wife Sarah, my littlelion Daniel,
and my littleworld Juliet.

Essay 1

An Introduction to Photosloganeering

Alternative Title:
C'mon, Paul Auster, that's your fucking
author photo? I mean, *seriously?*

While Susan Meiselas, president of the Magnum Foundation, was seated in her office on West 27th Street finalizing details for the "Photography, Expanded" symposium and Geoffrey Batchen was sitting in his office at Victoria University in Wellington, New Zealand researching the implications of photography's reproducibility and Geoff Dyer was watching Andrei Tarkovsky's *Stalker* for the one-hundred and fifty-first time on an old TV/VCR at his home in Cheltenham, England, failed photography theorist Carlos Spencer-Bayard was sitting in *Rafael's Silver Cloud Lounge* thinking about (.) (.) But the man known to his friends and family simply as "Ghost" was not ogling or fantasizing; he was philosophizing, or so he told himself. Haunted by photography and fueled by failure, Ghost was beginning to grow weary of his

Facebook account and its ever-present (.) (.) Every morning, he discovered a fresh batch of buxom photographs waiting for him; the timing and regularity of these deliveries – not to mention the doughiness of some of the photographs themselves – reminded him of bakeries baking loaves of fresh bread and delivering them all over town at the crack of dawn. *I'm so goddamn horny, the crack of dawn better be careful around me.* And it wasn't just his female friends. Somehow, during the past five years, Ghost had befriend-ed an exorbitant number of "chest puppies," as a man who takes pictures of his naked torso in a bathroom mirror are known in local gay vernacular.

Were the Facebook accounts of other photography theorists so saturated with (.) (.)? Did Abigail Solomon-Godeau have to suffer through photo-after-photo of swimsuit-clad vacationers (a genre Ghost dubbed "bosoms on the beach"), party animals ("bosoms boozing"), or couples enjoying an evening on the town ("classy cleavage")? Did Rosalind Krauss' Facebook friends in-undate her account with mirrored selfies taken after outrageous acts of exercise ("Muscular Christianititties")? Did Victor Burgin even have a Facebook account?

From the sky we look so organized and brave. This Jason Is-bell line, slightly altered, always reminded Ghost of Facebook: *from the sky we look so organized and fun.* Good-bye, Thoreau's quiet desperation. Good-bye, Hobbes' nasty, brutish shortness. Good-bye, Wilde's sad world of melancholy puppets... Hello, SUGA-LUMPS!

But Ghost was suspect. He knew these people. He knew who they were and how they lived. And he knew that although their lives were no longer quiet, the majority of his Facebook friends were living lives of chesty desperation.

Carlos Spencer-Bayard took a sip of his Jameson on the rocks and smiled. *Lives of chesty desperation*: that was a good phrase, he thought extracting a pen from his pocket and reaching for a nearby bar napkin.

To Ghost, Facebook was both a burlesque and a burka; while seductively exhibiting ample acreage of flesh, it concealed every inch of a person's personality; in other words, you could know intimate details about what a person *looked* like, but nothing else. On Facebook, people were both naked and veiled.

Both a burlesque and a burka: good phrasing.

Both naked and veiled: that too.

As a devout Nietzschean, Ghost knew the importance of good phrasing. A man could eke out an existence from good phrasing, a meager academic stipend, cold mountain walks, and an occasional skinnydip. "Do with profound problems as with a cold bath," Herr Professor advised in *The Gay Science*: "quickly in, quickly out."

From his years of skinnydipping into the topic of photography, Ghost knew that while traditional art lives in whitewalled institutions (museums, universities, art galleries), photography lives in the world. Images are everywhere, of everything and wherever images go, imagetheory must follow. Thus an imagethinker is a scholar of the cultural kitchen sink: nothing is verboten. Song lyrics, silly quotes, cumbersomeportmanteaus, run*onandonandon* sentences, snippets of poetry (both bad and good), fictional narrators, bar napkins scrawlings: everything is permissible under Imagereality's secular perspectival sun. In fact, perspectivism was the key to unlocking photography's labyrinth. Ghost had initially learned about perspectivism from reading Nietzsche; from reading Harold Bloom, he had learned about Shakespearean perspectivism and how it differed from Nietzschean perspectivism; and from reading Bloom's arch-nemesis, Michel Foucault, he had learned how perspectivism often tumbled into the turmoil of unreason and silence: this tumbling explains why photographs are so often surrounded by silence.

> *Silence is something to be shared*
> *When you learn what it's worth...*

[What song was *THAT* from? It wasn't Jason Isbell...]

So why could Ghost not share photography's silence? Why did he insist on continuing to skinnydip into the topic of Imagereality, when doing so resulted in nothing but haunting failure and humiliation?

Contemplating these questions, Ghost took another sip of Jameson, allowing a single ice cube to tumble into his mouth.

[*Crunch*]

This was a twice-told tale. Nietzsche and photography, photography and unreason: like ice from an empty glass, Ghost had crushed these topics between his teeth before; in fact, he had delved so deeply into Imagereality's relationship to madness that he had been touched by the very blueflame he sought to analyze.

It had begun with a tiny crack in his consciousness; the more he thought, the more this crack grew, spidercrawling its way across his mind like a fissure across a windshield. Before long, he found himself standing outside the world; he could observe the pleasing domestic tableaus that surrounded him, couples conversing coyly about their shared future, children playing atop fields of grassy pleasure, elderly couples reading in recliners or watching television. From where he stood, everything looked so warm, so inviting; but he could only see the warmth, he couldn't feel it. He was a man apart. It was as if he was separated from the world by a pane of glass.

Another slippery cube of ice slid past his lips and was ground into coldgravel by his teeth.

[*CrunchCrunch*]

Photography: he could care less, he told himself. He could; but instead, he cared so much, so phenomenally. Why?

Mad or not, Ghost believed that he understood something about photography that successful photograph theorists could never understand. And that something was this: since it begins with the unattainable desire to capture reality, every photograph is a little failure. Thus the study of photography is the study of failure. To truly understand the medium, an imagethinker must be intimate with failure.

Consider Roland Barthes' *Camera Lucida: Reflections on Photography*. This beloved book, the cornerstone for so much of photography theory, is an undeniable failure. Upon publication, it was denounced in *Artweek* as a "sketchy outline of an incomplete thought." In *Art Journal*, it was accused of being "positively harmful to a proper, and more profound, understanding of the medium." Barthes had conceived of the book as a palinode, a poem in which the poet retracts something said in a previous poem; in this regard, the book was a phenomenal success. *Camera Lucida* was a sensual earthquake, whose aftershocks demolished the author's earlier Semiotic-driven theories on photography. As a replacement to these theories, Barthes sought to capture "something like an essence of the Photograph." It was here that the book became a failure, and this failure, Ghost believed, was what inevitably led to the death of the author.

A month after *Camera Lucida* was published, Roland Barthes was walking home from a ritzy luncheon given by the future President of France, François Mitterrand. As he stepped from the curb to cross Rue des Écoles, he was knocked down by a passing laundry van. Unconscious and bleeding from the nose, he was taken to the Salpêtrière hospital, where he died almost exactly one month later. Ay, but here's the rub: Barthes' doctors swore that there was nothing physically wrong with him; having sustained no serious injuries from the accident, he simply died from anguished languishing.

Staring into the softblackness that nightly engulfed his bedroom, Ghost often thought about Roland Barthes lying in his hospital bed at Salpêtrière. He thought about the anguish, the languishing; he thought about how, for months prior to his accident, Barthes had been fond of repeating Michelet's phrase: "Aging, this slow suicide"; he thought about the looks on the faces of the befuddled nurses as they fluttered and fretted around Barthes' bedside; and he thought about the decisive moment when the famous Frenchman finally decided, *"C'est tout."* A doomeager imagethinker, who had failed in his quest to capture the essence of photography? During the blackest hour of the darknight, Ghost often thought of himself and Roland Barthes as bosom buddies.

[*CrunchCrunchCrunch*]

His glass was almost empty.

No matter how much of failure's "slow suicide" he had to personally endure, Ghost could not stop believing that the act of analyzing a photograph articulates something essential about who we are. In this regard, it mirrors the act of interpreting Shakespeare. According to Harold Bloom, Shakespeare's perspectivism reached its apotheosis in *Antony and Cleopatra*. If you want to see Cleopatra as a horny, hooknosed Egyptian Hillary, you can do that; or if you want to see her as a crass vamp whose antics would shame Priscilla, Queen of the Desert, you can do that too; or if you want to see her as a regal ruler, whose passion was so pure that it captivated an entire continent, you can do that too; whichever perspective you choose says nothing about Cleopatra herself, but speaks volumes about who you are.

The same kind of perspecitivism is apparent within photography. To prove this, Ghost allowed a single image to leap into his consciousness: Yves Klein's *Leap Into the Void*. This selection did not surprise him, as he had been carrying Klein's enigmatic image around in his head for over twenty years. You could dis-

miss *Leap Into the Void* as a manipulative hoax, or you could see it
as pure, meaningless pluck, or you could celebrate it as not only a
great work of art, but the perfect illustration of how to approach
the topic of photography: rushing towards failure and plunging
potentially into madness with rapt confidence and pitch-perfect
aplomb, not falling or stumbling, but *leaping*. With such a leap,
Carlos Spencer-Bayard hoped to show himself, and the world,
who he really was.

    [*CrunchCrunchCrunchCrunch*]

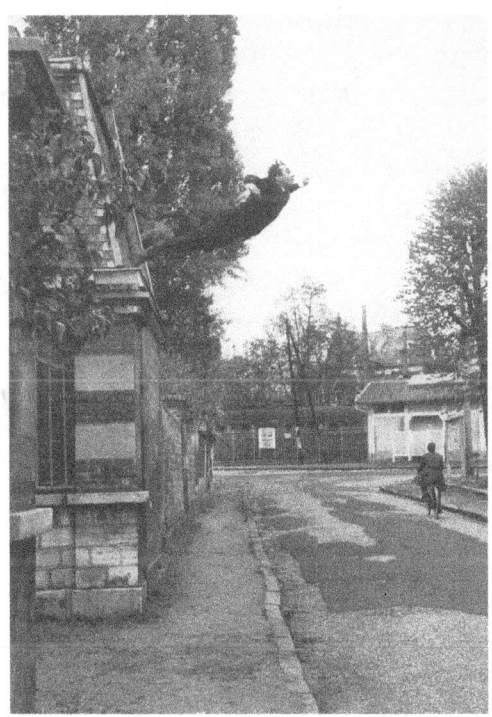

2

ALFRED FUCKING STIEGLITZ!

He had done it again! He had used the verb *analyze* in relationship to Imagereality. No one *analyzes* Imagereality: people *wrestle* with Imagereality. Images are slippery and nearly impossible to subdue, thus imagetheory is less akin to scholarship than sport. A visual equivalent for this phenomenon is Lewis Hine's *A "Wrestling-Club" in a Social Settlement in One of Our Large Cities*. Gazing upon the image, it would be easy to assume that the boy standing fourth from the left, leaning forward with his fists clenched atop his thighs, would be the strongest wrestler of the group, as he exhibits the most impressive physique, but Ghost knew that wrestling was not about physique, it was about technique. The same could be said for imagetheory. Approach the topic with too much erudition and an imagethinker risked sounding like Walter Benjamin philosophizing over Mickey Mouse; approach it with too much casual flippery and risk banishment to the blogosphere, which is a cold, sober solar system of skim reading. Stylistically speaking, the perfect literary format for wrestling with Imagereality would be the aphorism, as images are *visual aphorisms*. But nobody reads aphorisms these days, Twitter notwithstanding.[1] To avoid the trap of working in a dead genre, Ghost had invented a new technique: photosloganeering, or as Ghost liked to think of it: *Satori* speak. Concise, insightful commentary. Snapshots. A burst of illumination in ample *italics* and **bold**.

----

1   Nietzsche would've killed on Twitter!

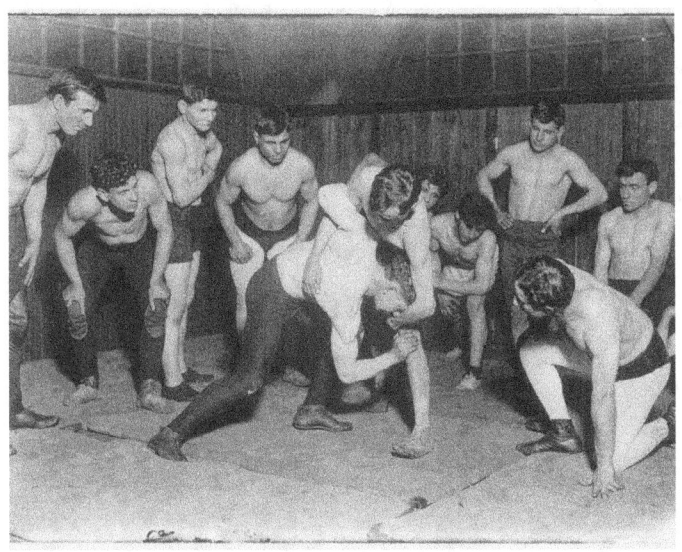

Of course, the peril of working in a dead genre is not the only dilemma every imagethinker faces, there is another, darker dilemma: the overtakelessness of *Camera Lucida*. In her strange-fascinating book *Nox*, Anne Carson defined overtakelessness as the sensation of some entity that "cannot be got round," and thus is destined to remain beyond understanding.

In his quest to learn the essence of Imagereality, whenever Ghost arrived somewhere, intellectually, he couldn't shake the sensation that Roland Barthes had already been there; no matter where he found himself, Ghost noticed the words *"Roland était ici"* scrawled in elegant script nearby. It felt like he was *chasing* the fleet-footed Frenchman; over time, Ghost realized that such a sensation is essential to understanding Imagereality. **Image-reality is an elusive pursuit.** Every photographer is a perpet-ual pursuer, a constant chaser. Visual truth, breathtaking beauty, fleeting flotsam, irrefutable evidence, the decisive moment, ruin porn, the ethereal within the everyday, the essential within the ever-evolving: a photographer's pursuit never ends, for the minute a photographer stops *chasing* is the moment he ceases to be a photographer. Thus the perfect emblem for a photographer is a man forever rushing to catch something. This realization reminded Ghost of Henri Cartier-Bresson's *Derriere la Gare Saint-Lazare*. Whenever Ghost saw this image, in his imagination, he erased Cartier-Bresson's figure, replacing him with Klein's image from *Leap into the Void*. This act of mental manipulation made the image much more enjoyable. Ghost snickered, thinking: *"Sacrebleu, that's one helluva flop de belly!"*

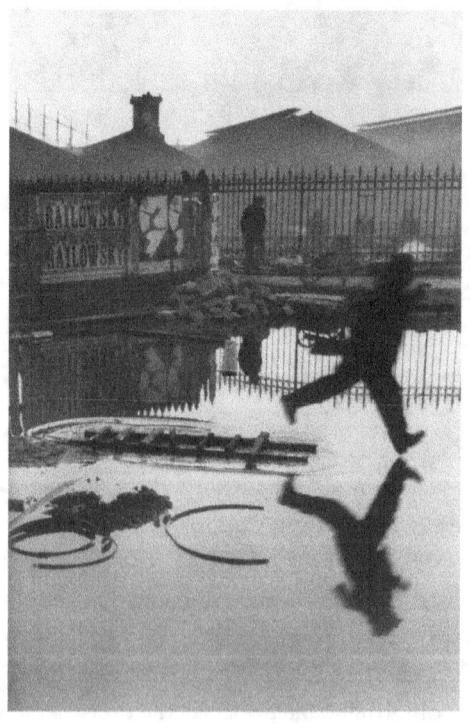

To be forever *chasing* means to never experience fulfillment. This explains why Imagereality is haunted by feelings of unfulfillment. Even as they multiply at an exorbitant rate, images do not fill the world: they empty it. Understanding Imagereality means understanding how to find fulfillment in unfulfillment. So what then is an imagethinker? Is he not a chaser of the chasing, a pursuer of the pursuing? Such ridiculousness reminded Ghost of the crying child who chases his inattentive, chickenchasing mother in Shakespeare's Sonnet 143:

> *So runn'st thou after that which flies from thee,*
> *Whilst I thy babe chase thee afar behind*

Should this spatchcocking[2] of the Sonnets and Imagereality be too surprising? Shakespearean scholars have been wrestling with the Sonnets for a millennium. Plus, the Bard is the quintessence of overtakelessness; he is always intellectually ahead of his readers. And perhaps most importantly, the Sonnets, like photography, are about *possession*, both real and imaginary; and as Shakespeare documented so painfully, with enough burningchurning twistingturning, the desire for possession becomes obsession. **Imagereality = obsession.**

3

Upon declining his PhD acceptance to both the University of Auckland and Victoria University in Wellington, Carlos Spencer-Bayard never intended to return to the topic of Imagereality. Imagereality was in the past; he was a novelist now, or so he told

---

2   Spatchcock: (v) the overlaying of two or more disparate entities within a work of literature. The word comes from *Ulysses*. Stephen Dedalus uses it in the library scene, musing, "Why is the underplot of *King Lear* in which Edmund figures lifted out of Sidney's *Arcadia* and spatchcocked on to a Celtic legend older than history?"

himself. Such foolishness embarrassed him now. How could he have been such a fool? How could he have forgotten one of Imagereality's core principles? **With Imagereality, the past *becomes* the present.**

Ghost's return to Imagereality was sparked by an unexpected act of liontaming. One afternoon, while attempting to blunt his son's desire to destroy his living room, Ghost had lifted the wildchild onto his lap and reached for the nearest book. Instead of picking up *Sheep in a Jeep* or *The Pout Pout Fish* or Richard Scarry's beloved *Cars and Trucks and Things That Go*, he grabbed the George Eastman House Collection's *A History of Photography from 1839 to the present*. The trick worked; the act of flipping through the book soothed the savage babybeast. The next afternoon, Ghost discovered his littlelion calmly standing at the base of the rocking chair pointing to the book, pleading: "Flo-dose." Once again, Ghost scooped up the book and the babyboy, positioned them both on his lap, and began flipping through the history of photography. Soon, this routine became one of his son's favorite afternoon activities.

Ghost quickly learned that he and his littlelion had wildly different tastes in photography. No matter how hard he tried, Ghost couldn't get his son interested in Buel's Gallery (Pittsfield, Massachusetts)'s *Top Hat*, which he thought would be a fantastic image to use on the cover of an imagetheory book; and no matter how hard he tried, Ghost couldn't share his son's excitement over Frederick W. Brehm's *Police Officers with Horses, Motorcycles, and Police Van*, which never failed to elicit joyful shouts of "POLICE GUYS!!" and "MO'STACHES!!" from his son.

But there was one photographer whose work both Ghost and his son enjoyed: Lewis Hine. Ghost admired Hine's work for its progressive social themes, while his littlelion loved the photographs because they were so baby-centric. Every time he saw an image of a poor, grubby child laborer toiling away in some dingy

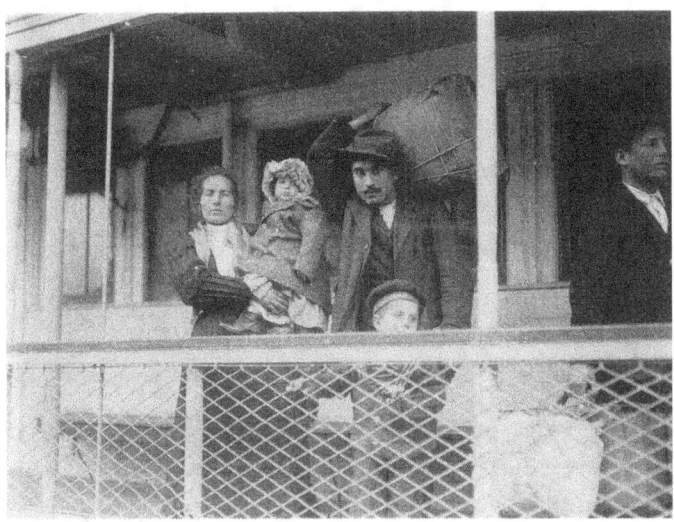

factory, he gleefully exclaimed: "Ba-*BEE*!" Because he knew his son enjoyed the images so much, Ghost often lingered over the five pages devoted to Hine's work; during this lingering, one of Hine's images began haunting Ghost: *Italian Family on Ferry Boat, Leaving Ellis Island.*

What Ghost found so haunting about this image was how much the young Italian family resembled his: the tranquil baby-girl-in-arms, the preciously dressed two-year-old babyboy, the sternweary mother, and the father who was carrying the weight of his family... *upon his back*. Every time he spied the image, Ghost felt like calling out: *Ahoy, comrade*! *I un-der-stand*!

And there was something else that haunted Ghost about the image, its date: 1905. Assuming that she lived a long life, the babygirl in the picture had witnessed amazing advancements in technology: from Ellis Island to email, from ferry boats to Facebook, from the Statue of Liberty to status updates, from tiny woolen coats to (.) (.) With each advancement came new levels of acceptance towards Imagereality, which rode atop technological progress like a boat upon the waveswaveswaves. Ghost saw all of this in Hine's image. Imagereality is Futurism *in reverse*; it allows the future to envision itself in the past.

4

— Hey Steinbeck, ready for another Jameson?

Glancing up from his scrawlsheet, Ghost recognized the face of his favorite bartender.

— Yeah. Thanks, Drew.

As a rabid rugbyhead, Carlos Spencer-Bayard carried an imaginary rugby pitch around in his head at all times; whenever he met someone new, he immediately placed them on this pitch. Because of his height, imposing bulk, and unruly beard, Drew reminded Ghost of Wellington loosie Brad Shields. And while discussing imaginary rugby likenesses, Ghost was happy to note that his own physique resembled three-time IRB Player of the Year, and notorious kiwi heartthrob, Dan Carter.

Over the course of his many trips to *Rafael's Silver Cloud Lounge*, Ghost and Drew had struck up a friendship over their shared interests in art, music, and Ghost's sister-in-law.

— I haven't seen A. Flynn Fox around much lately, Drew said as he slid a dram of Irish whiskey across the bar.

— Me neither, Ghost replied.

— I wonder what she's been up to, Drew mused, trying to sound casual.

— I think she's been going to *Brothers Drake* almost exclusively.

— Yeah, I know she likes that place.

— What are your thoughts on *Brothers Drake*? Ghost asked, taking a sip of Jameson.

Drew shook his head disapprovingly.

– Not my kind of place.

– Yeah, me neither, Ghost concurred. The place is weird. It's like a cult where they brainwash people into thinking douchebags are fun to talk to and mead is drinkable.

– Yeah, mead's not any good, Drew agreed.

– I'd rather drink warm PBR.

– Yeah, but instead you drink the PBR of Texas: Lone Star.

Ghost grimaced.

– Good point. When it comes to booze, I'm a renowned anythingarian.

– Well, if you happen to see Flynn, tell her I asked about her, okay?

– Yeah. Sure thing, Drew.

As Drew receded from view, returning to the bar's crowded, noisy center, Ghost was left alone once more with his Irish whiskey, scrawlsheet, and his imagethinking.

5

What was it about *Leap into the Void* that Carlos Spencer-Bayard found so enchanting? Initially, Ghost had been drawn to the formal aspects of Klein's flamboyant figure: the upturned chin, the spiky hair, the splayed arms, the tippytoe still touching the ledge; but as he matured, Ghost became more interested in the image's other features: the quiet French street, the quaint crooked curbstones, the odd A-shaped poles in the background, and the oblivious cyclist, forever frozen mid-pedal, on his morning ride. Ghost also enjoyed the fact that *Leap into the Void* was not photofamous; it would be awkwardly out-of-place within the George Eastman House Collection's *A History of Photography from 1839 to the present*. Photofamous images often left Ghost cold; for example, he could think of nothing clever or insightful to say about Dorothea Lange's *Migrant Mother* or Robert Capa's *The Falling Soldier*.

But there was something else about *Leap into the Void*, something elusive, something *je ne sais quoi*. Ghost discovered a whisper of this something in Peter Schjeldahl's review of Klein's 2010 retrospective at the Hirshhorn Museum:

> *I trace Klein's character, in part, to a legacy of French Romanticism: the positing of some Absolute, by which ideas that gratify the mind are presumed to construe reality. (That always boggles me, as a pedestrianly pragmatic American: I'm not sure if what I'm missing flies beyond the feeble grasp of my intelligence or, simply, isn't there.)[3]*

Leap into the Void had something that other images didn't have, although Ghost found it difficult to explain exactly what that something was: a Frenchman might call it *romance*; Peter Schjeldahl called it "some Absolute"; the ancient Gnostics might call it *pneuma* (spark); while Ghost's mother might say that the image had a mischievous glimmer behind its eyes. In *Camera Lucida*, Roland Barthes called this something *punctum*, while Ghost called it… *something*. Under normal circumstances, Ghost might've been dismayed by his inability to describe this phenomenon; after all, the inadequacy of language was a major theme of his novel, as was apparent in the fact that he had coined so many "portmantypos" that his original manuscript overwhelmed Word's Spell Check. (Who knew Spell Check had a maximum capacity?) But Imagereality is different. Ghost comforted himself by repeating the Nietzsche quote that appears on the inside cover of Harold Bloom's *Shakespeare: The Invention of the Human*: "That

---

3   True Blue: a Yves Klein Retrospective, *The New Yorker*, June 28, 2010.

for which we find words is something already dead in our hearts. There is always a kind of contempt in the act of speaking." Ghost suspected that a similar thing could be said about Imagereality: *"That for which we can photograph is something already dead in our hearts. There is always a kind of contempt in the act of photographing."*

Anyone who considers Imagereality a language is mistaken; Imagereality is not a language, it's a way of *communicating*. Ay, but here's the rub: the inability to find words for something that is *alive in your heart* exactly mirrors the silence that surrounds everything else; for example, Ghost could not explain why he preferred the work of Edward Weston over Alfred Steiglitz, he could only juxtapose Stieglitz's *The Steerage* (a perfectly fine photograph) with Weston's *Pepper No. 30* (Damn, that's one SEXY PEPPER!), or Stieglitz's *The Terminal (New York)* (again: perfectly fine) with Weston's *Excusado*, which Ghost found both exquisite and hilarious.

> **Weston's wife:** *Excusado*, Edward… [knock, knock, knock]… I need to use the bathroom…
>
> **Weston:** [muffled] I'm in here.
>
> **Weston's wife:** *Excusado*, Edward… [knock, knock, knock]… What are you *doing* in there?
>
> **Weston:** [muffled] I'll be out in a minute, dear!
>
> **Weston's wife:** EDWARD!!!… [POUND, POUND, POUND]… Are you photographing the toilet again?
>
> **Weston:** DAMN IT WOMAN, JUST GIVE ME A MINUTE!!!

After this imaginary exchange, Ghost envisioned Weston's poor wife having to crouch down outside the bathroom door in the discomforting pose of *Nude, 1936.*

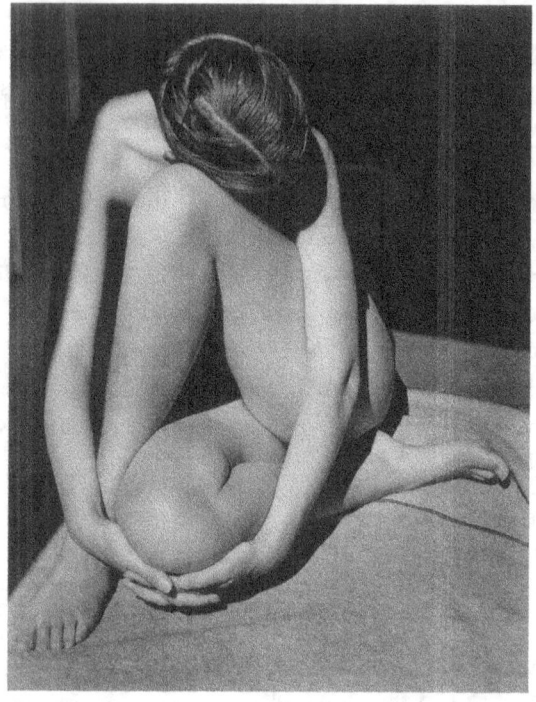

Gazing upon *Excusado* also reminded Ghost of the rumor that Weston kept a daily journal of his bowel movements. Ghost found this rumor fascinating: he couldn't seriously contemplate Weston's work without thinking about it. Why would anyone do such a bizarre thing? And how many different adjectives could a person use to describe bowel movements? And practically speaking, where did Weston keep the journal? It had to be next to the *Excusado*, right? But wouldn't family members or dinner guests notice the oddly placed notebook (and perhaps even thesaurus)

leaning against the base of the toilet and casually flip through it? What would *they* think? Wouldn't any relationship and/or dinner party be ruined upon learning that the third of May, 1928 at 7:53 A.M. was "magnificent" and "heroic," and the day after "verdant" and "swift"? [4]

Of course, another reason why Ghost was thinking about Weston's *Excusado* might've been because he was currently potty training his son, which was an endeavor he would categorize with the adjectives "herculean," "wildly frustrating," and "muchomessy." In fact, the only aspect of potty training that he enjoyed was when his babyboy whispered to him, "let's go plop the quiet ploppers."

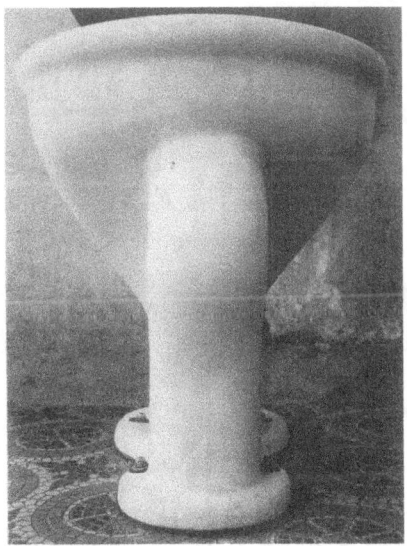

---

4   Ghost didn't know if these specific adjectives appeared within Weston's potentially-nonexistent journal; the Weston Family Photographic Trust had repeatedly ignored his requests to do "doo research" in their archives.

6

That for which we can photograph is something already dead in our hearts. There is always a kind of contempt in the act of photographing.

To Carlos Spencer-Bayard, Edward Weston's work possessed an undead heart; it pulsated and shimmered as it fought to stay alive in his consciousness, and the same could be said for *Leap into the Void*. Of course, not everyone feels this way about Klein's image; *Leap into the Void* is seldom mentioned in any discourse regarding the history of photography, and when it is, it is inevitably dismissed as pure fakery. No one can deny that *Leap into the Void* is not technically a photograph: it's a photomontage created by splicing together two photographs. Ghost suspected he should care about this, but he didn't; to him, the image *felt* real, feral even. In Ghost's opinion, *Leap into the Void* is both a photograph and not; thus it is a perfect example of what Ghost called a "both and not."

Ghost grimaced slightly. The idea of a "both and not" was dangerously close to dialectics, and Ghost was extremely distrustful of dialectics. This distrust stemmed from the fact that he was not entirely sure what the word meant; in the dictionary, dialectics is defined as logical argumentation; in an article on Walter Benjamin and the Frankfurt School, Alex Ross defined the idea as:

> *The word "dialectic," as elaborated in the philosophy of Hegel, causes endless problems for people who are not German, and even for some who are. In a way, it is both a philosophical concept and a literary style. Derived from the ancient Greek term for the art of debate, it indicates an argument that maneuvers between contradictory points… {Dialectics} come naturally in the German language, whose sentences are themselves*

*plotted in swerves, releasing their full meaning only
with the final clinching action of the verb.*[5]

Ghost thought of dialectics as conversational pingpong,
and he was amazed at how many people loved to argue logically,
especially his wife. Whenever he offered any opinion or expressed
any idea, his wife would pick up her imaginary pingpong pad-
dle and *Wack!* some part of it back to him. Ghost would then
attempt to restate his original statement... *Wack!* He would try
to elaborate.... *Wack!* Substantiate... *Wack!* Reiterate... *Wack!*
Explicate... *Wack!* Elucidate... *Wack!* Illuminate... *Wack!* Such
exchanges left Ghost exhausted and confused; he could never remember what he had been trying to talk about before he was
pulled into a pointless twenty shot dialectical pingpong rally à
la Federer v. Nadal c. 2008. Ghost suspected that his hatred of
dialectics was one of the things that had initially attracted him
to the study of Imagereality: Imagereality is the anti-dialectic *par
excellence*. **It is impossible to argue with a photograph.**

But wait!

While scrutinizing *Excusado*, Ghost spied something
scrawled along the toilet's pristine porcelain surface: *Roland était ici.*

From *Camora Lucida*: "the photograph is undialectical." But
what Barthes failed to mention was while it is impossible to argue
with a photograph, it is also impossible to completely agree with a
photograph. The reason for this strange negative doubling is that a
photograph is both truth and not; or to phrase it differently, a photograph is neither a truth nor a lie, **a photograph is an *untruth*.**

....

5   The Naysayers: Walter Benjamin, Theodor Adorno, and the critique of pop culture, *The
New Yorker*, September 15, 2014.

7

At the far end of the bar, the front door to *Rafael's Silver Cloud Lounge* squeeeaked open and a young couple walked in. In the reflection of the long horizontal mirror that hung behind the bar, Ghost watched the couple as they sat down on barstools and began chatting with Drew.

The name A. Flynn Fox was Ghost's sister-in-law's *nom de internet*. When Ghost told Drew that he didn't know what she had been up to lately, he wasn't being been entirely truthful; or to put it another way, his answer was both truth and not. Although Ghost didn't know what she had been up to lately, as he thought it was impolite to inquire too frequently about the social engagements of one's sister-in-law, he did know one thing she was doing for certain: avoiding Drew. After their initial handful of dates, the courtship ended abruptly and Ghost's sister-in-law stopped patronizing *Rafael's Silver Cloud Lounge*. When he finally asked his wife if she knew what had happened, she informed him, rather bluntly, that they "hadn't hit it off." And that was that. Period. Full stop. System shutdown. Strike3. Bigbrickwall. Ghost could've inquired why they "hadn't hit it off," but he chose not to, even if his wife knew the reason, Ghost was sure that he wouldn't be able to understand it. When it came to anything involving relationships, Ghost never understood anything, and thus the one question he learned never to ask was *why*.

Glancing back into the mirror behind the bar, Ghost casually observed the newly arrived couple: he was watching some meaningless college sporting event on TV, while she was smartphonescrolling. Squinting, Ghost observed the couple's sameness: same age, size, fashion, quaffedness, whiteness, and straightness, and by this Ghost didn't mean their teeth, which were undoubtedly extremely white and straight. Ghost had no difficulty envi-

sioning the couple's backstory: they met in college; their courtship involved alcohol and casual sex; as graduation neared, they
started to domestically intertwine. Why not? It was easy, comfortable. More than anything, the couple radiated comfort; even
their casual disinterest with each other appeared comfortable.
Whenever Ghost observed such couples, and it was a common
habit of his, he always felt a tinge of envy: he had *never* felt comfortable with anyone.

For many years, Ghost attributed his uncomfortableness
to the fact that every relationship is really a doubling, and thus
there are four people in every relationship: YOU (interior), YOU
(exterior), ME (interior), and ME (exterior). This explains why
relationships are so confusing: nobody can ever be sure exactly
who is talking to whom. Ghost magpied the idea of relationship
doubling from Harold Bloom's theory that both "intensely erotic
relationships" in the Sonnets were "at least a doubling (Southampton *and* Pembroke, Mary Fitton *and* Emilia Bassano Lanier
and Lucy Negro)."

While flipping through the George Eastman House Collection's *A History of Photography from 1839 to the present*, Ghost
was shocked to discover the perfect visual personification for his
theory in Larry Silver's *Head Stand, Muscle Beach, Santa Monica,
California, 1954.*

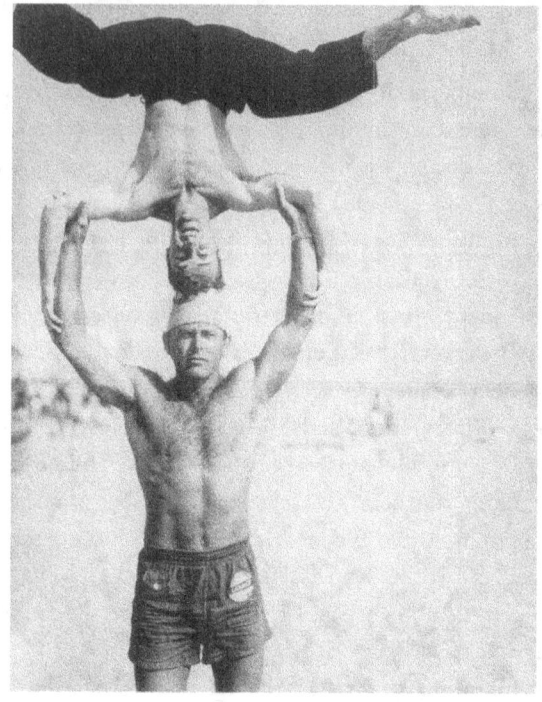

The SELF (exterior) is the bottom figure: strong, confident, and exhibiting high levels of probity; the SELF (interior) is the top figure: loony, unpredictable, and not fully in the frame.

Ghost found the theory of interior and exterior selves comforting, but upon returning to Ohio, another idea slowly crept into his consciousness: what if some people did not have a SELF (interior)? What then? While contemplating this, echoes of Elliott Smith spun through Ghost's consciousness:

> *You're just some dude*
> *with a stilted attitude*
> *that you learned from TV*

Without interiority, people resemble the output from a 3D printer: feed a photograph into the machine and... [*sputter spit sputter sputtersputter spitspitspit*]... *Voila!* a three-dimensional person! Without interiority, what a person looks like *is* who they are.

While scrutinizing Silver's image, Ghost noticed something odd scrawled across the bottom man's chest. It appeared as if the man had fallen asleep in the sun and some mischievous fellow - I wonder who? - had written something in suntan lotion across his bare chestflesh. The writing was faint, but if he squinted, Ghost could make out the words: *Roland était ici.*

From *Camera Lucida*: "The photographic look has something paradoxical about it which is sometimes to be met with in life: the other day, in a café, a young boy came in alone, glanced around the room, and occasionally his eyes rested on me; I then had the certainty that he was *looking at* me without however being sure that he was *seeing* me..."

8

WILLIAM FUCKING SHAKESPEARE!

He had done it again! He had mentioned the Sonnets in relation to Imagereality. Nobody wants to talk about the Sonnets, especially imagethinkers. In a *New York Times* review of Neil L. Rudenstine's *Ideas of Order: A Close Reading of Shakespeare's Sonnets*, a book which Carlos Spencer-Bayard devoured in three days, Glyn Maxwell groaned, "I would take the least of the plays over the whole blooming [sequence]." *Reeeally*, Ghost thought, *Titus Andronicus? Henry VIII?* Ghost sometimes suspected that he was the only Bardolator alive who actually *enjoyed* the Sonnets. Sure, lots of people enjoy cherrypicking individual poems, but what Ghost particularly enjoyed was the sequence's problematic narrative. This enjoyment stemmed from a number of reasons: first, the narrative offers insight into a topic that obsessed Shakespeare during the most productive years of his life[6]; second, Ghost commiserated with the Shakespeaker of the Sonnets' plight, which stems from his inability to understand other people; and third, reading the Sonnets is a delightful education in *schadenfreude*. When asked the 'desert island' question, James Joyce responded, "I would like to say Dante, but I would have to take the Englishman, for he is richer." Fair dinkum, but what if you couldn't fit the entire *Complete Works of William Shakespeare* into your suitcase? I mean, you're traveling light, right? What if you could only take *two* books? Of course, the first book would be *Hamlet*, but what about book #2? As painful as it would be leaving *Othello* ashore, Ghost would take the Sonnets, as reading the Sonnets might ac-

....

6   In *Shakespeare: The Invention of the Human*, Harold Bloom dates the sequence as beginning in 1589 and ending one year before the Bard's odd semi-retirement in 1609.

tually make a person feel good about being on a deserted island, farfarfarfarfar away from the perpetual cycle of desire and despair, love and self-loathing associated with relationships.

But there was something else, something stranger. The Sonnets reminded Ghost of Imagereality, as portions of the narrative are heavily *photographic*. As Oscar Wilde so brilliantly illustrated in his dialogue *The Portrait of Mr. W.H.*, the Shakespeaker is in possession of a painting of his beloved Fair Young Twatwaffle. This painting was commissioned as a way to fix the young man's beauty and thus exempt it from the ravages of Time; such an irrational desire mirrors the photographic urge. Lines such as:

> *Then the conceit of this inconstant stay*
> *Sets you most rich in youth before my sight,*
> *Where wasteful Time debateth with Decay*
> *To change your day of youth to sullied night;*
>   *And all in war with Time for love of you,*
>   *As he takes from you, I engraft you new.*

and

> *But thy eternal summer shall not fade,*
> *Nor lose possession of that fair thou ow'st,*
> *Nor shall Death brag thou wand'rest in his shade,*
> *When in eternal lines to time thou grow'st.*
> *So long as men can breathe or eyes can see,*
> *So long lives this, and this gives life to thee.*

appear to speak directly to Imagereality. "Engraft you new" is what photographs do, and as anyone who has ever gazed longingly upon an image of an absent loved one, photography also "gives life to thee."

Furthering the connection between Imagereality and the

Sonnets is the Shakespeaker's struggles to understand the difference between outward appearance ("show") and inner reality. And
there's more: the sexual frenzy associated with the Dark Lady with
the Hellvagina mirrors the overt sexuality of modern visual culture; every time he turned on the television, Ghost perceived the
Dark Lady with the Hellvagina *everyfuckingwhere*. And finally, like
Imagereality, the Sonnets are anti-dialectical; in fact, they are so
anti-dialectical that they often appear *anti*-anti-dialectical; that
is, it's impossible to argue logically with the Sonnets because it's
impossible to figure out anything to argue with them about. No
one wants to talk about the Sonnets: they're pointless. Early in his
book, Rudenstine quotes W. H. Auden's famous grumble: "more
nonsense has been talked and written, more intellectual and emo-
tional energy expended in vain, on the sonnets of Shakespeare than
on any other literary work in the world." Talking nonsense and
expending critical energy in vain? This, of course, is an imagethinker's *spécialité*.

So what *are* the Sonnets? Carlos Spencer-Bayard found the
best way to answer this question was by detailing what the Sonnets are not: they are not a chronicle of agony, because it's never
clear whether or not the Shakespeaker ever feels any agony over
the sequence's many betrayals, aggressions, and transgressions;
and the Sonnets are not a chronicle of loss as the frequent language of financial dealings reminds the reader that the Shakespeaker is never in possession of anything resembling ownership:
no "world-without-end" bargains are ever agreed upon, no con-
tracts signed, no laws broken, no promises rendered invalid, and
no accusations of perjury substantiated. No, the Sonnets are a
chronicle of *turbulence*. The Shakespeaker's determined resolve, his
almost stoic sense of *c'est la vie, c'est la guerre,* mirrors the mindset
of an experienced traveler on a bumpy flight; hopefully, the plane
will land soon, but until then, there's nothing you can do but grip

the armrest tightly and hope for the best. Furthering this analogy is the fact that there is only one direction to the gravitational pull of the Sonnets: *downward.*

> *He went down, down, down*
> *and the devil called him my name.*
> *He went down, down, down,*
> *hanging on the back of a train*

"No one emerges in a posture other than prone," Harold Bloom remarks of the Sonnets in *The Anatomy of Influence*, "no other 'love poems' are so finally forbidding."

The destructive nature of the Sonnets is driven by a single, haunting question: can anyone ever really know the true nature of another person? This question haunted Carlos Spencer-Bayard, and Imagereality only exacerbated the dilemma. Images are strange; every time he gazed upon an image of himself, Ghost saw a *stranger.* Images of himself always made Ghost feel uneasy: it was what he looked like, not who he was; in other words, it was both him and not.

Pound

Pound

Pound

{Squeeeeeeeak}

A single image leapt into Ghost's consciousness. He knew the image well: it was an old high school basketball image of him. Having achieved a modicum of notoriety as a basketball player, Ghost's photograph appeared frequently in his local newspaper. In this particular image, Ghost was mid-air, having just Moses-Maloned an offensive rebound. What made the image strange was the fact that he was staring directly at the camera. Scrutinizing the image in his memory, Ghost noticed something odd; in the upmost right-hand corner, next to his school's logo of a bobcat paw, the words *Luv Ya Blue* had been replaced by a cartoonish cursive scrawl: *Roland était ici.*

From *Camera Lucida*: "All I look *like* is other photographs of myself, and this to infinity: no one is ever anything but the copy of a copy, real or mental..."

After his basketball career was over, Ghost never really thought much about his aversion to photographs of himself, but with the publication of his novel, this aversion flared up anew. When his publisher requested an author photo, Ghost suddenly found himself, once again, confronting the *strangeness* of Image-reality.

Why would readers want to know what he *looked* like when reading his book showed them who he was? Adding to his unease was the knowledge that, within his novel, he had openly mocked Paul Auster's "darkbrooding eyes" in one of his old author photos. "C'mon," Ghost had written in the annotated version of his novel, "that's your fucking author photo? I mean, *seriously?*" Auster's author photo practically purred, *Come hither, pussycat.*

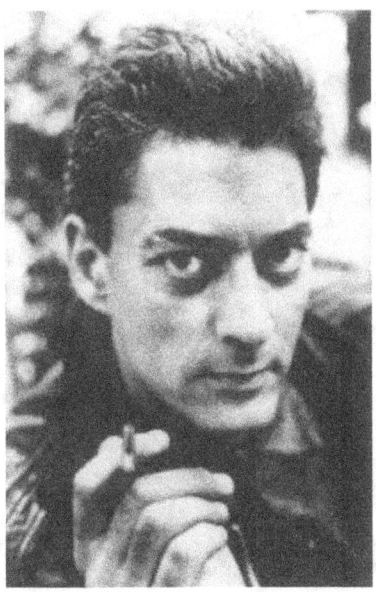

Once an author had mocked another author's author photo, didn't he leave himself open to like-minded mockery? To avoid such mockery, in his own author photograph, Ghost tried not to look too darkbrooding; he tried not to flash the kind of Fuck-MeEyes so ubiquitous in Hollywood headshots; he tried to look casual, relaxed; and echoing Harold Bloom's sediments on Shake-speare, he tried to look like someone with whom you could have a relaxed drink, but this wasn't easy. In the end, Ghost simply aped an old Dan Brown author photo that he had unearthed on Google Images. To Ghost, Brown's author photo exhumed friendliness, warmth (that fireplace, those layers!), and undislikeablity; also, Brown's author photo scored extremely low on what Gary Shteyn-gart in *Super Sad True Love Story* deemed "fuckability."

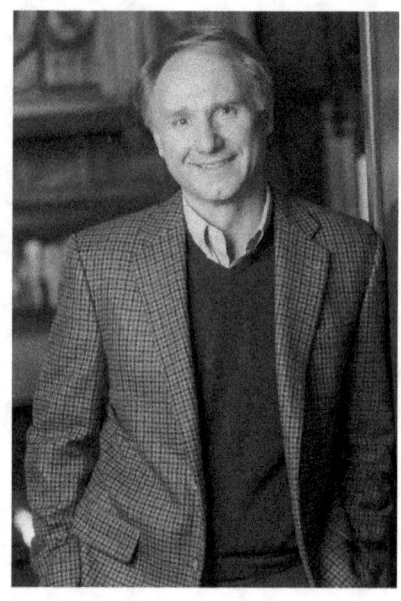

Of course, Shteyngart's own author photo from *Super Sad True Love Story* was Super Sad True Creepy. Who takes their author photo outside in the middle of winter, as opposed to posing in front of a warm fireplace? And wasn't it a tad aggressive to stare into the camera while walking directly towards the photographer? *Baby, it's cold outside*, Shteyngart's stare suggested, *come curl up with THIS*:

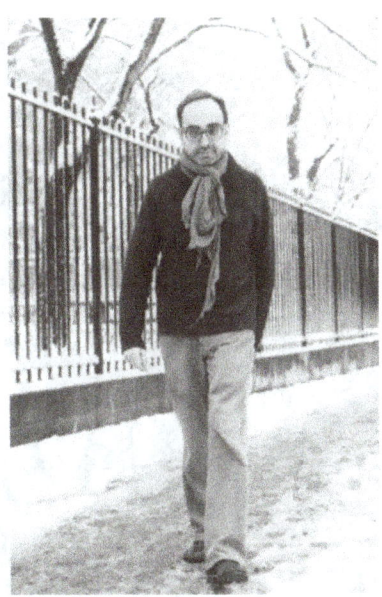

Walking towards the photographer with an intent stare was apparently a popular author photo trope; in the author photo for Jeffrey Eugenides' *The Marriage Plot* this trope reached its apotheosis. O, that stare! That pirate-y facial hair! That perfectly half-opened vest! The particulars of the figure were so intriguing that Ghost almost forgot to notice the surroundings. Where the hell was Eugenides and what the hell was he doing? He looked like a well-dressed, erudite hobo taking a casual stroll down a deserted railroad track outside of Detroit. And where exactly was he walking to? Toledo?

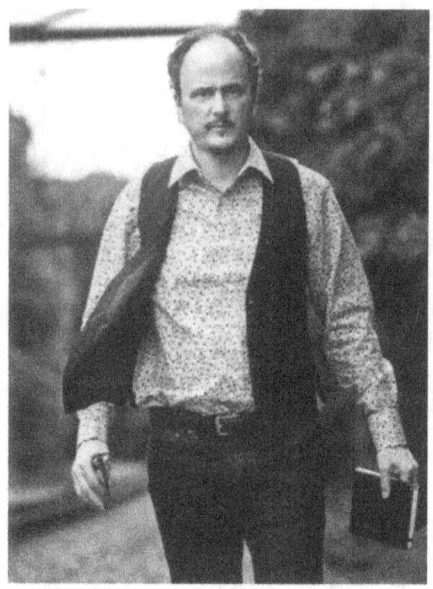

While deciding between reading *Super Sad True Love Story* and *The Marriage Plot*, Ghost felt like he was caught directly between these two authors, who were rapidly approaching him in opposite directions with the determined intensity of the two rival dancing gangs in Michael Jackson's *Beat It* video.

At the same time he was fretting over his author photo, Carlos Spencer-Bayard was also attempting to write a synopsis of his novel that would appear on the book's back cover. Ghost thought of this synopsis as the novel's author photo. Having no idea how long a back cover synopsis should be, Ghost composed a synopsis that was entirely too long, which was actually a smart move, as his publisher simply cut this original offering down and added the phrase: "a love of literary acrobatics worthy of David Foster Wallace."

[Grimace]

Ghost was aware that his publisher thought of him as davidfosterwallacesque, he was also aware that the comparison was intended to be a compliment, but in his opinion, he was both davidfosterwallacesque and not. For one thing, Ghost had never actually read any of David Foster Wallace's books; also, there was a worrisomely foreboding element in being compared to a novelist who was so famously doomeager. But *bumbo clatt*, David Foster Wallace was smart; the idea of a "both and not" is actually his, as it comes from his essay on Roger Federer titled *Both Flesh and Not*.[7] Within this essay, the author counselled: "You more have to come at the aesthetic stuff obliquely, to talk around it, or- as Aquinas did with his own ineffable subject-to try to define it in terms of what it is not."

Attempting to embrace his status as davidfosterwallacesque, Ghost considered apeing one of his author photos, but a quick Google Image search paralyzed him with fear: scrolling through a batch of David Foster Wallace's author photos was a painful reminder of photography's ability to make madness visible. In the author photo for his debut novel, *The Broom of the System*, the author appears young and healthy; while reading *The Marriage Plot* – Ghost had opted for the erudite hobo over curling up with the Shteyngartian koala bear – Ghost's enjoyment was greatly enhanced when he envisioned Leonard Bankhead as looking less like Adam Duritz and more like this:

---

7 *Both Flesh and Not* is also the title of a posthumous collection of the author's essays.

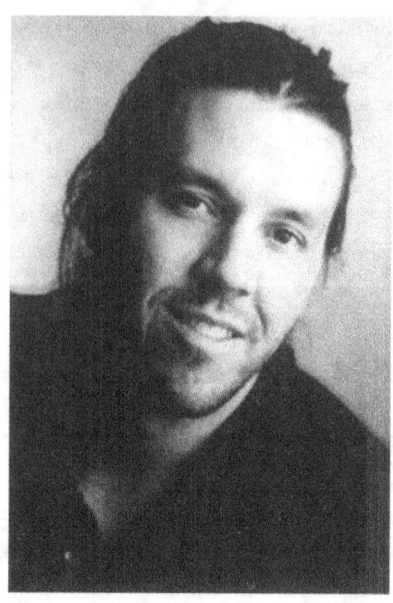

Handsome bloke, right? The author photo for *Both Flesh and Not* is very different: gone is the gregarious grin, the engaging gaze, and the charming, messy mop of hair; in short, gone is the youthful romanticism of a yearning young man. In the author photo for *Both Flesh and Not*, David Foster Wallace appears weary, tired. His stare is particularly unnerving; imagine a photographer asking someone who is staring at him like *that* to put on a fancy scarf or a paisley patterned shirt and pose on a snowy sidewalk or a deserted railroad track. He hadn't even taken the time to fix his bandanna, the size of which makes his head look *gigantic*. Staring at this gigantic headwrap reminded Ghost of how Wallace claimed that the only reason he wore bandannas was because of the idea that they were keeping his head from exploding. But his head *had* exploded. And knowing this, Ghost was not particularly happy with his publisher's comparison: he had no desire to "bandanna up." But Ghost did like Wallace's glasses. They looked comfortable. Lightweight. In fact... [grimace] They were the same glasses Ghost wore.

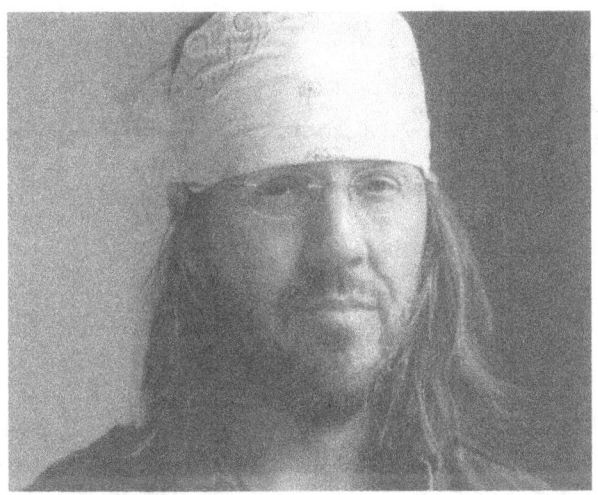

9

While scrutinizing other author's author photos, it was important to note that Ghost wasn't particularly happy with his own author photo, but this unhappiness had nothing to do with the photograph itself- it was a perfectly fine photograph- but rather with his face. First: his smile. Awkward. Forced. It was his sober smile, not his *real* smile. But his sober smile was, undoubtedly, more photogenic; his *real* smile made him look slightly unhinged, but this unhingedness conveyed a great deal about who he was and why he wrote the way he did. Second: his head. Small. Shorn. Without his *real* smile, his head appeared too skull-like, reminding him of Mitya's cry from *The Brothers Karamazov*: "It is I, per-

haps, who am Yorick. Yorick now, that is, and later- the skull."
Like a figure out of a James Ensor painting, the skull needed the
smile. Ghost was a grinning skull, but no one would know this
from his author photo.

Originally, Ghost envisioned the photoshoot for his author
photo taking place at *Rafael's Silver Cloud Lounge*, which seemed
appropriate seeing how a large portion of his novel had been written there, but a blizzard derailed these plans, and the photoshoot
ended up taking place in his parents' house. Had Ghost been photographed at *Rafael's Silver Cloud Lounge*, here is what his author
photo might've looked like:

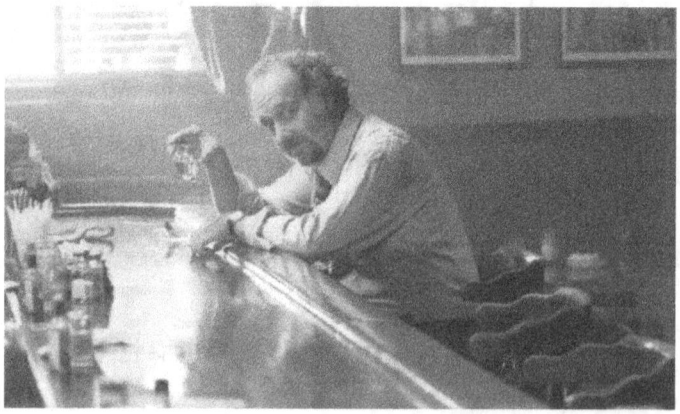

Remove Paul Giamatti from the image and replace him
with the figure who appears within Ghost's author photo *et voila!*
... his *true* author photo.

And still, didn't this imaginary photomontage only convey
his ME (exterior)? What about his ME (interior), what did that
fellow look like? This was a difficult question to answer. The next
time he flipped through the George Eastman House Collection's
A History of Photography from 1839 to the present, Ghost kept this

question in his mind... his mind, his dark, collapsible mind... filled with the desert of thought, the night of now, and the sudden surge of illumination. *Satori.* There ME (interior) was: Ansel Adams' *Moonrise, Hernandez.*

10

– Another Jamesons? Or do you want to switch over to Guinness?

Carlos Spencer-Bayard stopped scribbling for a moment to contemplate the question.

– I'll switch, Drew.

– Your pour?

– Yeah, do you mind?

– Of course not, I'm just glad it's not Lone Star.

A moment later, Drew appeared with an unopened can of Guinness and an empty pint glass, both of which he left in front of Ghost. Like any good bartender, Drew knew his regulars. Ghost quickly popped open the can, tilted the glass, and poured until three-quarters full. He then grabbed the nearest candle and inched it closer to watch the blackmagic happen.

Ghost took pouring his Guinness seriously. Once, in Detroit, he had almost been 86ed from an Irish pub for questioning the bartender's pour. Normally, he was very non-confrontational, especially with female bartenders, but she totally buggered his pour: straight in, no tilt, no pause, no clue. Who poured a Guinness like *that*, especially in an Irish pub?

Glassgazing, Ghost watched the steady blackness rise. A beautiful, drinkable kinetic composition Rothkoed before his eyes: velvety deepblack underneath slow sandy caramel underneath a frosty creamtop. But the blackmagic was just beginning. Once his Guinness had finished Rothkoing, Ghost poured the remainder of the can into his glass. The resulting dark cascade reminded Ghost of Democritus' description of the downward whirlwind of atoms: tumbling and swerving while forever fallingfallingfalling.

As a child, Ghost had mistakenly believed that physical deterioration was the most unpleasant aspect of aging, as premonitions of achy joints, sore knees, arthritis, and a hip replacement (or two) haunted him nightly. After playing a single season of Midget League Baseball – he wasn't very good – Ghost became resigned to the fact that he would eventually need Tommy John surgery. While in high school, he scrutinized the chapter on disease in his health textbook like a man ordering sushi from an à la carte menu: two Palinopsia rolls, a piece of Sciatica sashimi, and some Kluver-Bucy Syndrome. Upon reaching adulthood, Ghost realized he was wrong, physical deterioration is NOT the most unpleasant aspect of aging; erectile dysfunction is a foolish toy when compared to the cascading darkness that continually envelopes adult life. Love, loss, betrayal, bereavement, disillusionment, diminishment: the sky gets darker and darker until all is consumed by the darknothingness of night. And the darkest hour of the blacknight comes with the unavoidable realization that death eventually sweeps everything away, even the most inconsequential things: it sweeps away books you have yet to read, novels you have yet to write, dreams that only live in our dreamconsciousness, and songs you hate but can't stop singing. Death also sweeps away our favorite images. This is what Ghost saw when he gazed upon *Moonrise, Hernandez*: unavoidable, uncontrollable, inexplicable darkness. For him, this darkness was the photograph's Barthian *punctum*.

   [*Grimace*]

   Punctum was Roland Barthes' word for the element within a photograph that "pierces the viewer." Personally, Ghost never liked the word *punctum*. To him, it conjured up the scene in *Moby -Dick* where the wounded whale's heart bursts, causing a stream of blood to erupt from its blowhole. Live long enough and every whaleheart is assaulted by suffering to its burstingpoint. *There ain't no cure for that*. And yet writers appear to enjoy a perverse relationship to suffering: the more profoundly a writer suffers, the more profoundly he writes. A quick glance at Ghost's bookshelf supported this theory: Shakespeare (erotomania… or was it genophobia?), Cervantes (penury & loss of a hand), Joyce (penury & exile), Nietzsche (penury & probable virginity), Dostoevsky (firingsquad fakery), Melville (more penury), Lucretius (possible lovepotion poisoning), Orwell (neckwound), and Beckett (pimpwound).

The darknothingness of night waits to embrace us all. Whenever Ghost found himself obsessing over this unpleasant eventuality, he recited to himself his favorite Aram Saroyan poem:

> night
> so daylight

This perfect little poem reminded Ghost that the only way to achieve illumination was by travelling through darkness. For Ghost, this too was apparent within *Moonrise, Hernandez*. But there was something about the image that always bothered Ghost: those damn crosses.

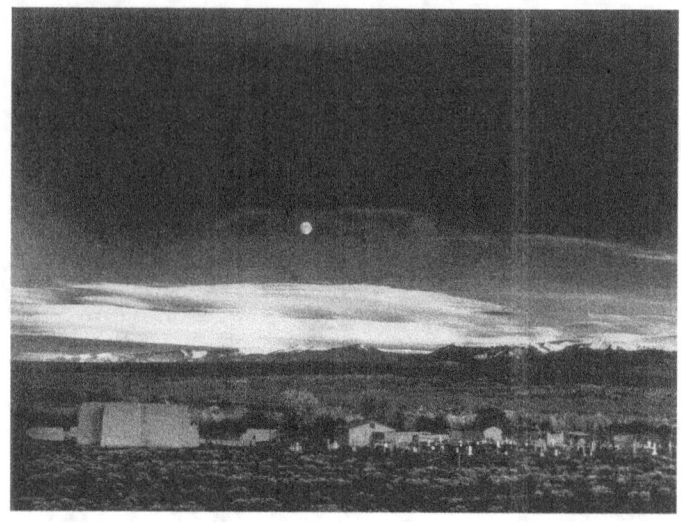

11

Religion and Imagereality have a queer relationship. On the surface, it appears that the two entities are worlds apart: religion focuses on the invisible and the immaterial, while Imagereality is preoccupied with the visible and the material. Within religion, ancient rituals, objects, and symbols possess *gravitas*; Imagereality eradicates *gravitas*. Religion is sacred and exclusive; Imagereality democratizes and trivializes. F. Holland Day's *The Seven Last Words* or Gabriel Harrison's *The Infant Saviour Bearing the Cross* are so trivial and *gravitas*-less that they almost appear ridiculous; whenever Ghost gazed upon such images, he thought of people dressing up like Jesus for Halloween, and in the spectrum of Halloween costumes, dressing up like Jesus is pretty pedestrian.

The topic of religion seldom appears within any discussion of the history of photography. Ghost himself might never have connected the two disparate topics had he not stumbled upon the following passage in Geoffrey Batchen's essay 'Desiring Production':

> *In the introduction to his authoritative tome The Origins of Photography, Helmut Gernsheim went so far as to describe the timing of photography's invention as "the greatest mystery in its history": "Considering that knowledge of the chemical as well as the optical principles of photography was fairly widespread following Schulze's experiment {in 1725} . . . the circumstance that photography was not invented earlier remains the greatest mystery in its history. ... It had apparently never occurred to any of the multitude of artists of the seventeenth and eighteenth centuries who were in the habit of using the camera obscura to try to fix its image permanently."*
>
> *Why 1839 and not before? Why, for example, didn't any of the great thinkers of the past — Aristotle, Leonardo, Newton — come up with this idea, even if only in the form of textual or pictorial speculation? This is the question that continues to haunt the history of photography's invention.*

So why hadn't Leonardo da Vinci invented photography? He possessed all the necessary tools: knowledge, curiosity, and chemicals. The thought of capturing images on a chemically enhanced surface should have captivated him, but for some reason it didn't. Ghost believed that Leonardo never invented photography because he never *wanted* to invent photography. And why not? Ghost's theory was that Leonardo da Vinci, not to mention all of Renaissance Italy, wasn't religious enough to invent photogra-

phy. "If God did not exist," Voltaire once quipped, "it would be
necessary to invent him." Ghost thought, "If God did not exist,
it would have been impossible to invent photography." Religion
readied the world for the invention of photography by teaching
it how to *make believe*.

The cornerstone of religion is belief, and belief is a funny
thing. Like Imagereality, belief is both truth and not. Ghost suspected that no one really believes those silly stories about Adam
and Eve, that wily snake Satan, Job's bursting boils, or the Im-
maculate Conception: it was all *make believe*. Ghost found it difficult to contemplate any religious *make believe* without remembering Nietzsche's unforgettable cry: "What appalling paganism!"
Nietzsche is a bridge between Imagereality and religion, as many
of his observations on religion are also true for Imagereality. For
example, in *The Anti-Christ*, Nietzsche accuses theologians of attempting to "look at reality from a superior and foreign vantage
point," of reducing reality to the "mere 'appearance,' of a menda-
ciously fabricated world... honored as reality," and of demanding
a "picturesque effect... of the truth." He also denounced Christi-
anity as a "whole world of fiction... rooted in *hatred* of the Natural (of reality!); it is the expression of a profound vexation at
the sight of reality;" and as for the Christian conception of God,
Nietzsche pronounced it a "deification of nothingness." Would
such language be out of place in a discussion of Imagereality?
Could images, especially digital images, not be aptly summarized
as "nothingness," and could our collective obsession with photographic truth not be considered a "deification of nothingness?"
And yet, Imagereality has fooled the world into *believing* it is true.
But here's the funny thing about belief: if you choose to *make
believe* something is true, it *becomes* Truth. And Truth, by nature,
is anti-dialectic. Ghost didn't mind religion, he just didn't enjoy
talking about it; conversely, he didn't enjoy talking about athe-

ism either. While listening to an atheist rally against the stupid-
ity of religion or a Christer denounce the shallowness of atheism,
Ghost often found himself contemplating William Blake's assertion: "Everything Possible to be Believed is an Image of Truth."
Imagereality is an Image of Truth. An image is Truth if you
want it to be true, if you *need* it to be true; in other words, an
image is Truth, if you *make believe* it is true.

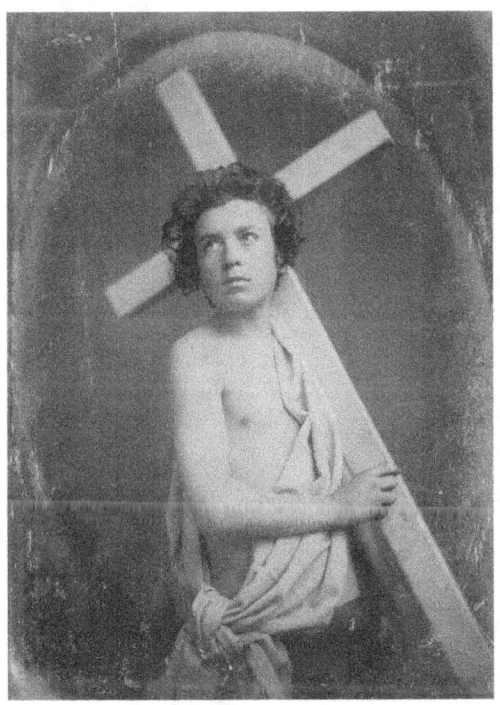

12

The only thing that disturbed Carlos Spencer-Bayard about William Blake's "Everything Possible to be Believed is an Image of Truth" was the verb tense: *to be Believed* not *to Believe*. Like belief, Imagereality only exists in the Past Perfect. This realization made Ghost extremely uncomfortable, as he did not enjoy the past. The past is problematic, the past is occupied territory; as such, entering it is *dangerous*. Ghost was amazed at how many people, his wife included, were oblivious to this fact; such people appeared perfectly content not only to enter the past, but to *live* there. The present is a prison: the past is perfect. Ghost suspected such perfectness was why so many people chose to live in the past; also, the past is controllable. The same thing cannot be said of the present, which is filled with swearing, sweating, swerving, mistakes, misunderstandings, misprisions, misspellings... the list is endless. Whenever he thought of the present, Ghost recalled Hans Jonas' description of the ancient Gnostics as experiencing the "intoxication of unprecedentedness." The perfection of the past is *sobering*, while the present is overbrimming with *intoxication*.

While writing his novel, Ghost became intimate with *intoxication*. Novels should be intoxicating: they should seduce, glitter, gather, and beguile. Nonfiction can inform and enlighten, but seldom does it touch upon what Michel Foucault, in *The History of Madness*, calls "the sensible drunkenness" of the world. Madness is a notoriously slippery subject for any author; within his *très grand* tome, Foucault employs a wealth of creative phrasing to encapsulate the moment when reason fails, logic falters, and the human consciousness is left flailing within an abyss of confusion as the world roars forward as if nothing is amiss. With each new phrase – other favorites included "animal unreason" and "dazzlement" – Ghost envisioned translator Jonathan Murphy shaking his head in disbelief and muttering under his breath: *"Encore, Michel? Sacrebleu!"*

Gnostic intoxication, the sensible drunkenness of the world, only exists in the present. Charles Olson once drew a distinction between "the act of the instant," as opposed to "the act of thought about the instant."[8] Imagereality is an act *about* the instant; it is not *of* the instant. Furthering Imagereality's remove from "the instant" is the fact that images, like memories, can so easily be manipulated. Such manipulation often occurs when people seek to augment the Cult of the Past, or as Ghost liked to think of it: the Cult of the Lost Cause. With its blurry edges, singlepoint perspective, and purposeful omissions, the past resembles a retouched photograph.

This realization sparked a humorous photo-centric memory. In this memory, Ghost and his wife were taking an evening stroll around the West End of Portland, Maine. The moment was both pre-children and pre-Rumsfeld. As was frequently the case during such walks, they were casually gossiping about friends and family.

– My sister is having trouble with her boyfriend, Ghost's wife announced as they travelled down West Street towards the Western Promenade. This announcement did not surprise Ghost, as he knew his sister-in-law often had boyfriend trouble.

– The Lounge Singer? Ghost replied. All Ghost knew about his sister-in-law's most recent boyfriend was that he worked in a piano bar; on the food chain of desirable employment for a boyfriend, Ghost considered piano bars sleaze bottomfeeders.

....

8   'Human Universe,' in *Selected Writings of Charles Olsen,* Robert Creeley (ed.). New York, New Directions, 1966, p. 54. Ghost first encountered this quote in Wystan Curnow's essay 'We'll Take Manhattan: Repatriating Len Lye' from the exhibition catalogue for the Govett-Brewster Art Gallery's exhibition *Len Lye: The New Yorker.*

– Yes.

– What's the matter? Ghost asked as they entered the Promenade and turned towards Western Cemetery.

– Well, she doesn't know if he's a widower or not.

– *WHAT*?!! How can you date somebody and not know if he's a widower or not? That kinda seems important.

– She says he doesn't like to talk about it.

– You mean, he's a widower and doesn't like talking about it, or he doesn't like talking about whether or not he's a widower?"

– She doesn't know.

– How do you date a person and not know that?

– I know, that right there is the problem.

As their conversation meandered onward, Ghost found himself unable to stop thinking about the 'IS HE A WIDOWER, OR IS HE NOT A WIDOWER' question. When they returned to their apartment, he made an unexpected request.

– Is the Lounge Singer on Facebook?

– I assume so.

– Would you log into your account and show me a picture of the guy?

– Why, Ghost's wife asked skeptically.

– I just want to see what the guy looks like.

– I doubt you'll be able to tell if he's a widower or not just by looking at the guy.

– *WHAT*?!! That's absurd, that's not why I want to see a picture of him.

– Why else would you want to know what he looks like, Ghost's wife asked with growing skepticism.

– Because every time we talk about the guy, in my mind, all I see is that cheesy *Saturday Night Live* skit of Bill Murray singing the theme from *The Love Boat*.

Apparently, this request was deemed acceptable, as Ghost's

wife sat down at her laptop and logged into her Facebook account. Clicking on her sister's FRIENDS tab, she scrolled down until she recognized the Lounge Singer's name. *CLICK*. She opened his Facebook page. *CLICK*. She maximized the first picture she found.

— There, Ghost's wife said matter-of-factly. What do you think? Think he's cute?

Ghost leaned over his wife's shoulder to get a better look at the image.

— What's up with *THAT CAT*? Ghost blurted out without thinking.

— It's probably just his cat, Ghost's wife said with rising irritation. You're not supposed to be looking at *THE CAT*. You're supposed to be looking at him.

— How can I not look at *THAT CAT*? It's fucking HUGE!

— So?

— Wait a minute, Ghost said leaning closer to the screen. That picture's been photoshopped.

— How can you tell?

— Look at the cat's ear: it doesn't line up with the picture's border. Plus, pussy's blurry from being enlarged.

For a moment, both Ghost and his wife stared at the screen in awkward silence. Ghost's wife finally broke the spell.

— You don't think... [her voice trailing off]

— I don't think what? Ghost replied although he suspected he knew what his wife was thinking, as he was thinking the exact same thing.

— You don't think he... [her voice trailing off again]

This time, Ghost finished his wife's thought.

— ... Photoshopped a picture of a giant cat over a picture of his dead wife? Is that what you were going to ask?

Ghost's wife nodded, which allowed the awkward question

to hang in the air like a giant, fluffy photoshopped cat. What kind of widower photoshops his dead wife out of a photograph? Wasn't it more logical that the cat was just covering up an obnoxious ex-girlfriend? And still, who does that? Maybe the cat wasn't covering anything at all. Maybe the guy just wanted a picture with his cat and the damn thing wouldn't sit still. It was impossible to know.

– Well, said Ghost's wife irritably.

– Well what?

– Do you think he photoshopped that cat over a picture of his dead wife, or not?

– Are you really expecting me to answer that?

By the look on his wife's face, Ghost instantly knew the answer to this question. Staring again at the picture, Ghost could only think of one thing to say...

– THE LOOOOOVE BOAT, he crooned in his loungeist loungesinger voice.

The truth is always perspectival: photography only knows a single perspective. Thus Imagereality is only an Image of Truth. With the truth comes responsibility, but the same thing cannot be said of *untruths*, which are completely devoid of responsibility. *Untruths* are irresponsible. **Imagereality is irresponsible.**

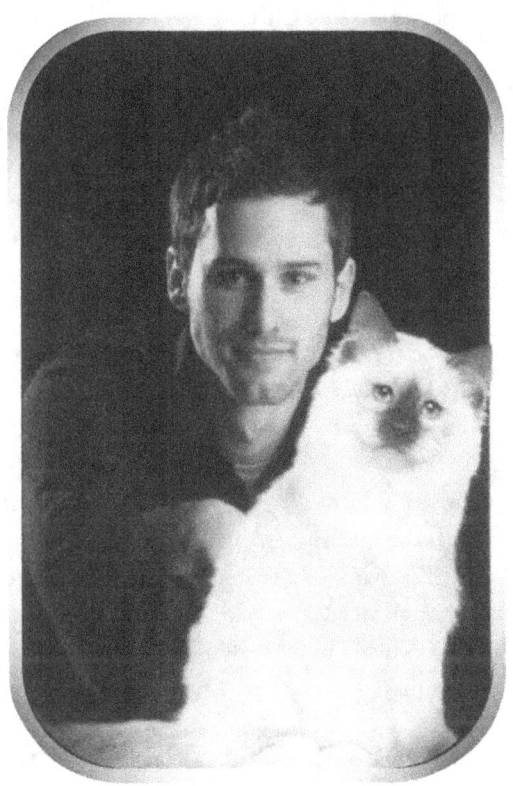

13

Exiting *Rafael's Silver Cloud Lounge* through the side door, Carlos Spencer-Bayard emerged onto the street. Darkness engulfed him. The night was a symphony of deserted streets. Glancing skyward, Ghost observed the greatest of all unphotographs: the nightsky. Shuffling to his right, Ghost played *Where's the Moon, There's the Moon*, a game he had invented based on the title of a book of poetry by Dan Chiasson. As he located the glowing orb in the darkstillness, Ghost thought of the moon as a giant flashbulb, illuminating everything and nothing, the sleeping and the dead. There were times when Ghost thought of Imagereality as some kind of natural phenomenon akin to moonlight or snow:

Yes, the newspapers were right: photography was general all over the world. It was falling on every part of the dark central plain, on the treeless hills, falling softly upon Hernandez, New Mexico and, farther westward, softly falling into the dark mutinous puddles of Paris. It was falling, too, upon every part of the Cimetière de Urt, that lonely church-yard on the hill where Roland Barthes lay buried.

Curving through the carless intersection of East Blenkner and South 4th Street, Ghost passed German Village's only authentic German establishment: *Juergen's Traditional Bavarian Bakery*, which was so authentically German that no one ever went there. Ghost himself had only been there once. Being wrongfooted by the bakery's strange menu, eerie vibe, and total emptiness, he had ordered a hot chocolate; his wife refused to order anything, later claiming, "that place was *creeeepy*." Its creepiness only increasing at night.

Passing *Juergen's* front door, Ghost glanced inside. In its illuminated emptiness, the interior appeared almost otherworldly: imported German foodstuffs, strange baked goods, odd decorations, old tables and chairs. The interior struck Ghost as the kind of place Friedrich Nietzsche might've frequented. This thought reminded Ghost of Stefan Zweig's description of the philosopher at mealtime:

> *Carefully the myopic man sits down to a table; care-fully, the man with the sensitive stomach considers every item on the menu: whether the tea is not too strong, the food not spiced too much, for every mistake*

in his diet upsets his sensitive digestion, and every
transgression in his nourishment wreaks havoc with
his quivering nerves for days. No glass of wine, no
glass of beer, no alcohol, no coffee at his place, no
cigar and no cigarette after his meal, nothing that
stimulates, refreshes, or rests him.

As he neared Beck Street, Ghost glanced up at the moon again. *Parallax.* Slowing his steps, Ghost allowed the darknight to encircle and *become* him. A familiar feeling began to well up in his heart. *All's ill around my heart*, a ghostly voice whispered from the grave. It was unavoidable.

FAILURE

It was happening again: he was doing it again. He was trying to understand Imagereality by understanding what Imagereality is. He knew better. **The only way to understand Imagereality is by understanding what Imagereality is *not*.**

Essay 11

Roland Barthes ♥ Annie Leibovitz?
Y or N (Circle One)

Alternative Title:
"Honey, I put the B on eautiful, don't switch it to itch,"
said the drag queen.

Carlos Spencer-Bayard had never thought about Susan Sontag's crotch before. Why would he? He was neither an ardent reader of her work nor a crotchophile. To him, crotches – even famous ones – just looked like any crotches. But here he was, staring obediently at the crotch belonging to the author of *Notes on Camp*. There was really no way to avoid it; there she was, lying spreadeaglebeagle on a clean white couch, her left hand directing the viewer's gaze towards her sleeping crotch. The image was part of an exhibition of Annie Leibovitz photographs at the Wexner Center. While dutifully trudging through the show, sleeping Susan was the first piece that caused Ghost to pause. Was she really asleep? Her pose appeared extremely uncomfortable; it looked more like she was doing Irish Yoga, i.e. she was passed out. Perhaps she had fallen asleep while reading, on the floor near the couch rested a pair of glasses atop what appeared to be a magazine. Ghost narrowed his eyes to read the magazine's cover: *Sports Illustrated's Complete Guide to the WNBA*.

[snicker, snicker]

Ghost loved making Susan Sontag jokes. Once, while drinking scotch in a bar in Portland, Maine, Ghost had been accosted by an angry Sontagian, who demanded to know how his research differed from Saint Susan's.

– It's art history, not Cultural Studies, Ghost answered offhandedly.

– Art history falls under the categorical reach of Cultural Studies, the angry Sontagian countered.

– Yeeeeah, so does the WNBA.

This was undoubtedly a rude response, but what did he care? He was already three Taliskers into the evening, and his irritation levels rose steeply whenever any conversation boofed into the swampy bog of Cultural Studies.

He liked Susan Sontag, both *On Photography* and *Regarding the Pain of Others* were referenced heavily within his Master's thesis. He admired her inquisitiveness, sensitivity, and her courage, and by this, he didn't mean her intellectual or physical courage, he meant her *photographic* courage. Being in a relationship with a photographer is brave, as there's always a camera lurking around every corner, but being in a relationship with a portrait photographer who photographs celebrities when you yourself are a celebrity is especially brave.

Returning to the crotchshot, Ghost wondered if these were the clothes that Sontag wore around the house? Had she written *On Photography* in a grey sweatsuit? Ghost knew that the poet Kay Ryan wrote in her pajamas, but he expected Sontag's housewear to be more formal. Of course, the casual housewear in which she was photographed looked much better than the outfits he wore around his apartment. Ghost grimaced thinking about an image of him asleep in his housewear appearing in a museum; in his imagination, he envisioned himself sprawled out on his couch, his baggy cargo shorts at "rapper level," i.e. lowlowlow, his socks outrageously mismatched. Ghost was weird about socks, his current sock craze being for colorful kneehighs with dunking basketball players on them, which he wore mismatched to make it appear that there was an intense game of 1-on-1 occurring on his opposing shins. But without a doubt, the ugliest article of his housewear collection was the black Hawaiian shirt that his parents had purchased for him on Captiva Island. The shirt contained quite the bestiary: rabbits, giraffes, hippos, and flamingoes all frolicking around a large, fiery whitebearded wizard, who Ghost dubbed the "Beast Master." The shirt was hideous; and still, Ghost wore it everyday. But he had strict rules when it came to his hideous housewear: he never wore any of it outside of his apartment, and he made sure to ghost out of the room whenever a camera appeared.

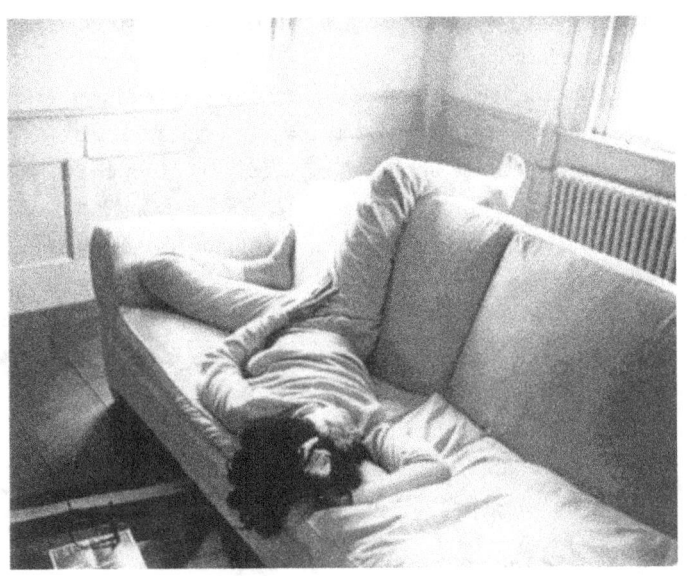

2

— Is that Patti Smith?

A group of squawkers surrounded Ghost, scrutinizing the crotchshot.

— Nope, one of the squawkers responded after reading the wall label.

— Who is it?

— Somebody named Susan Sontag.

— Who?

Move along, squawkers, Ghost thought, *no one über-famous to see here.*

Ghost had never seen the Wexner Center this crowded: rumor was that the exhibition was tripling the institution's attendance estimates. Standing directly in front of the Sontag photograph was a tiny mental oasis in the otherwise throbbing, over-crowded exhibition.

After the squawkers were gone, Ghost recalled his favorite quote from *On Photography*: "The photographer's insistence that everything is real also implies that the real is not enough." *C'mon Susan*, Ghost thought, *when has reality EVER been enough?* Humans have been augmenting reality for millenniums. Imagereality, and its accompanying daily avalanche of images, is just the latest augmentation. Reality, of course, is a drinkwater word.[9] And any offshoot of a drinkwater word is a tricky concept. Here's another example: Talkreality, also known as Squawkreality. Ghost's wife was such a squawker that she had acquired the pet name 'Rumsfeld.' Any question, no matter how mundane, was an invitation for a bewildering burst of Rumsfeldian rhetoric. For example:

Ghost: Do we need milk?

Rummy: Not if it's a large container; I can't get through an entire large container of milk by myself. It's just too much milk.

Ghost: OK... [pause] I'm making out a grocery list... [pause] Do we need milk?

Rummy: I don't know. It depends on if there's any in the refrigerator or not.

Ghost: Right... [pause] Could you check, seeing how you're holding the refrigerator door open right now?

Rummy: Of course there's milk in here. But what I don't know is when it was opened.

---

9   Drinkwater word: (adj) Any word that attempts to describe something so obvious that it renders description impossible.

At this point in the conversation, realizing that it would be impossible for his wife to either confirm or deny the fact that they did or did not need milk, Ghost rose from the kitchen table, brushed past his wife, reached into the refrigerator, shook the milk container gently, and discovered that it was nearly empty.

– We need milk... Rumsfeld, Ghost announced on his way back to the kitchen table.

In addition to Rumsfeldian rhetoric, Ghost identified two other defining features of Squawkreality: speaking *towards* people, instead of *to* them – Ghost called such interactions "press conferences" – and incessant justifications. Ghost's wife was a grand justifier; she could justify *anything*, no matter how outrageous. Squawkreality necessitates lengthy justifications: reality doesn't. Anything that exists in reality doesn't need any justification, it just is. The confusing thing about Squawkreality is that it so blatantly contradicts Nietzsche's theory "that for which we find words is something already dead in our hearts. There is always a kind of contempt in the act of speaking." Was it possible that Nietzsche was wrong? Ghost's wife certainly felt no contempt in the act of speaking; instead, the act of speaking appeared to give her great comfort. In fact, the argument could be made that she *only* felt comfort while squawking. The issue was anxiety. Ghost suspected that his wife's brain was a giant spinning wheel that created anxieties in order to control them, but these anxieties, like all anxieties, aren't real: they only exist when spoken aloud. Within Squawkreality, the act of self-overhearing is a form of self-representation: anxiety needs an audience. The same thing can be said of Imagereality. **Imagereality is an anxiety that needs an audience.** Images manufacture the illusion of control, but this is only an illusion, an unreality. And like anxiety, unreality is unhealthy: **Imagereality is unhealthy.**

3

Turning away from the Sontagian crotchshot, Carlos Spencer-Bayard ghosted up the Wexner Center's central ramp, feeling slightly bemused. Here he was surrounded by glamorous movie stars and gorgeous celebrities and all he kept thinking was: *look at all of these fucking has-beens*! **Imagereality turns everyone into a has-been**. Every image is a reminder that, visually-speaking, our best years are behind us. This realization reminded Ghost of Samuel Beckett's quote: "Perhaps my best years are gone. When there was a chance of happiness. But I wouldn't want them back. Not with the fire in me now." *Ignition*: that's what Ghost asked of an image; images should ignite a fire inside you. Most images are a cold milk bath, but a select few *ignite*. And if anyone doubted this assertion, Ghost would direct their attention to Jane Bown's photograph of Beckett himself; whenever Ghost encountered this image, he thought: *now there's an author photo*!

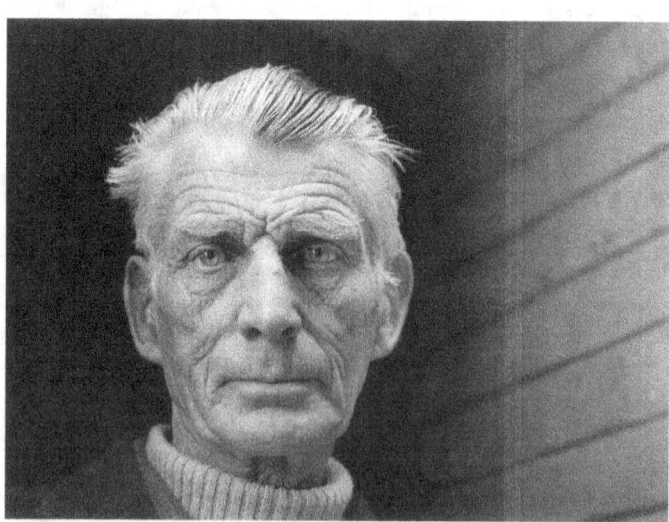

At the very northernmost end of the Wexner Center stands a large, two-story glass wall that separates the museum's calm solitude from the outside world. Because of the museum's location within The Ohio State University's campus, this wall offered unprecedented vistas of slouching college students and their neverending trudging. To class: trudgetrudgetrudge. Back home: trudgetrudgetrudge. To the bar: trudgetrudgetrudge. Back home: trudgetrudgestumbletogether. To the health clinic: trudgetrudgewince. Back home: trudgetrudgeblush. Whenever he visited the Wexner Center, Ghost inevitably gravitated towards this wallwindow. As he observed the steady trudging, Ghost wrestled with his conflicting emotions towards Annie Leibovitz. The problem with Leibovitz's photographs were that they didn't live in the world. Gorgeous celebrities? Elaborately staged backdrops? Multi-million dollar make-up? What world did these photographs belong to? Certainly not his. For one thing, his world included *darkness*. **Imagereality is a new chiaroscuro**: the lightest light against the darkest dark. Imagereality is bright and beautiful; people take photographs of things they want to see and remember, but lurking just outside the circumference of every camera's flash is the world, and the world emanates darkness.

So what would be the ideal unLeibovitzian image? The first image that leapt into Ghost's consciousness was of the singer Rihanna after she had been assaulted by her boyfriend Chris 'BeatHerDown' Brown. The story behind this image was almost otherworldly: two mega-celebrities, an exclusive pre-Grammy party, a fight *in a Lamborghini*. But the image that emerged from the assault was shockingly of *this world*. Here was an unLeibovitzian image: a celebrity unposed, unadorned, and ugly. After a moment, a second, more palatable, image materialized in Ghost's mind: Weegee's *The Critic*. The two glamorous operagoers were Leibovitzian, while the leering old drunken hag was *of this world*.

While researching the image, Ghost was surprised to learn that Weegee's image, like all of Leibovitz's work, was staged; Weegee's assistant had located the old hag at *Sammy's Bar* in the Bowery, transported her to Lincoln Center, and propped her up for the shot. Ghost was less surprised by the posed nature of the image as by the knowledge that Weegee had an assistant. *Wow, Weegee had an assistant?* Ghost thought upon learning the image's backstory, *what a shitty job that must've been.*

> *WANTED: Photographer's assistant. Must be will-*
> *ing to work all hours of the night, sleep in an auto-*
> *mobile, and bribe police officers; applicant must also*
> *feel comfortable around corpses, perpetrators of domes-*
> *tic violence, drunks, streetwalkers, homeless families,*
> *circus performers, and murderers. No prior experience*
> *necessary.*

Darkness surrounds every photograph. Ghost thought of this darkness as the *unphotographable*. The *unphotographable* is what people don't want to photograph, because they don't want to see and remember it: ugly moments of loneliness, physical abuse, drunkenness, and despair. Glancing through the George Eastman House Collection's *A History of Photography from 1839 to the present*, an imagethinker might mistakenly believe the world is a brightbeautiful place, but every so often the darkness of the *unphotographable* bursts through Imagereality's façade and a photograph captures it.

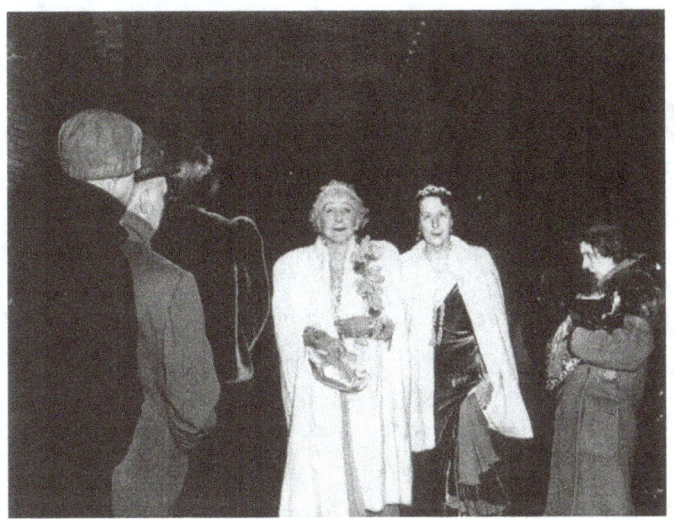

4

Slowly, Carlos Spencer-Bayard's attention turned back to the collegiate trudgeparade. It was December and a thick covering of snow whiteblanketed the ground; of course, this didn't stop students from wearing short-shorts, mini-skirts, and hoodies instead of proper winter coats. He even saw a few flip-flops, though most wore Uggs. It was Ohio: of course he saw flip-flops. The longer he observed any large group of Ohioans, the more apparent it became that he was living in a foreign country; this was an odd realization seeing how he actually *had* lived in a foreign country, and still he couldn't quite shake the sensation that he was more of a foreigner in Columbus. Who are these people? Why did they look so comfortable, so *satiated*? Why were they such slowmoving creatures; didn't they have anywhere they wanted to be? What was the deal with all those calf tattoos? Who saw those, pets? *My Miniature Schnauzer just loves your Celtic cross calf tattoo*! Why were so many people who obviously didn't do yoga – "Irish yoga" not-withstanding – wearing yoga pants? And what exactly are yoga pants? Extra long biker shorts? Extra tight Hammer Pants? And perhaps most importantly, why did everyone look so much like an eager cocker spaniel? *Love ME LoveME LoveME LoveMElove-MEloveMEloveME* the eyes of these shaggy, needy creatures plead-ed. But who were *YOU* and why did *YOU* feel so unfulfilled? Staring out of the Wexner Center's wallwindow, Ghost was struck by an overwhelming sensation of sameness, especially *on the in-side*. Without inwardness, appearance is all and calf tattoos are the verbose statements of character. **Imagereality is our interiority now.** In *Beyond Good and Evil*, Nietzsche cautioned that if you gaze long enough into an abyss, the abyss gazes back into you; the longer we stare vacantly into images, the longer Imagereality's vacancy stares into us. **Imagereality hollows us out.** *Empty/Emp-tiness*: that was a good way to describe Ghost's feelings towards Annie Leibovitz. He did not dislike her work. How could he? Her photographs were beautiful images of beautiful people. But Leibovitz's entire leviathan oeuvre was completely ignitionless. While viewing the exhibition, Ghost never could quite shake the sensation that he was flipping through a magazine at a barber-shop while awaiting a haircut. Sigmund Freud's couch... *FLIP*. Scantily clad Scar Jo... *FLIP*. Hunter S. Thompson drunk on a plane... *FLIP*. (With so much flipping, how could an imageth-inker *NOT* be flippant?) The question every image must answer is: *Who gives a damn?* Leibovitz's answer to this question was ob-vious: her images are cultural documents. As such, they are the provenance of Cultural Studies, and as Ghost had learned from reading Walter Benjamin, Cultural Studies is an exercise in *empty/emptiness*.

From *The Work of Art in the Age of Mechanical Reproduction*: "To pry an object from its shell, to destroy its aura, is the mark of a perception whose "sense of the universal equality of things" has increased to such a degree that it extracts it even from a unique object by means of reproduction."

At first glance, the connection between Leibovitz and Benjamin appeared bizarre, but upon further reflection, it made perfect sense. Benjamin had been a cousin of Hannah Arendt's first husband; when the young couple moved to Paris in 1933, Benjamin befriended the young philosopher; after Arendt relocated to New York City, she befriended a young Susan Sontag; of course, Susan Sontag – and her crotch – eventually befriended Annie Leibovitz.

The more Ghost contemplated *The Work of Art in the Age of Mechanical Reproduction*, the more he began to see Walter Benjamin everywhere in Leibovitz's photographs: posing in blueface next to John Belushi, standing diminutively next to Wilt Chamberlain, roostering on stage with the Rolling Stones; but more than anywhere, Ghost saw Benjamin in Leibovitz's images of bodybuilder/actionhero/governor/buffoon Arnold Schwarzenegger. In his imagination, Ghost saw a shirtless Benjamin smoking a cigar while astride a white horse, skiing in Sun Valley, Idaho, nakedassing around a hotel room, and wearing a snaptight blackspeedo while flexing his intellectual muscles. *Hasta la vista, Vichy*!

Although it is heresy for an imagethinker to admit this but for years, Ghost considered *The Work of Art in the Age of Mechanical Reproduction* to be nonsensical gibberish. To him, the essay appeared pertinent to every genre of art *except* photography. Ghost only began to appreciate the essay, and its pivotal sentence, upon becoming a parent. As a parent, Ghost read pages upon pages of children's literature: *Highlights* magazine, *National Geographic Kids*, Richard Scarry's *Busy, Busy World* books, Sandra Boynton's

Greatest Hits, The World of Eric Carle, Skippyjon Jones, The Gruffalo, Anna Dewdney's *Llama Llama* books; soon, Ghost's apartment was overbrimming with what he called 'the paper playground.' Many of these books and magazines were filled with not-quite/quite-shite poetry. Here was an example:

My Best Friends
by Heidi Bee Roemer

Dexter and Shelby
are warm and shaggy.
Their tongues are wet.
Their tails are waggy.
We fall asleep,
and we snooze just a little-
Dexter and Shelby
and me in the middle.[10]

With every not-quite/quite-shite poem, Ghost's appreciation for *real* poetry grew more distant. Afraid that his babyboy would grow up thinking poetry was nothing but silly rhymes and childishness, Ghost began reading Shakespeare's Sonnets out-loud to him. This was when *satori* struck: the reproduction of simple rhyming couplets in children's literature was *emptying* real poetry of its aura. Benjamin's essay had nothing to do with *mechanical* reproduction, it was concerned with production; or rather, *overproduction*. It would be easy to think that photography never possessed an aura, especially when viewing such vacuous/glamorous cultural artifacts as Annie Leibovitz's images. While traversing

---

10 *Highlights High Five*, February 2015. Never in his wildest dreams did Carlos Spencer-Bayard ever think that he would be footnoting *Highlights High Five*, or as his son called it: "*Highlights...HIGHFIVE!!!*"

the Wexner Center, Ghost found himself constantly reminding himself that photography did once have an aura, but that it had been obliterated long before he was born; in fact, photography's aura had been obliterated long before Annie Leibovitz was born; hell, photography's aura had been obliterated long before Walter Benjamin was born. Photography's aura was obliterated almost *immediately* after the first photograph was printed. When contemplating photography's auralessness, Ghost was reminded of profanity. For a small child, every "fuckbomb" is a momentous event. During his second birthday party, Ghost's littlelion recounted to his *entire* extended family how, earlier that morning, his father had said "Fuck!" when the garage door wouldn't operate properly, delighting everyone at the party, except Ghost. By the time a child reaches adolescence, "fuckbombs" have lost their aura. Of course, certain talented individuals, such as Richard Price, James Kelman, or Dick Cheney, can raise profanity to an art form, but for the majority of people, profanity remains deeply rooted in everyday utilitarian values. **Photography is akin to profanity.** Both are lighteningquick, straightforward, and slightly naughty.

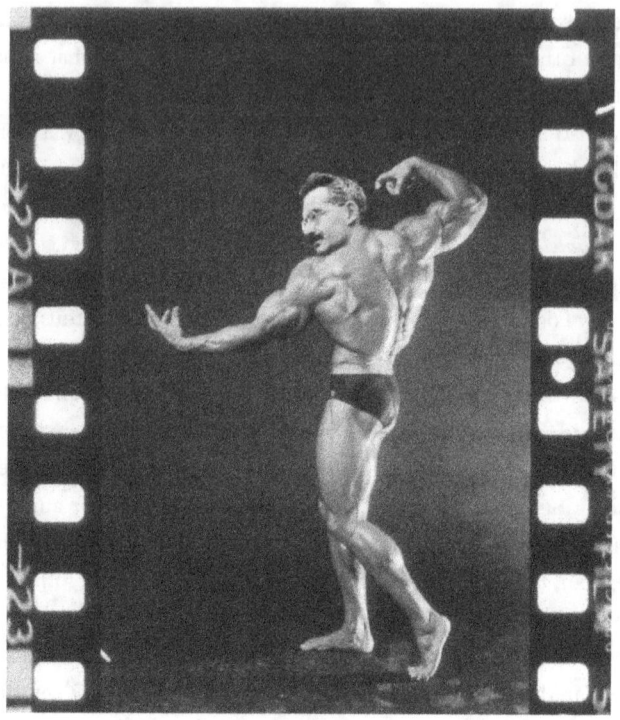

5

Turning away from the Wexner Center's wallwindow, Carlos Spencer-Bayard ghosted back into the crowd. His intention was to leave, but an image of a female baseball pitcher captured mid-pitch caught his attention. Somehow he had missed the image on his initial pass through the galleries. It was a pleasing image, nothing spectacular: southpaw, ponytail, stern concentration. The perspective was again surprisingly crotchcentric, but at least Ghost didn't see Walter Benjamin anywhere in the image. The photograph reminded Ghost of how every imagethinker has to learn how to hit two pitches: the curve and the knuckleball. The curve is the history of photography. The general mechanics of this pitch are always the same: it begins in the late 1830s and arcs into the present. Every photopitcher throws a slightly different curve; the pragmatic old-timer begins with Talbot, slopes through Muybridge and Adams, and hits the mitt with a *Struth*; the young phenom begins with Daguerre, whizzzs past Steiglitz and Stetchen, and ends with a *Wall*. To be successful, i.e. to make it to the BIG leagues, an imagethinker must anticipate what's coming and swing accordingly. Not so with the knuckleball, which is photography's relationship to reality. Once released, the knuckleball is impossible to control: its unpredictability frustrates and flummoxes. Does photography capture reality? Usurp reality? Replace reality? Augment reality? Is photography *real unreality* (Barthes)? Hyper-reality (Baudrillard)? Alien reality (Sontag)? Contemplating such questions can cause an imagethinker to fall behind in the count. Mustering up all of his strength, he takes a final sinewstretching, backspasming, bicepbulging, mightycaseyatbat swing…

STRIKE3!

Back to the dug-out, back to the minor leagues, back to the library, back to the books, back to Roland Barthes. Within the context of professional Imagereality – what Ghost liked to call the PhotoSox – Roland Barthes was the General Manager. Unlike a mere Head Coach, he was unejectable: no imagethinker can throw him out, because like Sigmund Freud, his theories are *inside us*. Being an imagethinker means having to continually come up with newclever things to say about Roland Barthes and *Camera Lucida*. Here are a few of Ghost's greatest hits:

> Similar to Hippolyte Bayard's famous *Le Noyé*, *Camera Lucida* is a self-portrait of a drowned man.

For many within {the photographic} community, Camera Lucida echoes the opening sentence of Ernesto 'Che' Guevara's published diary account of his time spent attempting to facilitate a populist revolution in the Congo: "this is the history of a failure."

Camera Lucida's confessional tone conjures up W.H. Auden's grumble about first-person poetry: "who the hell cares about Anne Sexton's grandmother?" Art historically speaking, who the hell cares about Roland Barthes' dead mother?

And here is Carlos Spencer-Bayard's newest Barthesian soundbite: **Imagereality is a form of Impressionism**. And thus, *Camera Lucida* is an *impression* of an impression of a sunset.

Impressionism is commonly thought to be a direct result of photography's invention: the two events are historically linked by the fact that the very first Impressionist exhibition was held in Nadar's photography studio on the Boulevard des Capucines. But to Ghost, Imagereality's relationship to Impressionism is less antipodal than commonly assumed. After all, what does a viewer garner from a photograph if not an *impression*? And what characterizes Impressionism – working *plen aire*, capturing the effects of light, and roughsteed speed – also characterizes photography. With every photograph, human nature is becoming more *impressionable*: Facebook is the *impression* of self, just as information is the *impression* of knowledge. Without depth, all is surface; Imagereality, like Impressionism, is all surface. Gaze long enough upon an Impressionist canvas and even the most loquacious art historian finds himself at a loss for language. You can't teach surface. You can't analyze surface. You can't delve into surface. **You surf and worship surface**. Surface worship consumes: it oozes and undermines. Face subjugates personality, as stereotypes obliterate individuality. Ignorance masquerades as knowledge, as complexity is swept aside by simplicity. The endgame for all of this consumingoozingundermining is that Existentialism (the philosophy of existence) is replaced by Impressionism (the worship of *impressions*). Existentialism exudes a fear of nothingness: Impressionism embraces nothingness with a blank stare.

Ghost used to lie awake at night thinking about Imagereality's knuckleball and why he couldn't make contact with it. In his imagination, he replayed the floating stillness of the pitch's mid-air magic. And then he didn't; the knuckleball simply disappeared, and not just from his midnight mind, it disappeared from the world.

Chivalry, cassette tapes, VCRs, ashtrays, old postcards, there is a name for such castaway junk: debris from a former age. Ghost stumbled upon this idea while reading Ernst Jünger's essay 'On Pain.' Within this essay, Jünger describes photography as an "expression of our peculiarly cruel way of seeing," and accuses the medium of standing "outside of the zone of sensitivity." Imagereality is cruel, cold, and insensitive; is it any surprise that it is capable of *murder*? **Reality is dead, Imagereality killed it.**

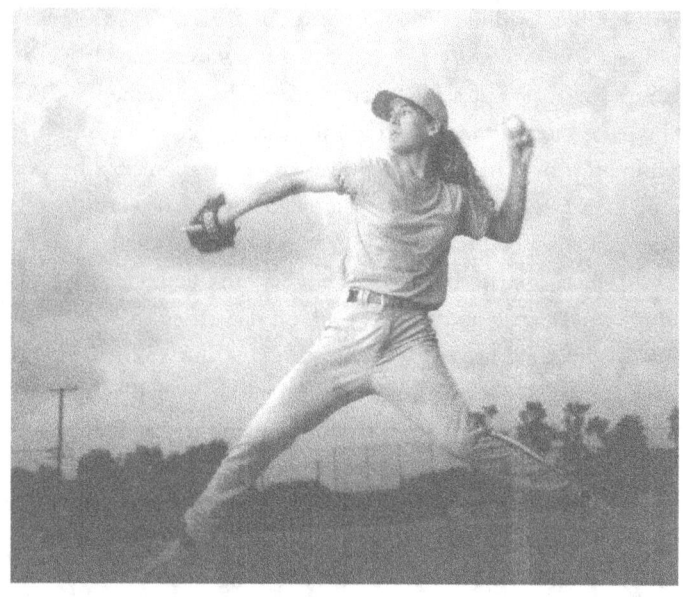

6

The final photograph in the Wexner Center's Annie Leibovitz exhibition was a close-up of President Barack Obama, but Carlos Spencer-Bayard knew that this was not the *final* image. Somewhere out in the world, at that very minute, Annie Leibovitz was taking a photograph. She would never stop, she would never retire. Unlike painters, who are prone to De Kooning-esque decline, photographers were free to click away until their dying day. Leibovitz's last photograph would be akin to an author's last words: "Here it is at last, the distinguished, unphotographable thing."

As Ghost began retracing his steps through the crowded galleries, a sudden question burst upon his brain: *What would*

Roland Barthes have thought of Annie Leibovitz? First off, Barthes detested whimsy; this immediately negated the majority of the exhibition, as whimsy was Leibovitz's *spécialité*. [STRIKE1] In *Camera Lucida*, Barthes also admitted to not being fond of color, saying: "I always feel (unimportant what actually occurs) that... color is a coating applied *later on* to the original truth of the black-and-white photograph." Leibovitz's seductive surfaces were like a chic kind of visual culture couture. [STRIKE2] So where was *punctum* to be found? Contemplating this question, Ghost paused in front of Leibovitz's portrait of a naked Keith Haring standing atop a coffeetable in the middle of a drab living room. Everything in the room, including Haring's naked body, was covered in the artist's signature sloppy graffiti scrawl. Haring's painted penis may have caught Barthes' attention, but Ghost seriously doubted that it would have qualified as *punctum*; after all, the word *punctum* is Latin for 'prick.' [Grimace] A little too obvious, *n'est-ce pas?*

The Wexner Center is strangely subterranean. As he ascended the institution's central staircase and surged into the bright-white wintersun, Ghost promised himself that he would return to the question of what Roland Barthes might have thought of Annie Leibovitz. But at the moment, he had other things on his mind. Carlos Spencer-Bayard was *thirsty*. Imagereality often made him thirst... for absinthe.

7

WHAT WOULD ROLAND BARTHES THINK? was a game Carlos Spencer-Bayard enjoyed playing immensely. *C'est vrai*, at first glance, Ghost might not have appeared very qualified for such a game – he was neither French, a homosexual, nor a Man of Letters – but over the years, Ghost had devised a clever technique for imitating the philosopher's perspective: absinthe.

Of course, Roland Barthes was not an absintheur, but Ghost felt that he should have been; absinthe was his birthright, but because of the liquor's global ban, Barthes had been robbed of the spirit. Devoid of *la fée verte*, Barthes found solace in a "new form of hallucination": *la photograph fée.*

   Imagereality and absinthe were intertwined in Ghost's mind during a particularly brutal winter spent in Portland, Maine. As the cold months piled on top of each other like snow on a parked car, Ghost decided to begin drinking absinthe again and bought a bottle of Lucid Absinthe Supérieure[11]. Drinking absinthe by himself in the middle of a snow-globe, Ghost questioned if his absinthe experience could be any less romantic. Yes, absinthe was again a presence in his life – he had procured his first bottle from Prague at the tender age of twenty-one – but associated with this presence was also a profound feeling of *absence*. Ghost didn't feel like he was celebrating absinthe: he felt like he was mourning it. At the time, he was reading Roland Barthes' *Mourning Diary*. One evening, greenglass in hand, Ghost stumbled upon the following sentence: "We don't forget, but something *vacant* settles in us." Within this sentence, Ghost heard echoes of Nietzsche's warning about gazing too long into an abyss. With Imagereality, viewers are able to indulge in the *impression* of presence, but this impression is an untruth. **Imagereality marks absence**. To mistake presence for absence is the very definition of a hallucination. With the invention of Imagereality, a great *absence* was released upon the world. While contemplating Imagereality's relationship to absence, *satori* struck. In his review of the Salon of 1859, Charles Baudelaire remarked, "an idolatrous mob... rushed, Narcissus to

---

11   Distilled in France using Ted Breaux's recipe, Lucid was the first absinthe to become legally available in the United States after the ban was lifted on March 5th, 2007.

a man, to gaze at its trivial image on a scrap of metal." The result of this mad rush was that "a madness, an extraordinary fanaticism took possession of all these new sun-worshippers." Baudelaire continued, ridiculing this mob of "mad fools" and mocking their belief that photography gave "every guarantee of exactitude that we could desire." Although he enjoyed Baudelaire's fiery rhetoric, Ghost never felt like he fully understood the poet's denouncement of photography, but now it made sense; of course Baudelaire hated photography, Baudelaire was an absintheur. Ghost had a name for the conflict between absinthe and photography: *joie de vivre* versus *joie de screen*. Strangely enough, he felt that absinthe was more *real* than photography. How could a photograph capture the spectrum and intensity of human existence? Unlike *la fée verte*, photography promises nothing but exactitude, and only a mad fool would believe that exactitude is a reliable guarantee of reality. Reality is a creation of the human mind: exactitude is created by a machine. Absinthe affects the mind by filling it with green-splendor: photography only entertains the eye. Absinthe liberates the mind: photography seeks to incarcerate it within a perspectival prison. With every photograph, thought becomes the slave of sight. **Images are idols.** Like all idols, images exist solely to be worshipped. But every act of worship is a vacant stare. Life is a turbulent swirl, how can it be comprehended with a vacant stare? Absintheurs are raconteurs: photographeurs are grunting mutes who communicate through images. Such communication is not a conversation, it is a slide lecture. As a result, to quote Susan Sontag, "our heads are becoming like those magic boxes that Joseph Cornell filled with incongruous small objects whose provenance was a France he never once visited."

Leaping French artists, grappling grapplers, Parisian puddle pouncers, Ellis Island immigrants, gorgeous toilets, beach-going headstanders, awkward author photographs, mountainous moonrises, babyjesuses, photoshopped felines, sleeping sirens in sweatsuits, chiseled Irish chaps, gay operagoers and heckling hags, ponytailed pitchers, migrant mothers, deadspanish soldiers, Iwo Jima, Hiroshima, Che Guevara... we don't forget, but something *vacant* settles in us.

There were only two images in the Wexner Center's exhibition that didn't leave Ghost feeling *vacant*. The first was *Celo, Bosnian army commander, Sarajevo, 1993*, and the second was the 2003 portrait of Susan Sontag that became the author photograph for *Regarding the Pain of Others*. Both images were sobering: adding to the second image's poignancy was the fact that it was Leibovitz's final portrait of her favorite model. **Photography is a solitary, sober endeavor.** As such, it is unabsinthe. *La fée verte* cannot be captured in a photograph, while photography is immune to the green fairy's charms. For one to live, the other had to die. Without absinthe, the world was vulnerable to photography's slavish devotion to exactitude. **The birth of the photographer was the death of the absintheur.**

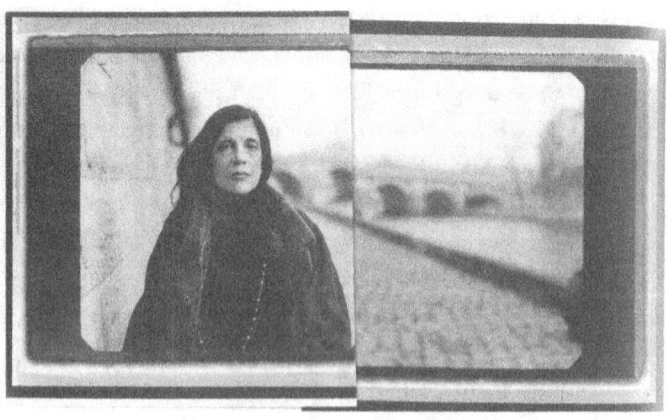

8

Feeling mentally fagged out, Carlos Spencer-Bayard lifted himself from the kitchen table, refilled his greenglass, and ghosted over to the couch. His preferred couchsitting position was very unSontag: he lay flat, his right leg perfectly straight, his left leg bent at the knee. Over the past hours, he had grown weary of Annie Leibovitz's *unreal, unintoxicating, unrecognizable* world. On the floor nearby, a thick tome of Eugene Atget's photographs beckoned: Ghost often enjoyed Atget's imagery while drinking absinthe. Picking up the book, Ghost began flipping. What he savored most about Atget's work was the sensation of being a photo-flâneur lost on the streets of turn-of-the-century Paris.

FlipFlipFlipFlipFlip

His mind began to wander...

[an imaginary *à gauche* at *l'angle de la rue de Seine et de la rue de l'Échaudé…*]

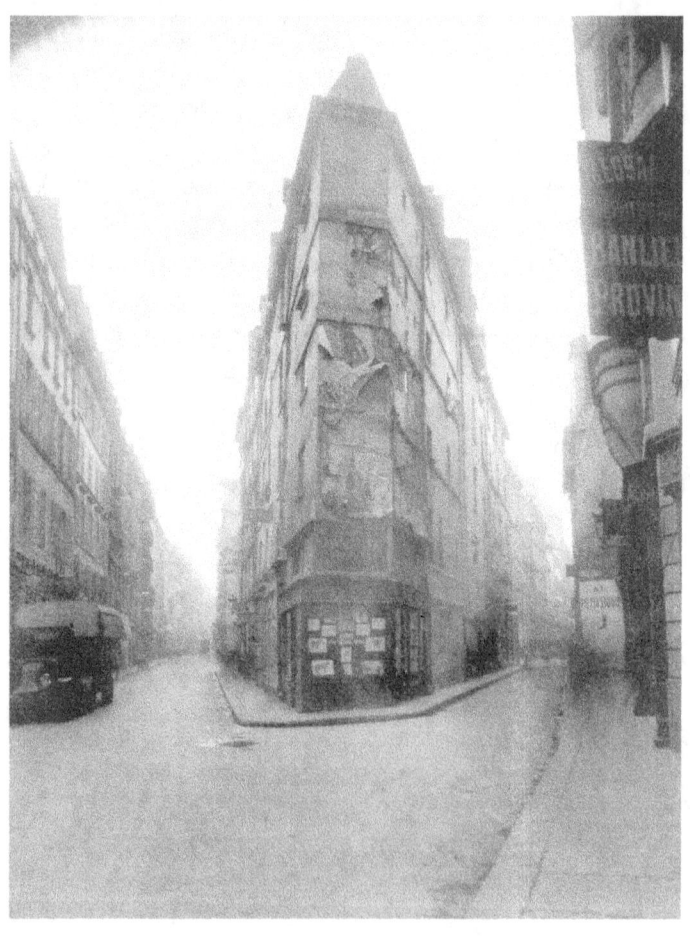

[an imaginary *à droite* at *Rue Pigalle*...]

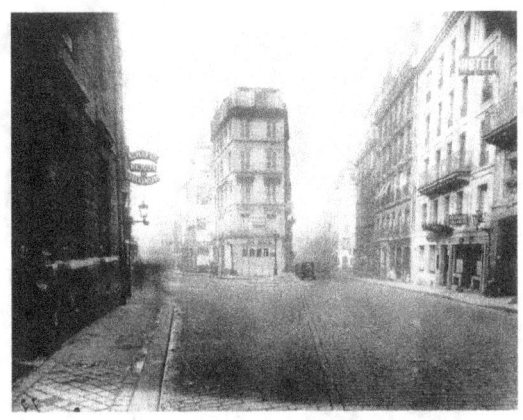

{*marche passé le Pavillon de Hanovre, construit par le maréchal de Richelieu en 1760, 33 boulevard des Italiens*...}

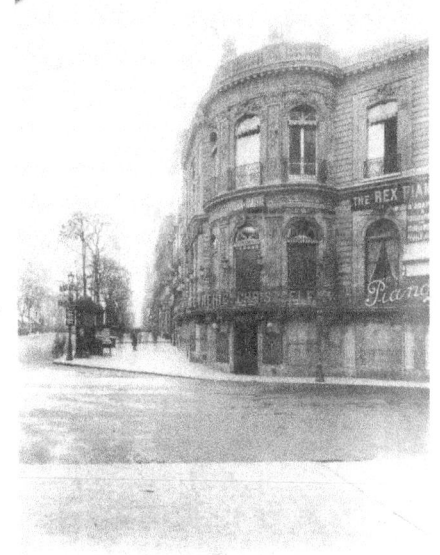

[*et voilà...*]

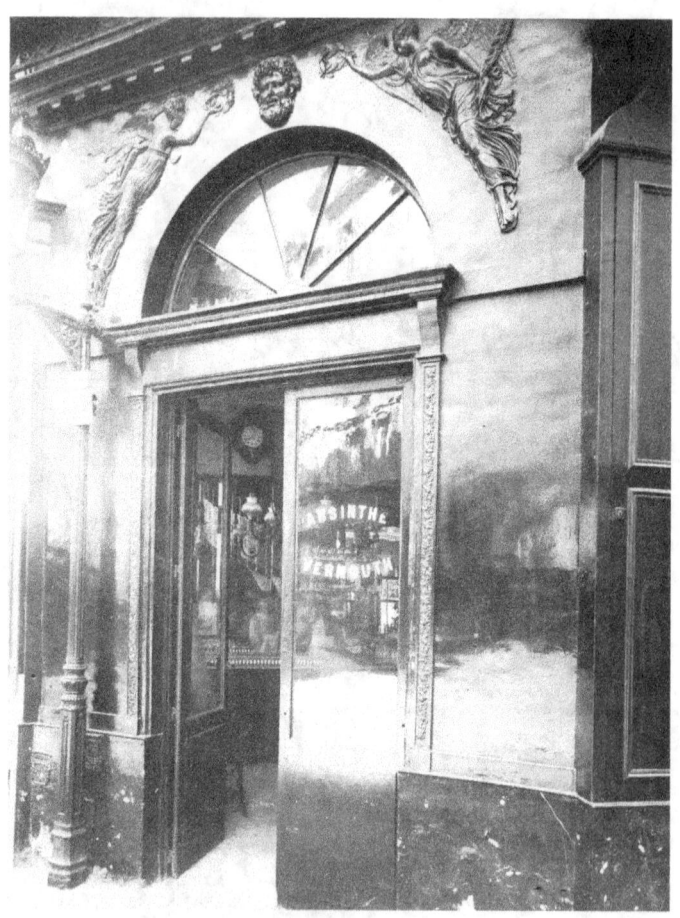

Absintheaven!

As his imagination strolled the deserted Parisian streets, Ghost felt that old familiar feeling: *FAILURE*. He was doing it again: he was *chasing* and nothing more. And once again, like a predictable plot twist in a mindless action movie, he had gotten himself lost, while his illusive prey got away – the villains' clichéd departure on a perfectly timed helicopter ladder. Imagereality cannot be understood through images: understanding Imagereality means *turning away* from images. *Camera Lucida*'s *overtakelessness* is a direct result of *turning away* from images. The second section of the book centers on an image of Barthes' mother, known as the Winter Garden Photograph, which the author refused to reproduce in the text. It is a frustrating omission, but then again, *Camera Lucida* is a frustrating text. Because of Barthes' refusal to reproduce the image, the Winter Garden Photograph has become the most oxymoronic of objects: the sacred photograph, the unphotograph *par excellence*.

The Winter Garden Photograph haunts *Camera Lucida*. It is impossible NOT to doubt whether the photograph ever existed; Barthes may have misremembered the image, or he could have conjured up the whole damn thing. Ghost once encountered the outlandish suggestion that Barthes had mistakenly confused the photograph with a photofamous image of four-year-old Franz Kafka. Since, in all his years wrestling with Imagereality, Ghost had never once seen a reproduction of the Winter Garden Photograph, he simply assumed that the photograph had either been lost over time or destroyed after the book was published. And since he never expected to see an image of the Winter Garden Photograph, Ghost was shocked to stumble upon a reproduction of it in *Mourning Diary*. *Sacrebleu*! There it was, the unphotograph, hanging haphazardly between a picture of a house and a gaggle of camels. It did exist!

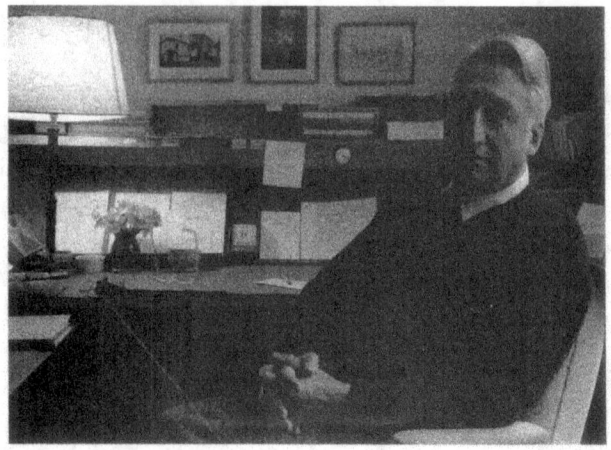

Roland Barthes at his desk in Paris, April 25, 1979. On the wall, three frames:
the house in Urt (left, reproduced in this edition); a picture of camels (right);
and the picture of Barthes's mother at age five in the Winter Garden (center).
This last photograph is discussed in *Camera Lucida*. (© François Lagarde)

9

As a former art preparitor, Carlos Spencer-Bayard often cri-
tiqued other people's picturehanging abilities, and the more he
scrutinized the image of the unphotograph, the more cringeworthy it became. Had Barthes himself hung that triptych? It looked
awful: the entire group wasn't centered between the lamp and the
corner, the photographs themselves weren't centered on each other, the spacing between each image was off, and finally, the whole
damn thing was crooked. Crooked photographs were as visibly
pleasing as wallmounted plumber's crack. *Arrgh*! What an utter
disaster! And this is to say nothing of the images themselves:
a photograph of your childhood home, a baby picture of your
mother, and a bunch of camels? [*Huh?*] Ghost suspected that the
flanking two photographs were afterthoughts, hung only to fill

the space: the bereaved author only had eyes for his mother. The only thing that made sense from the triptych was the placement of the Winter Garden Photograph: directly over the center of the desk, so Barthes could write while gazing upon the image. As if to reinforce this point, a single index card and a pen rested quietly on the desk.

What was written on that index card? Consulting his copy of *Mourning Diary*, Ghost discovered that there was no entry for April 25, 1979; in fact, there were no entries for that entire month. The closest entry was from March 29, 1979. It reads:

> *I live without any concern for posterity, no desire to be read later on (except financially, for M.), complete acceptance of vanishing utterly, no desire for a "monument"- but I cannot endure that this should be the case for maman (perhaps because she has not written and her memory depends entirely on me).*

At the bottom of the page, Ghost noticed a footnote for this entry: *The writing of Camera Lucida begins after this date; at the book's end, the dates of the text's composition are noted: "April 15-June 3, 1979."*

According to legend, Roland Barthes wrote one section of *Camera Lucida* per day. If this is true, on April 25, Barthes would've written the book's tenth section. His curiosity rising, Ghost consulted his copy of *Camera Lucida*, flipping to the book's tenth section.

Sacrebleu!

The tenth section of *Camera Lucida* outlines Barthes' famous *studium/punctum* divide. *Studium* is a "kind of general interest" in a photograph; "it is by *studium*," Barthes confesses, "that I am interested in so many photographs, whether I receive them as political testimony or enjoy them as good historical scenes." *Punctum* is any element within a photograph that disturbs the *stadium*; Barthes describes *punctum* as an "element which rises from the scene, shoots out of it like an arrow, and pierces me" and "that accident which pricks me (but also bruises me, is poignant to me)."

So that's where Roland Barthes wrote Camera Lucida, Ghost thought, scrutinizing the desk. He noted the small, tasteful vase of flowers and the tiny round clockface. *April 25, 1979.* Ghost was the same age as his littlelion; his wife hadn't even been born yet and neither had the internet, Photoshop, digital cameras, cellphones, Facebook, Flickr, Snapchat, or Instagram; and this is to say nothing of the rise of digital film, the death of analog, inkjet printers, glossy gossip magazines, hacked celebrity cellphone nudes, or the ability to order copious amounts of coffee mugs, teeshirts, and key chains adorned with personalized photographs from Shutterfly. Ghost smiled envisioning Roland Barthes drinking lukewarm oolong tea out of a mug emblazoned with the Winter Garden Photograph.

"Aging, this slow suicide." [sipsipsip]

Closing his eyes, a question crept into Ghost's consciousness: Was *Camera Lucida* debris from a former age? Was the cornerstone of imagetheory a charming relic? A period piece? A Polaroid camera? That old familiar feeling returned. Was the collective failure to understand *Camera Lucida* due to the fact that imagethinkers were looking for answers in the wrong place? As David Foster Wallace counseled, perhaps the book needed to be approached obliquely and defined in terms of what it was not.

Up from the couch...

Out the front door...

No more thoughts for Annie Leibovitz, no more glamour.

Left towards Fourth...

Pass beneath the canopy of neighboring Sycamore trees...

Glance skyward.

It was a dark, cloudless coldnight. The streets were wet and quiet: the moon shone luminously. *Parallax*. Two sentences from *Camera Lucida* materializing in his mind: he knew them well.

> *I would have to descend deeper into myself to find the evidence of Photography, that thing which is seen by anyone looking at a photograph and which distinguished it in his eyes from any other image. I would have to make my recantation, my palinode.*

10

Screeeeeeeeeeeeeeeeeech… **BANG!**

The front door to the South End Tavern announced Carlos Spencer-Bayard's arrival. For a straight bloke, walking into a dive-y gay bar is never **NOT** awkward, but the awkwardness increases tenfold if he happens to walk in while a drag show is in progress, which is exactly what Ghost did. Thankfully, the performer's attention was not focused on the door, but rather on a bachelorette party seated near the stage.

– Now don't get me wrong, sweetie, the drag queen was passive-aggressively purring. I *LOOOVE* straight people. I *LOOOVE* straight people as much as straight people *LOOOVE* comfortable shoes. Without straight people, honey, poor old *Payless* would go out of business!

Ghost grimaced. While he didn't shop at *Payless*, he refused to wear anything but comfortable shoes.

– And I *LOOOVE* weddings, the drag queen continued. Going to a wedding is like going to a **NASCAR** race: everybody's drunk, sitting on they ass watching a whole lot of nothing, and just hoping to see a **CRASH**! And are these pretty bitches yo' bridesmaids? I knew it! Now, how many of you pretty bitches are married? Let me see a show of hands... [gasp] I was right, you ARE some bitches!!! O Lord, look at that! Didn't none of you bitches tell this sweet, innocence girl about marriage? Y'all just gonna throw her in with the wolves, ain't you? OF COURSE, YOU ARE!!! Good for you!!! Didn't nobody tell you about marriage, right? Am I right? OF COURSE, I'M RIGHT!!! I know ALL about marriage. First rule of marriage: don't talk about marriage. Second rule of marriage: DON'T TALK ABOUT MARRIAGE!!! O yes, sweetie, that's a quote from a movie and it ain't *Casablanca*: the name of THAT movie is *Fight Club*. But it ain't like all marriages are bad. What's the name of that Hollywood troll with the big ass?

– YOU? a voice heckled from the darkness.

– PUH-*leeee*se, baby! I'm trying to do a show here. Don't be shouting out dumb shit: this ain't the Republican National Convention. Now, everybody knows that I have a big ass, but I'm twice the size of your average Hollywood troll. I'm a BIG woman. If you want to be with me, you better have BIG things: a BIG car, a BIG house, a BIG bed, a BIG "yes sir." Ya'll know what I'm talking about, I ain't gotta spell it out, do I? [pause] OK, I'll spell it out... W...O... [pausing suggestively with her mouth agape]...W. If any of you choirboys in the crowd tonight got BIG things, after the show, just come along to my undressing room. Miss Bride, does your man have BIG things? I hope so, because the BIGGER his BIG is, the BIGGER yo' half is going to be someday. KIM KARDASHIAN!!! That's that Hollywood troll's name! Just look at her and that big stiff dumpy old Kris Humphries. They got married and now they're both as happy as can be!

Ghost enjoyed drag shows for a number of reasons; first, he found drag queens hilarious and he felt infinitely more comfortable around them than regular homosexuals, who he just found confusing. Willful childlessness, gay or otherwise, confused him. To Ghost, the childless were like three-legged dogs: they *appeared* happy, blissfully unaware that they were missing something *essential*. Would *Camera Lucida* be less confusing if it wasn't so gay? Ghost was convinced that the only reason Barthes included Alexander Gardner's portrait of Lewis Paine awaiting execution for his role in the assassination plot of Abraham Lincoln and his cabinet was because he deemed the doomed Paine a hottie; in other words, he exhibited high Shteyngartian fuckability. This also explains why Ghost thought Barthes would've enjoyed Annie Leibovitz's *Celo, Bosnian army commander, Sarajevo, 1993*. Photography and fuckability: could the two ever be separated?

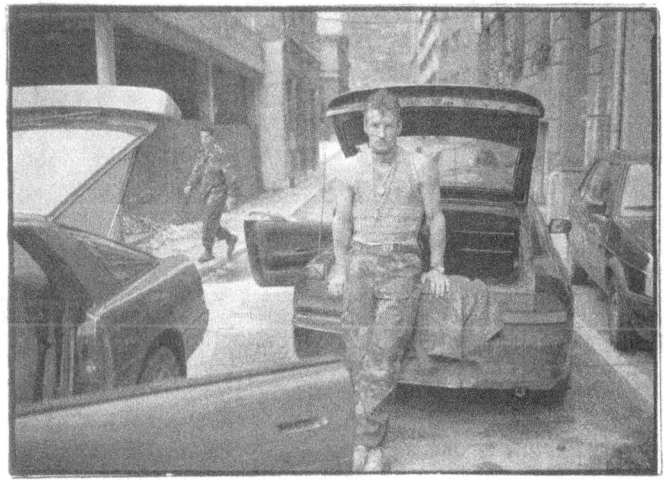

The second reason Ghost enjoyed drag shows was that they reminded him that one of Michel Foucault's definitions of madness was *dazzlement*. Drag shows exude *dazzlement*. There is also a great deal of *dazzlement* within Imagereality: people get dressed up and *perform* for the camera. In this sense, every image is a little drag show.

And finally, drag shows always struck Ghost as peculiarly Shakespearesque, as there was something undeniably drag about all of Shakespeare's female characters, especially Cleopatra. This is what makes the Sonnets so unique within Shakespeare's oeuvre; the Fair Young Twatwaffle could've easily been a character out of one of Shakespeare's early plays, but the same cannot be said of the Dark Lady with the Hellvagina: she is strictly nonfiction. As a Sonnetologist, Ghost was fascinated by the Dark Lady with the Hellvagina, but he cared less about who she was – her true identity is inconsequential – and more about what she did: she *shattered* Shakespeare. The Bard, who knew so much, was apparently blindsided by the intensity of erotic destruction. After this *shattering*, there was a crack in everything Shakespeare made. Friedrich Nietzsche experienced a similar *shattering* in the fall of 1882. Soon thereafter, he began writing *Thus Spoke Zarathustra*. It is entirely possible that Nietzsche would've written the book had Lou von Salomé not *shattered* him, but most likely it would've been a much different, much less painful text. Ghost thought the same thing could be said about Shakespeare's tragedies: he probably would have written them had the Dark Lady with the Hellvagina not *shattered* him, but they most likely would not have been so *shattering*.

The Droeshout Portrait of Shakespeare graced Ghost's copy of the Sonnets, but in his imagination, he replaced this image with Nietzsche's 1882 carthorse photograph. The Shakespeaker is Nietzsche, mischievously leaning into the arrangement that had been *his* idea in the first place; the Fair Young Twatwaffle is Paul Rée, handsome and somewhat stiff; the Dark Lady with the Hellvagina is Lou von Salomé, ready to lash her loving admirers. Without a doubt, there is something *mad* about the photograph. Six months after this photograph was taken, Nietzsche was *shattered*.

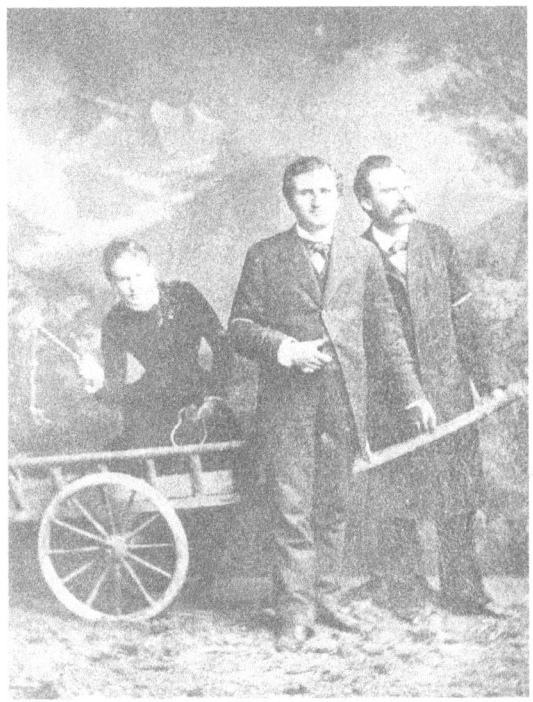

11

— What are you writing, sweetie?

— Just an essay on photography.

— Don't believe him, a voice came booming down the bar. All balls! He's writing something with a bite in it.

Ghost glanced up from his scrawlsheet to recognize an abrasive, yet convivial drag queen named Contessa (nicknamed: Cuntessa) seated near him around the bar's curve.

– O, I might like that. My name is Dorothy, sweetie.[12]

– Be careful, Dorothy, he's going to put us all in it, Cont/ Cuntessa continued. Me, you, and Tits McGee.

– O, I'm not sure all of me would fit into a book.

– He'll squeeze you into it, just like you squeezed into that dress.

– O Cuntessa, you bitch! [Dorothy put a hand over her mouth in mock shock] This dress is a perfect fit. The only thing that fits me better is oxygen.

– Like how it fills up a balloon?

– O, you're dreadful! [Turning back to Ghost] What do you think, sweetie? Is it too tight in the back.

[Spins around]

– It looks nice.

– He's not interested. He's just being polite, Cont/Cuntessa continued. He'll put whatever he really thinks into his essay.

– Well then, honey, put this into your essay, too: I put the B on eautiful, don't switch it to itch.

– How the hell would he ever put *THAT* into an essay on photography?

– O, he'll *squeeze* it in, that's how.

Like reality, *dazzlement* is a drinkwater word: it only speaks to what is dead in our hearts. Nietzsche would not have been a fan of drag queens. In *Ecce Homo: How One Becomes What One Is*, he warned "beware of all picturesque men!" which is a quote Ghost often recalled while scrolling through his Facebook feed. In January of 1889, *dazzlement* became Nietzsche's reality. It is almost as if he wrote his madness to life. A similar thing occurs in the Sonnets; as the sequence nears its conclusion, the word *madness*

....

12 If you ever meet a drag queen over the age of fifty, there's a 90% chance her name is Dorothy.

begins to appear with alarming frequency, culminating with the declaration:

> *And frantic mad with evermore unrest;*
> *My thoughts and my discourse as madmen's are*

Within *Camera Lucida*'s final two sections, some variation of the word *madness* appears fourteen times. Imagereality begins where *Camera Lucida* ends. The urge to capture something as undeniably elusive as reality is *madness*. Imagereality creates a wedge between itself and reality; in other words, contrary to prevailing opinion, Imagereality unmoors our connection to reality, offering not an exact replica of the world, but rather a haunting hallucination. And what begins in madness is destined for failure. **Every image begins in madness and ends in failure**. And since this is the curveship every image must travel, it is also the trajectory that every imagethinker must travel, since wherever images go, imagetheory must follow.

12

[Outside]
Overhead, a stirring of birds stirring a poetic memory.

> *i have found what you are like*
> *the rain,*
> *(Who feathers frightened fields*
> *with the superior dust-of-sleep. wields*
> *easily the pale club of the wind*
> *and swirled justly souls of flower strike*
> *the air in utterable coolness*
> *deeds of green thrilling light*
>
> > *with thinned*

> *newfragile yellows*
>
> > *lurch and.press*
>
> *-in the woods*
>
> > *which*
>
> > > *stutter*
>
> > > > *and*
>
> > > > > *sing*
>
> *And the coolness of your smile is*
> *stirringof birds between my arms...*[13]

Leaving the South End Tavern always made Carlos Spencer-Bayard uneasy. It was located in a rough neighborhood and Ghost was sure that any potential hate-criminals would be unmoved by his defense: "I'm not gay; I just go there for the *dazzlement*!"

To calm himself as he walked towards his apartment, Ghost repeated the opening lines to the E. E. Cummings poem, while continuing to contemplate Imagereality:

> *i have found what you are like*
> *the sea*

Ghost once penned an essay on photography that began: "The sea, the sea, the scrotumtightening sea. Photography is not simply all we see: photography *is* the sea."

> *i have found what you are like*
> *the unsun*

Imagereality is nothing like the sun. Its illumination is not *real* illumination: its enlightenment is not *real* enlightenment. It emits no warmth, no heat. Imagereality radiates nothing but a confusing, controlling darkness. **Imagereality is a black sun.**

> *i have found what you are like*
> *the birds*

---

13   Spellcheck HATES E. E. Cummings.

Since they live in the world, images resemble living organisms; thus, Imagereality is less a convergence of ideas and more a convergence of, say, birds. While living in Brooklyn, Ghost used to watch one of his neighbors train pigeons from the roof of his tenement building.

The birds, still stirring.

Glancing skyward, Ghost remembered his favorite passage from *A Portrait of the Artist as a Young Man*, altering it slightly in his mind as he walked:

> *What images were they? He stood on the steps of the library to look at them, leaning wearily on his ash-plant. They flew round and round the jutting shoulder of a house in Molesworth Street. The air of the late March evening made clear their flight, their dark darting quivering bodies flying clearly against the sky as against a limp hung cloth of smoky tenuous blue.*
>
> *He watched their flight; image after image; a dark flash, a swerve, a flutter of pixels. He tried to count them before all their darting quivering bodies passed: Six, ten, eleven: and wondered were they odd or even in number. Twelve, thirteen: for two came wheeling down from the upper sky. They were flying high and low but ever round and round in straight and curving lines and ever flying from left to right, circling about a temple of air.*

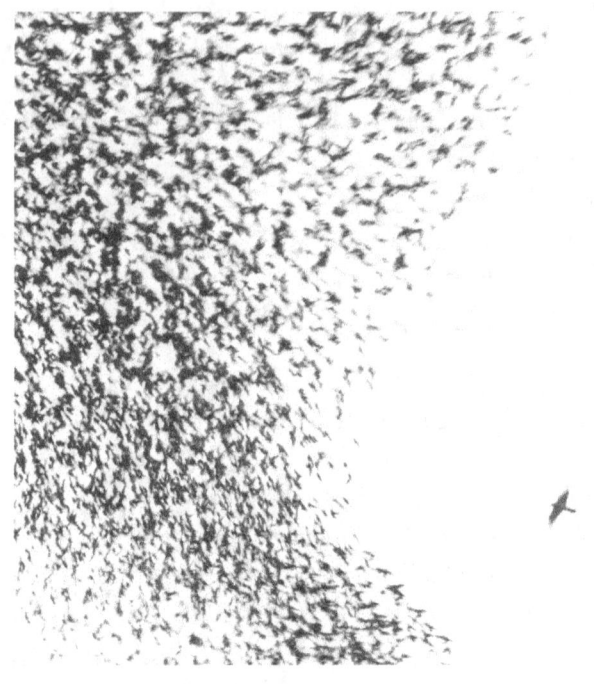

13

Dark was still the darkstillnight, the darting quivering birds were still dartquivering, and the moon was still *parallaxing*. Carlos Spencer-Bayard drunkenly drank in the darkness. The *dazzlement* was gone: all that remained was the lightless night. Pausing on his front porch, Ghost lowered himself so that his head rested lightly against the front door. A single word dartquivered through his restless mind: *endlessnessnessness*. The word was one of his favorite portmanteaus from the Bible of portmanteaus: *Ulysses*. In Sirens, while dining at the Ormond Hotel, a melancholy Leopold Bloom concludes a meditation on the soaring final notes of Simon Dedalus' rendition of the title song from Friedrich von Flotow's opera *Martha* with the word *endlessnessnessness*.

> *i have found what you are like*
> *Ulysses*

The connection between Joyce's magnum opus and Imagereality did not surprise Ghost, as the novel was one gigantic photographic panorama of what Joyce himself called "Dublin's street furniture." And yet, there is a difference: between 1880 and 1910, a Dublin photographer named Robert French, working for William Lawrence of O'Connell Street, took thousands of documentary photographs all over Ireland, including the façade of the Ormond Hotel.[14] French's photograph depicts what the hotel *looked like*: Joyce's poetry – Sirens is often mentioned as the most beautiful chapter in *Ulysses* – portrays what it *was like*. **Imagereality is unpoetry.** It cannot sing. From poetry's perspective, reality is enough; unlike Imagereality, poetry does not seek to become *total* reality.

[Grimace]

There was that word again: *reality*.

And here was Susan Sontag again: "the photographer's insistence that everything is real also implies that the real is not enough."

C'mon Susan, Ghost thought, *this is America*. Being American means *never* having to acknowledge limits: not to appetite, ambition, consumption, geography, power, income, the list is endless. *Limitlessness* is everywhere in American culture: car commercials, urban sprawl, gentrification, corporations, skyscrapers, the internet. *Limitlessness* rocketfueled the Space Race, paved the interstates, and underwrote America's most cherished cultur-

---

14 In 1942, the National Library of Ireland, another setting for a chapter in *Ulysses*, acquired the forty thousand glass plates of what is now known as the Lawrence Collection.

al clichés: from sea to shining sea, the American Dream, Stars and Stripes *Forever*. Imagereality plays an indispensable role in America's quest for *limitlessness*. The invention of photography may have been a French Revolution – *Liberté, égalité, photographié!* – but Imagereality is a strictly American enterprise. The connection between American culture and photography also occurred to Roland Barthes, as near the end of *Camera Lucida* he mused: "consider the United States, where everything is transformed into images: only images exist and are produced and are consumed. An extreme example: go into a New York porn shop; here you will not find vice, but only its *tableaux vivants*."

If the ancient Hebrew Blessing can be translated as "more life into a time without boundaries," the new blessing offered by Imagereality is "more images into a time without end." Yet there is something terrifying about *endlessnessnessness*, as whatever is endless can never end. Every day, thousands of new images must be birthed into the world: newspapers must have photo-journalism; magazines, glossy pictures; screens, content; books, author photos; albums, cover art; museums and galleries, exhibitions; art schools, students; Facebook, minute-by-minute minutiae; Twitter, tweets; Snapchat, naked selfies, sexting, naughtiness; and everything else must have advertising, advertising, *ADVERTISING*! Imagereality cannot end because it is required to sell things, explain things, amuse, entertain, entice, inform, arouse, and delight; the individual merit of these images themselves doesn't matter, as today's images will be washed away by tomorrow's. The *existence* of images is their primary importance. **Imagereality is industry.**

14

Because of its *endlessnessnessness*, essays on Imagereality are notoriously difficult to end. Imagethinkers aren't stupid: they know that today's imagetheory will be washed away by tomorrow's. Here is how *Camera Lucida* ends:

> *Mad or tame? Photography can be one or the other: tame if its realism remains relative, tempered by aesthetic or empirical habits (to leaf through a magazine at the hairdresser's, the dentist's); mad if this realism is absolute and, so to speak, original, obliging the loving and terrified consciousness to return to the very letter of Time: a strictly revulsive movement which reverses the course of the thing, and which I shall call, in conclusion, the photographic ecstasy.*
>
> *Such are the two ways of the Photograph. The choice is mine: to subject its spectacle to the civilized code of perfect illusions, or to confront in it the wakening of intractable reality.*

Cryptic shit, Carlos Spencer-Bayard thought as he watched the moon disappear behind the fluff of a fastcrawling cloud.

A whisper, a reminder: "You more have to come at the aesthetic stuff obliquely, to talk around it, or – as Aquinas did with his own ineffable subject – to try to define it in terms of what it is not."

Photography is a way to obliquely discuss something else, thus whenever people talk about photography, they are inevitably both talking about photography and not. *Camera Lucida* is no different. This explains why the book is so enduring; it's not about photography, it's about desire. The same thing can be said of the Sonnets: no matter how much suffering he is forced to endure, the Shakespeaker refuses to renounce his desire for either the Fair Young Twatwaffle or the Dark Lady with the Hellvagina; the sequence ends, the desire does not. Nothing exhibits more *endlessnessnessness* than desire.

15

The birds were gone now. Where did they go? To another tree, another neighborhood, another temple of air. As he stared out into the birdless sky, Carlos Spencer-Bayard realized that his posture perfectly mirrored that of the doomed hottie Lewis Paine in the photograph that Roland Barthes found so captivating.

Poor bloke, Ghost thought. *Bet on the wrong horse.*

Would Paine have avoided execution had John Wilkes Booth not been such an obsessive Bardolator? Five months before he shot the President, Booth performed alongside his brothers in a production of *Julius Caesar* to raise funds for a Central Park statue commemorating the three-hundredth anniversary of Shakespeare's birth. *Julius FUCKING Caesar*! The Bard *contaminated* the bold assassin, overbrimming him with desire. Poetry and desire: they were as inseparable as photography and fuckability. And just like in *Julius Caesar*, the conspirators hung together: Gardiner was there for that too.

Screeeeeeeeeeeeeeeeeeeech... **THUD**! the gallows groaned.

[Heavy curtain]

Photography is fleeting. Like people, places, and presidents, photographs come and go, as the unblunted lion's paws of Time devour us all. Proceed with passion, for without passion, photography makes ghosts of us all.

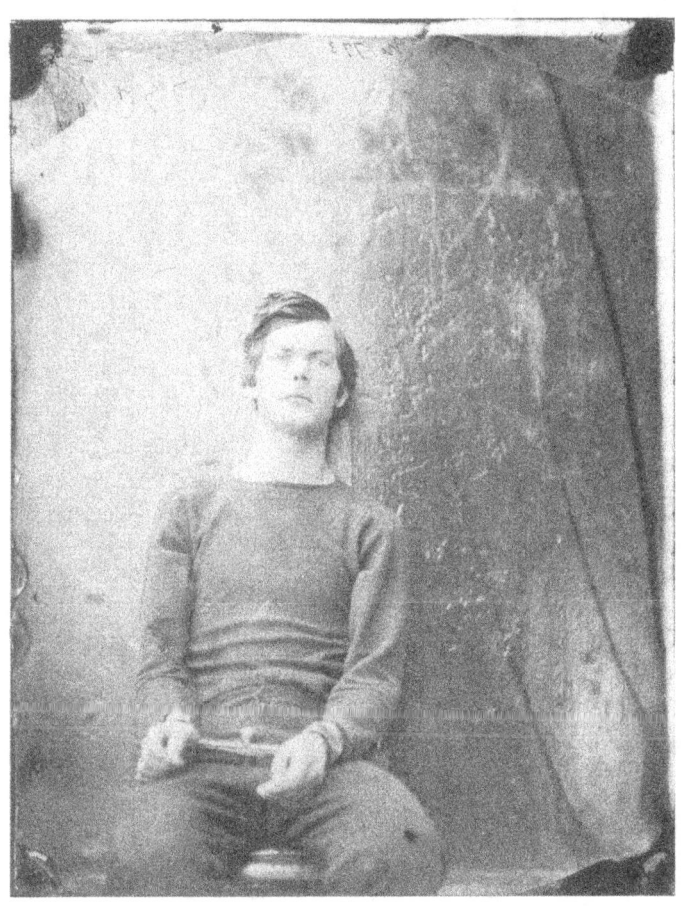

Essay III

ClockHead

Alternative Title:
Reflections on watching thirty-two hours of
Christian Marclay's *The Clock*

No one ever called Carlos Spencer-Bayard. This lack of tele-phonic communication was not because he was friendless, unpop-ular, or a bad conversationalist: he simply didn't like talking on the phone. For years, he had systematically ignored every phone call he had ever received. He ignored phone calls from family members, friends both drunk and sober, Denison University's te-nacious Alumni Fund, an aggressive bevy of telemarketers ped-dling a cornucopia of crapola, fundraisers for causes both worthy and dubious, and numerous political organizations and/or third party candidates whose petitions he had gleefully signed, will-ingly filling in his real phone number, knowing full well that he would never answer his phone when they called to follow-up and solicit funds; he also ignored phone calls from his bank, doctor, dentist, local library, and a host of property managers and landlords; and while he could never be sure about this because they refused to leave voicemails, Ghost also suspected that he had ignored hundreds (no: thousands) of phone calls from old girlfriends asking (no: begging, no: *pleading*) for him to take them back. Most recently, he had been ignoring phone calls from a pleasant, yet feebleminded-sounding old woman who kept mistakenly calling his phone number and leaving confused voicemails for someone named Stephanie.

Ghost ignored telephone calls to such an extent that he once changed his voicemail greeting to: "Hi. You've reached Carlos. I'm probably ignoring your call, but please don't take this as a personal insult: I'm phonephobic. Why not text me? Or better yet: email me." But after listening to this message on automatic playback, he decided that it made him sound too much like an A-hole, so he changed it back to his usual greeting: "Kia ora. This is Carlos. Leave me a message." Yes, this greeting was impersonal and perhaps perfunctory to the point of being banal, but he assumed that the combination of his first name and his Maori greeting would be enough to ward off wrong numbers, but after the recent spate of "Stephanie" messages, he was beginning to doubt this.

Another reason why Ghost decided to change his voicemail greeting back to his usual, boring message was because he wasn't entirely sure that his claim of being "phonephobic" was accurate: he had never been diagnosed by a licensed medical practitioner. He suspected that the reason for this diagnostic failure was because phonephobia didn't exist: he might have just made it up. The fact that no one ever questioned whether or not "phonephobia" actually existed did little to quell his doubts: Ghost suspected that his friends and family were too nice to nitpick his obvious behavioral quarks. Deep in his consciousness, Ghost even suspected that the human frontal cortex was biologically conditioned to never question any word ending with the suffix-*phobia* or -*phobic* (Had anyone ever questioned James Joyce's many phobias?) To test this theory, he had begun casually inserting the word "phallophobic" ("fear of dicks") into barroom discussions of celebrity lesbian couples.

Years of phonephobic behavior had finally yielded the desired result: Carlos Spencer-Bayard's phone had gone blissfully silent. So when his phone did happen to ring, like it did on this particular January morning, it was with quite the shock. This shock was more than just the casual surprise of an unaccustomed, unrecognized sound; years of phonephobia had resulted in the unintended side-effect that every seldom time Ghost's phone now rang, it filled him with deep dread. Why would anyone call a notorious phonephobe, if not to impart some kind of horrible news, like death, disfigurement, dismemberment, defenestration, or disembowelment? So now, whenever his cell phone began ringing, Ghost's first thought was: *who's disemboweled now?*

Bee dee da dee leedeedee DEE…

Bee dee da dee leedeedee DEE…

Why was his cell phone ringing on a cold Tuesday morning in January? Carlos Spencer-Bayard grimaced. In his mind, he envisioned the awkward exchange that was sure to occur if he made the mistake of answering his phone.

- Kia ora. This is Carlos.

- What?

- Kia ora.

- Key or what?

- No. Kia ora. It's a Maori greeting. It means "hello."

- Is this Carlos?

- Who else do you know answers his phone with a Maori greeting?

- O right, sorry. Hey, Carlos, I'm sorry to have to call you, but have you heard the news about [INSERT the name of a close friend, family member, college roommate, or high school basketball teammate]...

- No.

[Awkward pause]

- He's been disemboweled.

[Grimace]

- I'm so sorry to hear that. Is there anything I can do?

- He needs a bowel transplant, and we were wondering...

- *ME?*! You're asking *ME?*! Do you know anything about my bowels? If you did, I'm pretty sure no one would want my bowels...

The thought of somebody asking him for a bowel transplant sparked a rapid-fire burst of snickering, which momentarily quelled his rising dread.

Bee dee da dee leedeedee DEE...

Bee dee da dee leedeedee DEE...

His phone was still ringing...

Continuing to snicker, Ghost glanced over at his phone's message pad. *Unrecognized number.* This was a relief, as it meant that it was most likely a stranger who had been disemboweled. But then he noticed that the call was coming from the local 614 area code. [Grimace] A call coming from the local area code meant that if someone he knew *had* been disemboweled, it was most likely an extremely close friend or family member.

What a shame, Ghost thought, still ignoring the call. *That's no way to live, I tell ya. No way to live... gutless and all.*

Or the call could be for Stephanie. Impossible to know. When in doubt, best to just let the call go to voicemail.

None of this would have warranted much attention except for the fact that as Carlos Spencer-Bayard was snickering over the idea of casual disembowelment and deciding to ignore his cell phone on that January morning, he was also in the process of changing his six-week-old littlelion's diaper. As he was careening his neck to read his cell phone's message pad, he was simultaneously holding both of his son's softplump lumpy legs (or as he called them: his hammies) aloft by their ankles. And this would not have warranted much attention either except for the fact that, at that very moment, Baron von Fussmeister shot a "liquid missile" that traversed gravity's rainbow and splashed squarely onto his face. Of course, as his attention was focused on his cell phone, Ghost never saw this missile take flight, nor did he observe its direct hit. But he didn't have to: the lionroaring was enough to convey what had just happened.

As the "lion's roar" turned into the "teradyctla's cry," Ghost quickly looked down upon his son's now-urine soaked, redangry face.

"Shit!" he exclaimed.

Carlos Spencer-Bayard was not the kind of parent that shied away from swearing in front of his children. He saw nothing wrong with instilling the value of a good, well-timed cathartic curse word. In fact, Ghost found it odd when people didn't swear in times of stress; for example, the Book of Job. Why wasn't this distressing narrative as vulgar as your typical Martin Scorsese movie?

Job: Boils? *FAACK!* I'm *faacking FAACKED!*

Job's Wife: Are you still *faacking* maintaining your *faacking* integrity? Curse God and die, you boily *FAACK!*

This imaginary biblical conversation made Carlos Spencer-Bayard begin to snicker again. As he was snickering, he was aware that his son was still screaming and his phone was still ringing.

"SHIT!" he said again, with rising urgency.

Acting quickly, Ghost changed his son's diaper without further incident. He then used a damp gauze pad to tenderly wipe off his son's face, being sure to remove the glowing drop of urine that dangled from his earlobe like a gaudy hoop worn by a jaunty pirate. Once his face was dry and his diaper secure, Ghost scooped up the wailing infant and gently, yet firmly, pressed him to his chest. This action was meant to both soothe the child and muffle the screaming. As the screaming lessened in intensity, Ghost began bouncing the baby gently up and down in what he hoped was a pleasing manner.

And still, his phone continued to ring. The ringing phone and the wailing baby making an atonal, agonizing duet.

Carlos Spencer-Bayard decided that there was nothing he could do now: the call would just have to go to voicemail. This decision did not displease him in the least, as it was highly unlikely that he would have answered the call in the best of circumstances.

His cell phone sufficiently ignored and his son sufficiently attended to, Ghost casually detached his mind from the unpleasant particulars of his current situation and began his usual mental routine for calming himself during times of parental stress: composing a list of every player who had played for either the Chicago Bulls or the Los Angeles Lakers under head coach Phil Jackson. Other than the obvious (Michael Jordan, Scotty Pippen, Kobe, Shaq, etc.), this list included: Dennis Rodman, Luc Longley, Toni Kukoc, Bill Wellington, Bill Cartwright, Bison Deli (the nutcase formally known as Brain Williams), Steve Kerr, John Paxson, Brian Shaw, Rick Fox, Devean George, Samaki Walker (who Ghost had played against in high school), Derek Fisher,

Mark Madson, and Ron Harper (who had played for both the Bulls and the Lakers).

To be honest, Ghost had never been much of a fan of either the Chicago Bulls or Los Angeles Lakers; in fact, he cared very little about either franchise. He simply enjoyed reciting their rosters because, ever since the birth of his son, he had begun self-identifying with Phil Jackson. Within this identification, Ghost's wife was Kobe Bryant (young, headstrong, unyielding, and distrustful of teammates), while his son was Shaquille O'Neal (loud, jovial, gregarious at times to the point of irritation, and in need of constant attention/coddling.) His job as Phil Jackson was to exert a calm, zen-like presence. He often thought about this presence as he walked around his apartment with a stiff-legged gait, doling out advice that teetered dangerously between tantric wisdom and self-help nonsense. If such behavior was necessary for sculpting a successful basketball team, why should it be any different for a marriage? If the "Big Aristotle" and the "Black Mamba" could coexist, why couldn't his own apartment be an oasis of peaceful tranquility?

> *Bee dee da dee leedeedee DEE…*
> *Bee dee da dee leedeedee DEE…*
> *FAACK!*

His cell phone was still ringing!

His Phil Jackson meditational trick obviously not working, Ghost refocused his mind. He had *another* mental activity that calmed his mind during times of parental stress: Bardolatry. While continuing to slowbounce his wailing baby, Ghost tried to remember all of Shakespeare's plays in correct chronological sequence starting with… (he always picked one at random)… that charming stinker *The Merry Wives of Windsor.*

O that was a tough one!

Okay, here goes: *Henry IV (Part Two), Much Ado About*

Nothing, *Henry V*, *Julius Caesar*, *As You Like It*, and *Hamlet*. (After *Hamlet*, the progression was easy.)

As a curious circumnavigator of what James Joyce called the "Great Shapesphere," Ghost thought about Shakespeare nearconstantly, turning the topic over in his mind like a child playing with a wetpebble. As a Bardologist, what attracted him was the shape of ideas, rather than their weight. Anti-Stratfordian conspiracies? Post-Structuralism? Feminist fury? Ghost had no interest in such cumbersome, crookbacked concerns: what he was after was the kind of small strangebeauty that could be carried around in your pocket. For example, why wasn't everyone's favorite Shakespeare play printed on their driver's license? (His would read: HT: 5'10, WT: 165, HAIR: black, EYES: blue, PLAY: *Othello*.) And why was everyone so obsessed with learning other people's sexual orientation, as opposed to their favorite Shakespeare play? (*Coriolanus?* Now *THAT'S* queer!) And, in *The Western Canon*, why had Harold Bloom compared Shakespeare's "lackluster life" to Wallace Stevens? [Grimace] *Wally Stevens?* Yes, professionally-speaking, the comparison was valid, as both writers were successful businessmen; but Ghost doubted that Stevens was touched by Shakespearean fire, the defining feature of which was not its creative radiance, but its consuming destructiveness. What had Wallace Stevens ever destroyed? A pair of cufflinks? A starched shirt? Ghost enjoyed thinking of Shakespeare as more akin to Michael Jordan: both men came from rural upbringings, which they never quite left behind; both were shrewd in business, savvy in friendship, and ultra-competitive (Ben Jonson was the Bard's Karl Malone); in appearance, both were stable, loving familymen [*wink, wink*]; both exhibited a strange fondness for hoop earrings (yes, that earring in the Chandos portrait may have been a later addition; if so, who thought *that* was a good idea? *Sure, it's a nice painting, but you know what it needs…*); both men were emotionally shaken by the death of their fathers and ghostfathers (Shakespeare's ghostfather was Marlowe; Jordan's, Len Bias); and far from flamboyant, both men cultivated a cool disinterested-ness, which was so diamondtough that they were often perceived as being boring. Another wildly popular play? Another wily gamewinner? It was like they were sleepwalking, but this sleep-walkingness was a façade: the consuming destructive creativefire that raged inside both men burned deep below the surface. While it was unwise to allow yourself to be *touched* by Shakespearean fire, being near such fire, in small increments, could be enjoyable. Again, according to Harold Bloom, Shakespeare was "someone with whom you could have a relaxed drink." Ghost could easily envision himself having such a drink with Michael Jordan; hav-ing a drink with Wallace Stevens sounded *dreadful*, as he would surely have droned on for hours about Life Insurance.

The thought of having a drink with Michael Jordan sparked a moment of *satori*.

Charles Oakley!

Had Oak Tree played for Phil Jackson, or had he been trad-ed to the Knicks before the "Gray Mamba" became Head Coach? Ghost couldn't remember. And where exactly in Cleveland had Oakley been born? Maybe he should Google Charles Oakley…

Bee dee da dee leedeedee DEE…

Bee dee da dee leedeedee DEE…

FAACK!

His phone was *STILL* ringing!

How many rings did it take for his voicemail to pick up? It had been so long since anyone had called him, let alone left him a voicemail, that Ghost had forgotten. He was not even entire-ly sure that he had ever programmed such information into his phone. Why would he? Since it was common knowledge that he never answered his phone, he assumed it was also common knowledge that he never returned calls. What was the factory preset on the number of rings before a call went to voicemail? Ghost had no idea. Fifty? One-hundred? Did the person who was calling him think he was in another state? Ghost imagined himself answering the call, breathless: *"Hi…*[Hhu Hhu]… *Sorry…* [Hhu Hhu]… *I had to run to get the phone…* [Hhu Hhu Hhu Hhu]… *I WAS IN PENNSYLVANIA!"*

[Silence]

The sudden cessation of both the ringing phone and the wailing baby left a violent silence, a reverberating absence of reverberation. A moment later, Ghost heard a loud *beeeeep*, which he assumed was an indication that a voicemail had been received. After this loud *beeeeep*, his phone returned to its usual deep slumber.

For Carlos Spencer-Bayard, one of the most bizarre aspects of parenthood was how much it magnified the elasticity of time. Activities that would routinely only take a moment or two, like washing a dirty dish or checking a voicemail, had to be put off *for hours*.

The sun had already been swallowed by the horizon when Ghost was finally able to check his voicemail to determine who had been so insistent about calling him earlier that afternoon. When he did so, he made a surprising discovery; actually, he made two. The first was that he still had a saved message on his phone from his dentist. How long had that message been there? Most likely, a long time, seeing how he couldn't remember the last time he was forced to endure a dental check-up. Ghost half-expected that his new voicemail was also from his dentist's office, but when the message leapt to life, he was greeted by an unfamiliar female voice. The voice's unfamiliarity was magnified by the fact that the message was garbled by a bad connection.

"Hi. This is a message for Carlos [*garble, garble*]… My name is Zoey [*garble, garble*]... I work for Ohio State University's Urban Arts Space [*garble*]... Twelve months ago, [*garble, garble*]... a job as an art preparitor [*garble, garble*].... hired someone else [*garble*]... resume on-file [*garble, garble*]... another opening [*garble*]... If interested [*garble, garble*]...Hired [*garblegarblegarble*]... start next Thursday..."

As Ghost's facial expression went from total bewilderment to sheer befuddlement to absolute dumbfoundry, the message garbled on, ending with the recitation of both a phone number and an email address.

When the message was over, an automated female voice spoke to him:

Press 1 to hear your message again. Press 2 to save. Press 3 to...

Pressing 1, Ghost suffered through the garbled message for a second time; this time, at the end of the message, he wrote down both the phone number and email address on the back of an envelope.

Press 1 to hear your message again. Press 2 to save. Press 3 to...

Before the automated female voice could finish, Ghost silenced his phone and gently placed it on his kitchen table. Behind this table stood a large group of windows whose strange shape always reminded Ghost of the Ghent Altar. One panel opened onto a narrow metal balcony that overlooked his landlord's tiny backyard. In Real Estate-speak, his apartment was a "carriage house." This phrase sounded oddly quaint, even regal: Ghost preferred to describe his living arrangement as "living over somebody else's garage." Had it not been winter, Ghost would have been staring down into the gentle, illuminated shimmerings of his landlord's pool. But as it was January and the pool had been drained and covered, Ghost found himself staring instead into a dark rectangular tarp that was held tightly in place by taunt plastic cables. On top of this tarp rested a light dusting of snow mingled with tiny, crystalized cobwebs of frozen water. Even in the peak of summer, his landlord's pool really wasn't much of a pool. To say that somebody was in possession of a pool instantly conjured up images of suburban grandeur, but this pool was small, tasteful.

[Grimace]

Perhaps not the best choice of words.

Tasteful hinted towards ingesting mouthfuls of water, and Ghost was hesitant to swim in his landlord's pool, much less accidentally drink from it. This was a profound statement coming from a man notorious for nightswimming in every available body of water, no matter how dirty or disreputable. Contemplating his nightswimming history, Ghost felt his mind floating away, as if carried by a gentle tide: Seneca Lake, Salt Fork, Lake Michigan, Lake Erie, Judges Bay, Waitamata Harbor, Torpedo Bay, Lake Lucerne, Casco Bay.

The tide turned, and Ghost began thinking about all the places in the world that he had never nightswam: Loch Ness, the Ganges River, the River Spey, Lake Silvaplana, whose waters licked the Zarathustra Rock as they had once licked Nietzsche's naked flesh (yuck, not a nice thought!), the poetically-named Lake Pontchartrain, the silly-named Lake Titicaca, Lake Taupo, the stretch of the Cote d'Azur where philosopher Dominique Janicaud had died of cardiac arrest after his morning swim (oh, another not nice thought!), Walden Pond, the Cambridge City Park Duck Pond, Great Salt Lake, Sandy Hook, Hurricane Sandy, Sandymount Strand. Wait, did people actually swim at Sandymount Strand, or did they just go there to have a go? He wasn't sure. Maybe he should Google that. Ghost knew that Stephen Dedalus refused to swim at Forty Foot Gentlemen's Bathing Place because he was a hydrophobe. Was Joyce a hydrophobe? Ghost couldn't remember. He knew about the author's cynophobia (fear of dogs), which he doubted anyone ever questioned; cynophobia was a pretty easy phobia to explain, especially in a country famous for those godawful ugly wolfhounds. But what about Joyce's keraunophobia (fear of thunder and lightning)? Surely, some people must've thought he made that one up.

Carlos Spencer-Bayard smiled. As a keen observer of the strangemotion of his own mind, he knew exactly what he was doing: he was trying to avoid thinking about the voicemail he had just received. He found the prospect of having been hired for a job that he had neither applied for nor interviewed for unsettling. It had only been forty-eight hours since he had started his current job, which technically was not a job. Until forty-eight hours ago, Carlos Spencer-Bayard had never spent any substantial amount of time with a child of any age, let alone an infant. Upon learning that his wife was pregnant, Ghost quit his job and spent the next seven months driving her to various doctor appointments, unexpected hospital visits, and numerous tests. When his wife finally returned to work, he did not. Did he want another job, a *real* job? Not particularly. But like any good Midwesterner, Carlos Spencer-Bayard felt that jobs were sacred; when you were offered one, you shouldn't refuse.

Exhaling loudly through his nose, which is what he did whenever he felt that life was imposing itself unjustly upon him, Ghost decided that he would call Zoey back and request an interview for the job that he hadn't applied for and didn't really want, but apparently already had. Of course, he would make this call during non-business hours, so he didn't have to actually talk to her. He would simply leave a message on her voicemail; he would then follow-up with an email, mentioning how email was the most reliable way to contact him.

In the meantime, Ghost decided it would be a wise idea to start prepping for a potential interview. A good place to start, he decided, was to refresh his knowledge of current exhibitions around town; if nothing else, such knowledge would make for good small talk. Snapping open his iPad, the first website Carlos Spencer-Bayard visited belonged to the Wexner Center for the Arts. And there it was: Christian Marclay's *The Clock*, on view January 27 – April 7, 2013. He would like to say that he couldn't believe his luck, but in reality, he could.

Carlos Spencer-Bayard's first exposure to *The Clock* came from a short review in the *New Yorker* by Peter Schjeldahl. After watching an hour and a half of the video at Paula Cooper Gallery, Schjeldahl declared himself "not an expert, just an enthusiast." Since he was living in Portland, Maine at the time and the piece was being exhibited in New York City, Ghost casually tossed *The Clock* into his ever-expanding mental accordion-file of intriguing works of art that he would probably never see in his lifetime. Because he found this repository so depressing to think about – "Hey, next time I'm in St. Petersburg, I should stop into the Russian State Museum to view Ilya Repin's *Bargehaulers on the Volga*!" – he tried not to spend too much time contemplating it.

Almost exactly one year later, a profile on Marclay by Daniel Zalewski appeared in *The New Yorker*. This time, there was a glimmer of hope. Near the end of the article, Zalewski recounts an exchange that occurred at the opening of White Cube's new Bermondsey gallery between Marclay and Sherri Geldin, the director of the Wexner Center. In this exchange, Geldin presses Marclay for permission to exhibit *The Clock*, citing the fact that the artist had already executed a clock piece for the Wexner Center back in 1990. "So you need to finish what you started!" Geldin playfully goads the reluctant artist. After reading this exchange, *satori* struck: Ghost was going to be able to view *The Clock* after all. The Wexner Center is nothing if not tenacious. At times, the tenacity of the WEX (as the institution is lovingly referred to by everyone in Columbus, except Carlos Spencer-Bayard) borders on the kind of desperation most commonly associated with single thirtysomething females.

This was not the first time Carlos Spencer-Bayard had said something slightly unflattering and/or downright rude about the Wexner Center; in fact, he had quite the history. When the institution bestowed the 2012 Wexner Prize on the notoriously profligate photographer Annie Liebowitz, he had decried the act as a "Bernanke-sized bailout," and denounced the accompanying exhibition as "too boring to fail." And in terms of a permanent collection, he was very vocal in his opinion that the Wexner Center was dwarfed by the New Concord Post Office. (Each institution owns only a single work of art, and the New Concord Post Office's mural *Skaters* by Clyde Singer is vastly superior to Maya Lin's *Groundswell*.)

Part of Carlos Spencer-Bayard's displeasure with the Wexner Center was purely semantic. He firmly believed that creative institutions should be named creatively: they shouldn't share a name with local hospitals. Just imagine the displeasure of suffering cardiac arrest, leaping into a cab, instructing your driver to take you to the Wexner Center, and ending up gazing into a rather banal, blueish pile of recycled automotive glass strewn with fallen leaves and garbage instead of an echocardiogram. And imagine how boring the artscape of the country would be if *every* museum was pedantically named after its primary donor: MoMA would be the Abby Aldrich Rockefeller Adamantine Ladies Museum; the Cleveland Museum of Art would be the Hinman Hurlbut Hall of Art; and the Museum of Contemporary Art, Los Angeles would be the Eli and Edythe Broad Art Museum, which, incidentally, *is* the name of a museum in East Lansing, Michigan. But now that the Wexner Center was bringing *The Clock* to Columbus, Carlos Spencer-Bayard vowed to never say another derogatory word about the institution.

With the exhibition opening in less than two weeks, Ghost didn't have much time to prepare. On their website, Ghost noticed that, once a month, the Wexner Center was scheduled to stay open all night to allow visitors the opportunity to view *The Clock* in its entirety. Using a calculator and a crude sketch of a clockface, Ghost calculated that he would be able to watch the entire twenty-four hour loop by viewing it in three hour increments during normal business hours and four hour increments during the museum's extended hours. In further preparation for his clockwatching, Ghost read everything he could find on both the work and the artist. What surprised him the most during his research was how every reviewer announced how long he or she had watched *The Clock*. Such announcements were so frequent that they appeared to be a prerequisite for writing about *The Clock*. According to his research, the undisputed heavyweight champion of ClockHeads was Zalewski, who watched *The Clock* in its entirety, mostly in Yokohama, Japan. The number one contender for the crown appeared to be novelist and photography theorist Geoff Dyer. In a short column in *Time Magazine*'s "The World's 100 Most Influential People" issue, Dyer announced that he had watched twenty hours of *The Clock* when it debuted at the White Cube gallery in London. By Ghost's estimation, the bronze medal for clockwatching went to Roberta Smith of the *New York Times*, who watched approximately six hours of the video at Paula Cooper Gallery. All three of these reviews could aptly be described as glowing; in fact, the grandiose title of Peter Bradshaw's review on *The Guardian*'s film blog summarized the praise that Marclay's video routinely received: "*The Clock*: the masterpiece of our times." (High praise indeed, especially considering that Bradshaw only watched an hour and forty-five minutes of the video at the Hayward Gallery in London.) Striking a similar hifalutin tone on the *New Yorker*'s film blog, Meghan O'Rourke hailed the video as "a signature artwork of our archival age." (O'Rourke logged an hour and a half at Lincoln Center, before she had to rush off to a doctor's appointment.) In all of his research, Ghost only unearthed one negative review. In this review, *New Yorker* film critic Richard Brody dismissed the work as a "mediocre, even trivial" spectacle. After watching two hours, Brody's major complaint was that Marclay "doesn't seem to love the movies."

Every review Ghost read struggled with the same thing: how to describe *The Clock*'s relationship to time. In fact, the topic popped up so frequently that, whenever a reviewer started pontificating on time, in the back of his mind, Ghost heard the chorus to Tom Waits' song of the same name.

"Time is the form and content, and, above all, the material" of all films, *The Clock* included. (Roberta Smith)

And it's Time, Time, Time...

The Clock exhibits an "obsessive preoccupation with the materiality of time." (Meghan O'Rourke)

And it's Time, Time, Time...

The Clock is a "provocative inquiry into the nature of time." (the Wexner Center's brochure)

And it's Time, Time, Time that you love...

"Adding the dimension of time infused Marclay's wit with drama." (Daniel Zalewski)

And it's Time, Time, Time.

As an experienced museumgoer, something felt amiss about all this timetalk. Never did art reviews mention the length of time that the reviewer spent in an exhibition. Why would they? Such mundane mathematics were irrelevant to the act of viewing a work of art. So why was every reviewer of *The Clock* so preoccupied with time?

Carlos Spencer-Bayard was intending to ponder this question on the eve of the exhibition's opening, as he poured himself a dram of Ardbeg and stretched his body across his comfortable softbrown couch. His wife and littlelion were asleep in the bedroom. But when he attempted to think about *The Clock*'s relationship to time, he discovered that his mind was tired and uncooperative. Complicating matters was the fact that it was Bobbie Burns Day, and he had just finished a dinner of haggis, neeps, and tatties. Ghost felt his thoughts slacken, as a cloud of *brainfogfag* descended upon him. Instead of contemplating the complex intertwining of time and creativity, Ghost found himself thinking about old Rabbie Burns.

Why did he love celebrating Bobbie Burns Day so much? He was not of Scotch descent, nor had he ever been particularly charmed by Burns' poetry. The answer to the question was simple, yet strange: he was hooked on haggis. He had first sampled the oft-disparaged delicacy while visiting the "most Scottish city outside of Scotland": Dunedin, New Zealand. The city was so Scottish, in fact, that it could boast of having a Bobbie Burns statue located in its very center. Ghost had been photographed seated on a park bench underneath this statue, looking, according to his mother, "very professorial." Only steps from this statue, along George Street, Ghost found a Scottish importer, and there in the window he had happened to notice a tiny, handwritten sign announcing: "Haggis available." Having recently read about haggis in *The New York Times*, Ghost couldn't resist the temptation. That evening, he cooked the gigantic sausage-on-steroids in the communal kitchen of his hostel, and found it was surprisingly delicious. If done properly, haggis bares a faint resemblance to stuffing; if done improperly, it tastes like taking buckshot in the face from Dick Cheney. The worst haggis he had ever sampled had been served at the Scottish Society of Southeastern Ohio's Bobbie Burns Celebration, where the "great chieftain o' the pudding race" arrived on his plate in a thick slice that resembled meatloaf. Even more disturbing than its size and shape was the haggis' odd gray color, which made Ghost suspect that the dish had been cooked years prior and kept in a dusty cupboard for *auld lang syne*.

Ghost found it humorous that his hankering for haggis predated his love of scotch. His first taste of haggis had been enjoyed with Wild Turkey. Only much later in his life did he swerve away from bourbon and beer. This year's Bobbie Burns Day selection, Ardbeg, was solid, but not spectacular. After years of drinking Caol Ila, Ghost's palate had gravitated away from Islay and ensconced itself in the Northern Highland region. Highland Park sat at the top of his list of favorites, just as it sat at the top of Scotland itself. Talisker, the "volcanic red" that came in the beautiful blue box, was a close second. After these two, Ghost favored Edradour (Perthshire), and Glen Garioch (Aberdeenshire). Rounding out his list of favorites…

SHIT!

He was supposed to be contemplating *The Clock*. Taking another sip of Ardbeg, Ghost focused his mind on the relationship between time and the experience of art.

As an activity, time gathers and passes. In this regard, it mirrors the physical experience of attending an exhibition. The gathering and exhibiting of works of art allows viewers to observe the passage of time as a concrete entity. Many exhibitions mark the passage of time visually. The most common way for an exhibition to do this is through a chronological floorplan. Within such an installation, different rooms denote different stages in an artist's career. Take, for example, Jackson Pollock's 1999 retrospective at Abby Aldrich Rockefeller Adamantine Ladies Museum. One moment, you're visually in 1943 staring at *She Wolf*'s godawful abstract teats, and two rooms later, you're in 1952 wondering how we let those bloody Aussies get their hands on *Blue Poles*. Or here's a better example: On Kawara's *Today* series, which is also commonly referred to as his "date paintings." Ghost's first significant encounter with this series occurred at the Govett-Brewster Gallery in New Plymouth, New Zealand on 26 March 2005. This exhibition began with **JAN. 9, 1966** and proceeded chronologically until **AUG. 7, 2005**. One of the joys inherent in the chronological installation of such work is being able to project events from a viewer's own life directly onto the walls. Gazing at the expanse of wallspace between 7 **NOV. 1976** and **MAR. 13, 1977**, Ghost thought: here is where I was born. And as his eyes lingered between 24 **OCT. 2004** and 20 **FEB. 2005**, he thought: here is where I moved to New Zealand.

Yet while such examples touch upon the "materiality of time," do they explain the *experience* of time? Not exactly. The experience of time can only be grasped through an act of measurement. In New Plymouth, what was the length of time that his eyes spent lingering? How many minutes? How many hours? Did he spend more time in this exhibition than, say, Georgio Morandi's 2008 exhibition at The Metropolitan Museum of Art, or William Kentridge's 2010 retrospective at the Abby Aldrich Rockefeller Adamantine Ladies Museum? Could anything be sillier than such considerations? Who brings a stopwatch to a museum?

But there's more: while *The Clock* is an exhibition, it's also a single work of art. Wasn't he being unfair to, say, the Akron Museum of Art's *Wall Drawing #1240, Planes/Broken Bands of Color* by Sol LeWitt, or the Hinman Hurlbut Hall of Art's *The Crucifixion of Saint Andrew* by Caravaggio (which, in Ghost's opinion, were the two greatest works of art in the state of Ohio) by lavishing a full twenty-four hours on *The Clock*? Just thinking about standing in front of a late Caravaggio for twenty-four hours made Ghost shudder, as he expected that the work's dark intensity would make a person go mad. And hadn't he always complained that video art selfishly demands too much attention? Within a museum setting, video art was like a spoiled only child. Was *The Clock* any different? (This explains why he enjoyed the work of William Kentridge so immensely: his videos are short enough to feel breezy, but substantial enough to spend hours watching.)

Pollock, Kawara, Morandi, Kentridge, LeWitt, and Caravaggio? Obviously, this was not the normal list of artists mentioned in association with *The Clock*. As a precursor, Zalewski mentioned Douglas Gordon's *24 Hour Psycho*, which slowly stretched Hitchcock's film until it reached twenty-four hours. Ghost's experience with *24 Hour Psycho* lasted all of two minutes, which he assumed was the average allotment of time devoted to a work that Zalewski himself dubbed "excruciatingly portentous." Zalewski also mentioned Andy Warhol's 1964 film *Empire*, which Ghost had never seen; in fact, Ghost had never seen any of Warhol's films. He would be willing to watch them, but he couldn't imagine what kind of venue would deem it worthwhile to screen eight hours of stationary footage of the Empire State Building. An ambitious arthouse theater? A deranged drive-in? The Insomnia Institute? He suspected every copy of *Empire* had become a stuffed owl perched upon a dusty storage shelf deep in the bowels of many a museum.

As he was pondering *The Clock*'s precursors, another name kept rudely elbowing its way into his consciousness: Matthew Barney. In the winter of 2010, Ghost had watched Barney's *The Cremaster Cycle* in its entirety at the Portland Museum of Art. When a friend later asked him to describe the experience, he compared it to having a colonoscopy and a root canal at the same time, which, if he wasn't mistaken, Barney himself endured in *Cremaster* 3. Or was it *Cremaster 4*? He couldn't remember. Ghost could never keep the series' convoluted sequencing straight. Chronologically, *Cremaster 4* was first, right? (Or was it *Cremaster 2*?) And the second movie was *Cremaster 1*, right? (Or was the second movie *Cremaster 4*?)

Even more upsetting than his inability to remember the cycle's correct sequencing was his inability to remember much of anything from the actual movies themselves. All he remembered were moments of random silliness: descending gonads riding motorcycles, muscular goatgirls dancing, a flying testicle-shaped thingy (or was it a flying vajayjay-shaped thingy?), and the afore-mentioned simultaneous colonoscopy and root canal. You get the point. His faulty memory was particularly disappointing because he had gone to great lengths to take notes during each movie, which was no easy task as they were screened in a dark movie theater. When he went back and consulted these notes in search of not only the correct sequencing but a simple reminder as to which movie he had enjoyed the most, Ghost discovered a bevy of crass barbs like: "enough with the feminist horseshit already!" (ten minutes into *Cremaster 1*), "this gas station sequence is boooooring" (thirty minutes into *Cremaster 2*), "I'm going to shove that whistle up somebody's ass!" (twenty minutes into *Cremaster 3*), and "Thank you, Mormon Jesus! It's finally over!" (end of *Cremaster 5*). *Cremaster 3*, which he was pretty sure was both the last movie to be filmed and the longest, received a particular-ly slanderous string of adjectives in his notebook: "excruciating" (after twenty-five minutes), "totally pointless" (forty-five min-utes), "utterly revolting and stupid" (fifty minutes), and "fuckall boring" (one hour and fifteen minutes).

While watching *The Clock*, Ghost was planning to revisit the darktheater notetaking technique he had perfected during *The Cremaster Cycle*. Would the results be as hostile and dismis-sive? (He knew that he could sometimes be accused of being an overly judgmental arthole.)

A single question haunted his homework: was Matthew

Barney *The Clock*'s ghostfather? For two very different works of art, the similarities were striking: both *The Cremaster Cycle* and *The Clock* are immense works of video art that exude outsized ambitions; because of their ambitious magnitude, both works have been compared to Richard Wagner's *Ring Cycle*; and, upon their debut, both works received near-universal, glowing praise. The major difference between *The Clock* and *The Cremaster* is that, since it debuted in 1994, *The Cremaster Cycle* has become a stuffed owl gonad in a jar of Vaseline perched on a dusty storage shelf deep in the bowels of many a museum. And he wasn't the only art historian to voice such an opinion; after initially being enamored with Barney's work, Robert Storr confessed to turning into a "self-described doubter." According to Storr, "the films are overly long, and the camera work is repetitive and often agonizingly slow." This quote appeared in Barney's 2003 *New Yorker* profile. Here's another quote from that profile: "longer than Parifisal, but not as funny." Could the same thing be said about *The Clock*? After all, it was four times longer than *The Cremaster Cycle*. That was a disturbing thought.

As he felt his mind starting to drift, another disturbing thought passed through Carlos Spencer-Bayard's consciousness: he hadn't taken a shower in over forty-eight hours. Rabbie Burns would be proud!

Before finishing his dram and journeying into the dark bedroom to join his wife and littlelion in dreamland, Ghost quickly reviewed his "survival pack" for *The Clock*: an oversized yellow notepad, four pens, two Chocolate Brownie Clif Bars, and two recent *New Yorkers* (everything he had read about *The Clock* mentioned lengthy lines and exorbitant wait times). To this list, he added one more thing: a shower. He didn't want to appear at the opening with anything worse than the feint odor of haggis clinging to his breath and body.

3:57 P.M. to 5:04 P.M.

Où est Gérard Depardieu?

Carlos Spencer-Bayard hadn't been watching *The Clock* for more than half an hour, *pourquoi le fuck* was he thinking about Gérard Depardieu? He was not a Gérard Depardieu fan; in fact, he wasn't sure that he had ever watched a single movie starring the iconic Frenchman who the *New Zealand Herald* once described as "having a face like a smacked bottom."

Twenty-three minutes ago, he had arrived at the Wexner Center. Like Phileas Fogg, Ghost was extremely punctual[15]. In fact, he was ur-punctual: he was early. Expecting a line, he arrived ten minutes before the opening was scheduled to begin. Upon descending the Wexner Center's staircase, he was pleasantly surprised to note that there wasn't a single other ClockHead in sight. He breezed past the Heirloom Café and was swallowed by the installation's shallow darkness.

The first face he recognized belonged to Julie Andrews, followed closely by Nic Cage. Well, this wasn't exactly true: the first face he recognized that afternoon actually belonged to the original ClockHead himself, Christian Marclay. On his way into the installation, Ghost happened to notice the artist, whom he recognized from the photograph accompaning Zalewski's article, seated at a table in the Heirloom Café. He appeared calm and relaxed, even though it was obvious that he was suffering through an interview with an OSU undergrad.

Moments after recognizing his first face (Julie Andrews), Ghost recognized his first movie: "Pineapple Express". In the clip, Seth Rogan wakes up in the driver's seat of a parked car next to James... *WhattheFUCKishisname?*

Not more than ten minutes into his first exposure to *The*

....
15   This reference will be explained later.

Clock, Ghost was experiencing one of the work's defining features; like those fancy laser pens in "Men in Black," *The Clock* wipes your memory clean. Upon entering the installation's darkness, your mind transforms into a *tabula rosa* for moving images to be projected upon.

No seriously, what the FUCK is that guy's name?

Normally, Ghost's memory-recall was sharp: Guillotine sharp, Kimputer sharp. It was so sharp that it was not uncommon for him to back-up other people's memory hard drives. He had even once corrected a friend's story about losing his virginity. "No, that's not right," he tactfully interjected while they were drinking together in a bar in Brooklyn. "It happened in the backseat of a parked car in a deserted parking lot in Caldwell."

I know that FUCKING guy. He did a real bang-up crap job of hosting The Oscars with Anne Hathaway.

Anyone familiar with Marcel Proust's beloved cork-lined room knows that remembrance necessitates stillness, as stillness allows the machinery of your memory to boot up. The longer the stillness, the more vivid the memory; but in a pinch, a momentary pause will do. Because of the surging nature of *The Clock*'s visual imagery, lingering stillness is impossible. *The Clock*'s imagery is as proleptic as Macbeth's murderous imagination.

It took Ghost over twenty-five minutes to remember the name *Franco*. And later, it took him over an hour to remember that the name of that Sofia Coppola snoozefest starring Scar Jo and Bill Murray was "Lost in Translation".

As he was struggling with his memory-recall, Seth Rogan and James *WhattheFUCKishisname* were engaged in a groggy dialogue about what time it was. This dialogue ended with Rogan yelling, "Four o'fucking clock? FUCK ME! No man, that's bad!"

Still snickering, Carlos Spencer-Bayard captured this quote on his notepad.

In the beginning, there was the Quote. The Quote was everywhere. The Quote was omnipresent. The Quote was king. Shakespeare, Poor Richard's Almanac, the Yahwist, Rhett Butler, Yogi Berra, Groucho Marx: quotes could be kidnapped out of any context and ransomed anywhere. (Heck, even Mark Twain's *name* was a quote.) *The Clock* is akin to a visual version of *Bartlett's Familiar Quotations*. Without viewing its imagery, a good way to appreciate the video's fragmentary, nonsensical nature was through a woven texture of quotes.

"Four-fifteen," a stern, matronly woman says to a younger woman, who appears to be some kind of teacher, "you're punctilious... and such a colorful frock!"

In between an image of a woman ironing clothes and a close-up of Tom Cruise, Ghost scribbled down his question regarding Gérard Depardieu. He then promptly wrote the phrase "funny sex scene: 2 people orgasming at same time" directly on top of it. (Drat, he had forgotten how difficult it was to write in a dark room!)

Où est le visage comme le smacked bottom?

As hilarious as the *New Zealand Herald*'s quote was, it too probably would have been swept from Ghost's mind by the forceful tide of forgetfulness had it not been for the fact that there was a New Zealand rugby player, named Aled de Malmanche, who looked as though some mad rugbyloving scientist had spliced Gérard Depardieu's head onto the Incredible Hulk's body. This strange amalgamation of strength and French cinematic sex appeal played hooker for the Waikato Chiefs. After four years and five test caps for the mighty All Blacks, de Malmanche was inexplicably dumped by the Mooloos. Bereft of options, he was forced to ply his trade in the Northern Hemisphere, where he donned the flaming pink jersey of Stade Français. (*Bien sûr!*) Ghost still thought about "Gérard" whenever he watched the Mooloos play, and so did his wife, who would inevitably ask, "whatever happened to that Gérard Depardieu-looking guy?"

The reason why Carlos Spencer-Bayard was thinking about Gérard Depardieu so early in his clockwatching was because so much of the video's dialogue was in French. But why did this surprise him? Born in San Rafael, California, Christian Marclay grew up in a suburb of Geneva. In *The New Yorker*, Zalewski describes Marclay's childhood as a "linguistic scramble." His mother spoke to him in English; his father, in French.

"It's 4:48," a police sergeant barks. "If he hasn't called back by 5:00, we storm the bank!"

At 5:04 P.M., after watching Jack Nicholson stare vacantly at a wallclock in an empty office, Ghost leapt from his seat, rushed through the Wexner Center's giftshop, ascended a narrow escalator, and hurried into the Mershon Auditorium.

The Lambert Family Lecture
(5:04 P.M. to 5:52 P.M.)

Carlos Spencer-Bayard hurried into the Mershon Auditorium just as the event's moderator was being introduced.

"… in addition to being a Curator-at-Large here at the Wexner Center, he is also a long-time faculty member within Ohio State University's Film Studies Program."

Lowering himself into an empty seat, Ghost groaned. *Film STUDIES Program?* he thought, dismissively. *Shouldn't that department be called the Film WATCHING Program?*

Like most art historians, Ghost harbored an intrinsic dislike of the academic discipline known as "Film Studies." To him, Film Studies majors were akin to homeschooled art historians. Whenever any conversation veered into a discussion of film, Ghost inevitably found himself thinking: *who needs robust critical discourse, when you've got… ADJECTIVES!?* To prove this point,

Ghost casually flipped through the Wexner Center's most recent brochure, compiling a quick list of adjectives used to describe the center's upcoming films: "most revered," "funny," "heart-wrenching," "nail-biting," "caustic," "profound," "great," "mesmerizing," "perfect," "Oscar-winner," "most penetrating," "black-and-white boldness," "haunting," "expressionistic," "unforgettable," "gripping," "effective," "poetic," "stylish," "most pointed," "humanistic," "surrealistic," "most alive," "indelible," "unnerving," "noir-ish," "moody," and "improvisational." And this was just from the first page: he hadn't even gotten to the description of "Thunderball"!

People who watch a lot of movies are not scholars: they're just people who watch a lot of movies. And the correct nomenclature for such people is movie buff. Was Ohio State's movie buff buff? Not when compared to Aled de Malmanche. Was he in the buff? Good heavens no! Nudity doesn't exist in the Midwest!

Almost immediately the lecture (which was really more of a conversation) launched into a discussion of "the archive." RED FLAG! *Never trust any American who quotes Michel Foucault*, Carlos Spencer-Bayard thought, fully aware that he himself was in the habit of quoting the celebrated Frenchman's theories on madness. Yes, he quoted them, but he never felt like he truly understood them. Adding to his distrust was the fact that his critical hero, Harold Bloom, hated Foucault with a passion that rivaled Superman's hatred of Lex Luther. In *The Western Canon*, Bloom denounced Foucault's "great flaw" as a "blindness toward his own metaphors, an ironic weakness in a professed disciple of Nietzsche." In other words, Foucault's "archive" is no more quantifiable than Freud's "unconscious." Foucault's "archive" is like Israel: it only exists if you want it to exist, if you *need* it to exist.

Christian Marclay appeared unwilling to be dragged into any grand cinematic discussions of "the archive." According to him, "the archive" consisted solely of conveniently located DVD rental shops around London. Ghost found this antidote delightful, as it reminded him of how whenever Harold Bloom heard someone pontificating on "the unconscious," he thought of his back. Now whenever Ghost heard someone discussing "the archive," he could think of Kim's Video and Music off St. Mark's Place.

Ghost couldn't help but feel disappointed with the lecture, which was light on enlightenment and long on longueurs. When the discussion turned to the legal ramifications associated with the appropriation of Hollywood movies [*snore!*], Ghost fled the lecture hall like Nietzsche fleeing Bayreuth. His rapid departure was made easier by the fact that he was sitting in the aisle seat in the very last row. He was no fool; like Clark Griswold parking his stationwagon at Wally World, he knew if he parked himself near the exit, he would be the first person out of the lecture hall, and thus the first person back into *The Clock*.

5:52 P.M. to 6:35 P.M.

At 5:54 P.M., as a clip of Napoleon Dynamite walking down a desert road slowly bled into "Citizen Kane," Carlos Spencer-Bayard started thinking back to something Christian Marclay had said during the Lambert Family Lecture. The most important thing about viewing *The Clock*, according to Marclay, was not the images themselves, but the viewing experience. For example, it doesn't matter how many times Ghost had already seen Michael Keaton versus Buster Keaton (two to nil), what really mattered were the decisions he was forced to make regarding his presence (when to arrive, where to sit, how long to stay, when to leave, etc.). With a normal moviegoing experience, these decisions are easy: you arrive before the movie begins (unless you're an inconsiderate A-hole), stay for the duration, and leave when it is over. But what happens when you encounter a movie that never begins or ends?

Deciding when to leave *The Clock* is especially difficult. This difficulty transcends the common desire of wanting to stay to see what happens. (Spoiler Alert: nothing happens in *The Clock*.) The discomfort of leaving *The Clock* is not mental, it's physical. As *The Clock* surges forward, the gravitational force of its neverending imagery presses viewers into their seats like a giant spinning centrifuge.[16] Even though he was excited to hear Christian Marclay speak, as 5:00 P.M. drew near, Ghost had great difficulty leaving *The Clock*.

There is a German word for this phenomenon: *sitzfleisch*.[17] Ghost first learned this word from Jeffrey Eugenides, who claimed that mastering *sitzfleisch* is an essential part of being a writer. Such mastery is also an essential part of consuming moving images. Mastering *sitzfleisch* in small increments is no great feat, as any combination of rapid imagery, color, and sound will hold our attention. Like a screaming child (as Ghost's was screaming in his bassinet next to him as he typed this) our attention *wants* to be held. When people seek out moving images, what they're after is a visual embrace. After the exhausting burdens of the workday or punishing discipline of the school day, people want to be held, they *need* to be held. This explains why so many people desire the embrace of moving images when they're tired, cranky, lazy, fussy, hungover, sick, or bored. (What other excuse did Ghost have for watching a two-hour interview between Dr. Drew and Bristol Palin in a hotel room in Waterbury, Connecticut?) Television today is akin to what Nietzsche once said about German music: it is beer for the work-weary masses.

....

16 Sometime between midnight and 4:00 A.M., such a centrifuge appears on a portable black-and-white television being watched by Korean teenager wrapped in a blanket.

17 Translation: the ability of sitting on one's flesh.

While consuming moving images, it is easy to forget the importance of the viewer, but this is not the case with *The Clock*. As Marclay explained during the Lambert Family Lecture, viewing *The Clock* means having to make choices: when to arrive, how long to stay, and when to sunder the embrace. Thus, within Marclavian Time, the viewer is not simply a passive consumer: the viewer is an active participant.

Be an active participant as opposed to a passive consumer? Didn't this go against the very definition of what it means to be a good Midwesterner? A good Midwesterner is a voracious consumer, who relishes the opportunity to do what he's told and buy what he's sold. He consumes cars from Detroit, beer from Milwaukee, whiskey from Kentucky, movies from Los Angeles, television shows from New York, ideology from Washington D.C., coffee from Seattle, cheap furniture from Sweden, foodlike substances from Godknowswhere, and everything else comes from China via Bentonville, Arkansas. To the rest of the country, the Midwest is a vast expanse of willing consumerism whose flat earth is covered with neatly arranged geometrical rows of money plants, each sprouting greenbacks like ears of corn. Local businesses, ambitious entrepreneurs, global corporations, and foreign companies battle to harvest this lucrative crop. And what's more: this crop wants to be harvested, it *needs* to be harvested. How can a good Midwesterner, so long schooled in the positive values of passive consumption, be expected to enjoy a work of art that requires active participation?

At 6:00 P.M., a distinguished looking gentleman with a brave moustache enters his house and bursts into song. Like Val Kilmer in "Tombstone" or Will Farrell in "Wedding Crashers," musicals are *The Clock*'s stealthy scene-stealers. After so much continuous imagery and nonsensical dialogue, songs are like explosions of auditory Technicolor. The chorus from this particular song repeats the line: "consistency is the life I lead." Teach a clock to carry a tune, Ghost thought, and would this not be its leitmotif?

Soon after this clip, it became obvious that the Lambert Family Lecture had ended, as a surge of people flooded the installation. Ghost didn't mind the crowd, but the white noise from the atrium threatened to overwhelm *The Clock*'s soundtrack. If you can't hear it, *The Clock* is not worth watching.

After watching a clip of Sean Penn and his magnificently sculpted facial hair awaiting execution in "Dead Man Walking," Ghost walked. Passing through the gala opening, he noticed that a line had formed to enter the installation. This made him nervous. Would he ever be forced to wait in line to view *The Clock*? If so, this could seriously bugger his carefully crafted schedule.

11:30 P.M. to 4:15 A.M.

Insomnia is a noose worn nightly. Carlos Spencer-Bayard didn't mind the sleeplessness – he could function on little or no sleep – what bothered him was the spoiling, unspooling of his mind. He even had a name for this nightly thought decay: nightmadness. For what is insomnia but a peculiar kind of madness? During the day, thoughts are turtle-like: slow, yet determined. But when the noose of nightmadness tightens, the turtle of thought is flipped onto its back. Frantic and flailing, this thought-turtle can go nowhere: the poor creature is totally overwhelmed by the helpless uselessness of sleeplessness.

As his body twisted and turned, rotisseriestyle, Ghost's thoughts would churn, straining against their constraints. Within this agitation, everything would jumble together: words, ideas, reality, unreality, reason, and unreason. This jumbling was the beginning of the nightly circus whose tent stretched across the flat, grassy pitch of his frontal lobe. Bad metaphors, inane activities, banal analogies, inelegant alliterations, and portly, pretentious portmanteaus all cavorted and gamboled around like tattooed swordswallowers and fatbearded ladies underneath a colorful tarp and taunt trapeze wires.

No, that wasn't quite right. Nightmadness isn't a circus; in fact, it isn't anything like a circus. It is not an unleashing of grotesque oddities: it's an escape into innocence. After the day's drudgery, the mind is finally free to be itself. It can be as silly-playfulcreative and unproductive as it desires, safe from the terrible damning logic of daylight.

The torment. The upturned turtle. The curious, nonexistant circus. The escape into innocence. Of course, none of these thoughts were any help when it came to drifting off to sleep. Not a jot.

In an attempt to calm his turningchurning mind, Ghost would lie perfectly still on his back and stare upward into the softblackness that engulfed his bedroom. While doing so, he would think about all the ghosts who haunted his thoughts doing the exact same thing. He envisioned Roland Barthes lying in his hospital bed at Salpêtrière, Walter Benjamin lying in despair at the *Hotel de Francia* in Portbou, Nietzsche lying insane in his room on Piazza Carlo Alberto in Turin, and Shakespeare lying in his "bestabed" in New Place awaiting the arrival of Ben Jonson and Michael Drayton, meticulously planning the merriment that the three friends would conjure up as part of his fifty-second birthday celebration.

Finally, Ghost would feel the loosening of his mind's grip on itself. The thunder of his thoughts would grow distant, as a heaviness settled in. When this happened, Ghost knew that he would soon be Sinbad the Sailor, Tinbad the Tailoring his way off to sleep.

Fatherhood added a new twist to insomnia, as it made him

feel like he was keeping watch over his family. His littlelion's crib was positioned only inches away from his side of the bed. While lying awake, Ghost enjoyed listening to the "Noisy Oyster" snort, sniff, sigh, and flipflopflip around in his crib, all under the blanket of babybliss. His son: the deepersleeper.

Hours after the opening gala at the Wexner Center had officially ended, Carlos Spencer-Bayard awoke in darkness, dressed noiselessly, and returned to *The Clock*. Upon his return, he was surprised to discover Ohio State's campus abuzz with activity. After bouncing up 4th Avenue listening to a rap song he had never heard before about popping tags and thrift store shopping, Ghost parked in the shadow of a nearby Starbucks and navigated his way past packs of partygoers prowling the streets, the level of inebriation high, the amount of clothing, especially among the female of the species, low. And blanketing this, according to his dashboard thermometer, the temperature was hovering just above twenty degrees Fahrenheit and dropping steadily, but this didn't deter the girls from sashaying around in skimpy dresses or blokes bouncing around in board shorts. Nobody appeared to be wearing a winter jacket, except him.

There were approximately twenty people watching *The Clock* when Ghost reentered the installation.

"Charlie, what time is it?"

"Eleven-thirty."

After a brief vista of a young Dustin Hoffman, Ricky Gervais appeared on-screen, lazily sprawled across a sofa watching television. His phone rings. It's an obese female friend, who is also on her sofa watching television. They're obviously both lonely and bored. After a moment of nonchalant chitchat, the woman poses a question: "which would you rather have: a bionic arm or a bionic leg?" They both choose the bionic leg, for different reasons. Just before the clip ends, Gervais' wistfully laments, "but a bionic arm would be useful some nights." (Cheeky, devil!)

"Twelve minutes to midnight," an equestrian John Wayne announces to his troops. "Bugler, sound the charge!"

Carlos Spencer-Bayard wasn't surprised to see The Duke make an appearance in *The Clock*, but he was surprised to see the Irish actor Stephen Rea, who once portrayed Leopold Bloom in a film version of *Ulysses*. (Would Poldy make an appearance in *The Clock*?) Rea's unexpected appearance reminded Ghost of another cinematic surprise: the cockshot from "The Crying Game." Was he the only person who had watched that movie and hadn't realized that she was really a he? How did he not see that cock coming? (Awkward phrasing that.) If that scene appeared in *The Clock*, this time he'd be ready.

If there's one moment in *The Clock* that every reviewer advocated was not to be missed, it was the midnight montage that culminated in the explosion of Big Ben. Like an iconic vessel in a series of Morandi paintings, Big Ben is undoubtedly *The Clock*'s heroic protagonist, appearing, by Ghost's count, fifty-three times. But Big Ben is not the only inanimate object to make numerous appearances within the video, other such objects include the Art Deco timepiece that anchors New York City's Grand Central Station, a giant wall clock in a strange, all-white boardroom, the clock at a crowded French train station (Ghost thought it was Gare Saint-Lazare, but how could he be sure?), the clocktower in "Back to the Future," and Nic Cage.

It turned out that Big Ben's midnight explosion was rather anti-climactic. Ghost was more impressed by a poetic, pre-midnight black-and-white image of a solitary man walking away from Notre Dame Cathedral.

Just before 12:15 A.M.'s montage of scary phone calls (remember those? No Caller I.D. How quaint!), Ghost was shocked to recognize a member of his extended film family: Kimmie Bauer.

For the sake of full disclosure, Carlos Spencer-Bayard had to confess something: he was a "frienemy" of film. He didn't particularly enjoy watching moving images, thus he didn't watch many movies, especially in the theater. (He suspected that his avoidance of movies irritated his wife to no end.) The last movie he watched in the theater was "That's My Boy" – an undeniable stinker – and that was over a year ago. Prior to that, it had been more than two years since he had visited a movie theater to watch "The Blindside," whose casual racism had made it even harder to watch than "That's My Boy." Ghost was adamant that his visual culture credentials not be judged by these two shitsandwiches: both trips to the movie theater were motivated by lengthy power outages in his apartment. And he enjoyed watching television even less than movies. The only television programs he enjoyed watching were New Zealand rugby matches and "24," both of which he had gotten hooked on while living in New Zealand.

But here's the thing: because he loved "24" so much, he had to ration out watching it. He watched one season per year, which usually equated to watching a new season in a new locale. He watched Season 1 while living in Auckland (it was as exciting as watching the Auckland Blues circa 2003); Season 2 at his parent's house in Ohio (not as exciting, but more intelligent, like the Canterbury Crusaders c. 2005); Season 3 in Park Slope, Brooklyn (unforgettable ending, just like the 2006 Super 12 Final between Canterbury and the Wellington Hurricanes); Season 4 in Portland, Maine (Um, sorry China: Jack's dead, just like the Waikato Chiefs were murdered in the 2008 Final). Most recently, he had watched Season 5 in Columbus. (Jack's back and the undead Jack is BADASS, just like the Chiefs of 2012). After such a peripatetic past, Ghost's fear was that he now had to move out of Columbus before he could watch Season 6.

A large part of the show's appeal was the unintentional humor inherent in its outlandish plotlines. Within the context of the show, these plotlines appear realistic, even commonsensical; but outside the context of the show, they sound utterly ludicrous. For example, Jack once infiltrated a Mexican drug cartel not once, but twice. (*"Holia, esta gringo looks familiar..."*) Obviously, nobody in the Salazar drug cartel had as good of a memory as China, who we learn at the end of Season 5 has a "Wery, Wery Wong Wemory." [God, Ghost loved that quote!] In Season 4, Jack (kinda) kills his girlfriend's ex-husband; one season later, he (kinda) kidnaps a different girlfriend's son. For a normal bloke, Ghost imagined, both of these occurrences would be a relationship deal-breaker, but not for Jack Bauer. In Season 5, we learn that both now ex-girlfriends are still pining away for Jack, which becomes obvious when one has to interrogate the other. (Awkward!) And things get even more awkward, a few episodes later, when Jack has to interrogate one of these exes only moments after learning that she has slept with known D-bag traitor, Walt Cummings, whose eyeball Jack once threatened to cut out of his skull with a pocket knife in front of the President of the United States. (And that was *before* he knew about their sexual entanglement!) And while discussing the show's infamous interrogation/torture scenes, who can forget the time that Richard Heller, under Sensory Deprivation Torture, confessed to... being gay! (*Holy Gitmo*! That must happen all the time to our military personnel while using Dick-Cheney-sanctioned torture techniques on suspected Al Qaeda operatives.)

If it's not obvious by now, Carlos Spencer-Bayard could prattle on about "24" for hours. (And to think, he hadn't even mentioned Dennis Hopper's ridiculous Serbian accent from Season 1!) This is one of the reasons why he didn't watch moving images: he couldn't turn it off. But this is not just aimless prattle, "24" does have a definite connection to *The Clock*.

Every episode of "24" begins with the announcement: "The

following takes place between the hours of [TIME] and [TIME]."
In Season 1, this announcement was followed by the terse declaration: "Events occur in real time." Of course, "real time" in
"24" is not real time, but it's darn close. For example, Richard
Heller's sexuality becomes a matter of National Security at precisely 4:32 A.M. And if anyone wants to watch Jack cut off his
daughter's boyfriend's hand with an emergency fire axe (and why
wouldn't you?) this happens precisely at 12:46 P.M. And "real
time" in "24" could easily become real time: all a viewer would
have to do is start Season 1 at precisely 12:00 A.M. on the day of
the California Presidential Primary. Being mindful to pause for
commercial breaks, the next twenty-four hours would occur in
perfect synchronicity. Of course, Ghost didn't recommend doing
this for a number of reasons: first, you would have to wait until
June 2020; and second, Ghost suspected that the intensity of the
show's subject matter would cause even the most diehard fan to
crack quicker than Richard Heller. (In Richard's defense, he did
courageously hold out for hours!)

The real time element of "24" was what made the show
unique. In this sense, the structure was more important than the
subject matter; in fact, the genesis of "24" illustrated how important the show's structure was to its appeal. The creator of the
series, Joel Surnow, first conceived of creating a television show
that took place in real time over the span of 24 hours before he
gave any thought to what the show would be about. Once he had
dreamed up the structure, Surnow struggled to think of what
would make characters stay awake for a full twenty-four hours.
His answer: a terrorist threat. Christian Marclay's answer: art.

"Not everybody's up at one o'clock in the morning, watching the porn channel," Woody Allen whines over the phone to

(maybe) Paul Rudd.[18]

Ghost harbored an intense dislike of Woody Allen's movies. (In his novel, he described Allen's movies as stinking worse than Staten Island.) Yet this was the second time during the night that he had laughed at one of his jokes.

At 1:07 A.M., Ghost sundered the visual embrace for coffee.

Unlike New York City, Columbus was a city that sleeps. Because of its somnolence, the city was devoid of all-nite diners. The closest thing Columbus had to an all-nite diner was *Buckeye Donuts*, which was located on High Street, four blocks north of the Wexner Center. *Buckeye Donuts* was not much of a diner; it was really just a takeout counter with a few seats clustered around a low, horseshoe-shaped bar. One look at the décor, menu, and cleanliness was all it took to realize that the establishment's main clientele was inebriated college students.

When Ghost arrived, *Buckeye Donuts* was marginally full of the collegiately intoxicated. His initial plan was to order a falafel gyro – he missed Brooklyn's all-nite falafel almost as much as he missed Yorkville's all-nite diners – but this plan quickly evaporated. The place was downright nasty. Almost everyone he saw was devouring large quantities of onion rings – clearly the safest menu solution. Plan B: order an 8oz coffee to go. He paid his eighty-nine cents, dropped the remaining eleven cents into the tip jar, and headed back to the Wexner Center. The entire roundtrip took twenty-seven minutes. He was clockwatching because he was in a hurry to get back to watching *The Clock*.

At this hour, walking along High Street near Ohio State's campus was actually akin to "watching the porn channel." Sex was everywhere. It was written on every exposed piece of flesh, underlined every interaction, and echoed in every argument. This

---

18   Ghost later realized that this was actually Paul Reiser.

carnal carnival reminded Ghost of that weird sex masquerade in Stanley Kubrick's final clunker "Eyes Wide Shut". Over the years, Ghost had come to realize that bingedrinking was a masquerade whose festive mask concealed the rustic and the rapist alike, and you never knew who was behind the mask until it was too late. Although he was once a colossal bingedrinker, he now found their cult utterly repulsive. If he were King of the Midwest, he would put bingedrinkers in public stocks, like medieval profligates. And while they pissed their pants and puked on their clever tee-shirts, he would invite anyone who has ever been hurt by bingedrinking (neglected children, battered spouses, victims of date-rape or drunk-driving) to tickle their feet with birch boughs, poke their bottoms with pointed sticks, and pelt them with rotten vegetables.

Back inside *The Clock*, the crowd had dwindled down to five people.

At 1:48 A.M., a humorous hypnotist intones, "You're feeling sleepy. You're thinking of going to bed."

Apparently, he was right. Soon after this clip, the crowd shrunk down to three.

At 2:00 A.M., an image of Don Cheadle as a radio DJ from the movie "Talk to Me" appeared on-screen. Six years ago, Ghost watched this movie in Manhattan at the United Artists Cinema at Union Square. It was his most recent trip to a movie theater that wasn't motivated by a power outage.

On-screen, a man urinates absentmindedly into a dingy gas station urinal. He glances up and spies something scrawled diagonally on the wall:

For Manly Love
Be Here
March 25th
At 2:15 A.M. *SHARP*

If you attended college anywhere in the Midwest during the late nineties, you shouldn't have to be reminded what movie this scene is from; but just in case a steady diet of bingedrinking and onion rings has totally waterlogged your memory, the answer is "Dumb and Dumber."

As comedic duos goes, Jim Carrey and Jeff Daniels dwarfed Steve Martin and John Candy in every category except total combined weight. Ghost was never a John Candy fan; he even went so far as to suspect that Chris Farley's career was helped immensely by the fact that John Candy showed the world how painfully unfunny a fat guy can be. After watching Steve Martin and John Candy attempt to barter their watches for hotel rooms, Ghost realized that "Planes, Trains, and Automobiles" would be a good subtitle for *The Clock*.

At 2:22 A.M., that subtitle could be changed to "Planes, Trains, and Automobiles (that stubbornly refuse to start)".

After a scene of Matt Dillon impersonating Charles Bukowski, a clip from Ghost's favorite movie of all-time, "Memento", appeared on-screen. The movie was Ghost's all-time favorite for a number of reasons: he loved the film's complex flashback/flashforward structure, its creepy noir-ish plot, and its creative casting (Joey Pants is unforgettable!); he also loved the fact that he had a (loose) personal connection to the director, Christopher Nolan. Nolan's mother and his mother were, according to his mother, the only two girls in Rocky River High School's class of 1960 who were not interested in becoming cheerleaders. After college, they reconnected in Chicago, where they were both living on Dearborn Street.

In the clip that appears in *The Clock*, Guy Pierce ("LENNY!") is burning some of his murdered wife's belongings, including an old alarm clock. As this scene is a rather nonessential part of the story, Ghost expected to encounter more of the movie later, but he was wrong: this was the movie's only appearance in *The Clock.*

Shortly after 2:30 A.M., the Salvador Dali-inspired nightmare sequence from "Spellbound" appears. While Ghost recognized the Dali imagery, he had never heard of the movie "Spellbound"; and of course, he had never watched it. He only recognized the sequence because it was mentioned in a blogpost by Daniel Zalewski on the *New Yorker*'s website.

As might be obvious by now, Ghost possessed a very paltry knowledge of movies and their stars. (His wife was much more knowledgeable about movies than he was.) So while he could easily recognize Jimmy Stewart and Raymond Burr from "Rear Window" and Gizmo from "Gremlins," he struggled to recognize the blonde actor who steps out of the pouring rain into a colorful New Orleans jazz joint. Since he looked like he could be the blonde Bond's older brother, Ghost was fairly certain that this actor was Steve McQueen, but he couldn't be sure because he didn't really know what Steve McQueen looked like[19]. But the same cannot be said of New Orleans. Even at this early hour, the city was unmistakable. The color, the sound, the electri*CITY*. Many times, Ghost had experienced a surge of electricity while stepping across the threshold into Mimi's in the Marigny, the Hi-Ho, or Siberia. With that single step, the blacknight was chased away by the wildcolor of the Crescent City. Such an experience dwarfed the deserted streets and the cat-having-a-seizure-on-a-piano soundtrack of "Eyes Wide Shut," or the dingy hotel room and depressively mopey dialogue of "Liver Wide Shut" (better known as "Leaving Las Vegas").

....
19 When he heard the name Steve McQueen, Ghost couldn't help but think of the follow-ing lyrics from Mark Kozelek's *Hey, You Bastard I'm Still Here:* "O, I can't help but think of my father and me when I see old movies with Steve McQueen."

The appearance of "Leaving Las Vegas" raised an interesting question: will *The Clock* include any real footage of Sin City, a city notoriously devoid of clocks?

As he was pondering this question, a black-and-white clip of the Wu Tang Clan's RZA and (maybe) GZA flashed across the screen. Ghost recognized the movie as "Coffee and Cigarettes," which he had watched while living in New Zealand. At the time, he remembered wondering why a director would compile such a magnificent cast (Jack & Meg White, Iggy Pop, Tom Waits, Roberto Benigni) and then force them all to speak such stupid, stilted dialogue? And who was the director of that movie? Was it Jim JZA or Wim WZA?

Sounded like time for more coffee…

Buckeye Donuts was substantially more crowded at 3:15 A.M. than it was at 1:15 A.M. Directly in front of him in line, an inebriated undergrad drunkenly belted out the chorus to *Radar Love* (How did a twentysomething know the chorus to *Radar Love*? Ghost's dad used to listen to that song on a cassette tape!) Behind him, another inebriated undergrad regaled his friend with a long, detailed story involving a text message about a blowjob that was sent to the wrong person and the desperate search to locate the unintended recipient's cellphone in hopes of deleting the text before it could be read. (Ghost loved overhearing undergrad conversations, especially when they sounded exactly like he expected them to sound. *A text message about a blowjob! Sent to the wrong person! Tell me more!*) As he ordered his 8oz coffee to go, Ghost realized that he was probably the only sober person in the joint.

When he returned to *The Clock*, the viewership was still three. It was not lost on him that, at this very moment, there were substantially more people eating onion rings at *Buckeye Donuts* than watching "the masterpiece of our time."

Nic Cage sighting #3 came at 3:33 A.M. This time, he

was reading *The Orchid Theft* in bed. After this clip, two of the three remaining clockwatchers disappeared into the morning. This only left Ghost and one other ClockHead. Alone in the dark, Ghost couldn't tell if his fellow ClockHead was a man or a woman, and he didn't want to stare to find out, as it would definitely be deemed creepy. But then again, maybe he should stare, or at least check his/her pulse. In the past four hours, Ghost had made three trips to the head and two excursions to *Buckeye Donuts*: his fellow ClockHead hasn't moved once. Perhaps he/she was, in fact, not a ClockHead, but a DeadHead. *How creepy would that be? Very.*

Or maybe he/she was just sleeping, Ghost thought, as a lengthy montage of people doing just that flashed across the screen. Trying to be nonchalant, Ghost glanced over and noticed that his fellow ClockHead was wearing one of those strange U-shaped airline pillows around his/her neck. *Was that really necessary?* He also noticed that his/her legs were propped up and stretched out across the sofa. There were few things that irritated Ghost more than people putting their feet up in public. Do people in other countries insist on doing this, or is it just a result of America's fierce love of "individualism," which is just a fancy phrase for the justification of selfish assholery? Americans will put their dirty feet on *anything*: bus seats, airplane seats, an art museum's sofa, an entire Arab country. Only a selfish, inconsiderate USAhole thinks such behavior is acceptable. As if to reinforce this belief, at 3:50 A.M., there was a clip of a man peeling off a pair of muddy boots in a military bunker. *Sacrebleu!* Could it be? *Gérard Depar...DAMN!* He couldn't tell! The clip disappeared too quickly! Before he could be certain, the scene walked off the screen like an emu out of a bedroom, which, according to Daniel Zalewski, was from Bunuel's "Phantom of Liberty".

At 4:05 A.M., Harrison Ford appeared huddled in an apartment building stairwell. A cat walks past. The outside door opens and a woman enters the building. Ford lights a single match and holds it to the face of his wristwatch. Ghost recognized the image from the cover of the Wexner Center's promotional material: seeing it was akin to spotting a celebrity on a crowded subway platform. Picking promotional images for *The Clock* couldn't have been easy. How can you promote something that is, on one hand, saturated with imagery; but on the other, completely devoid of an iconic, unifying image? To rectify this, every article Ghost had read on *The Clock* reproduced the same eight, rather banal, film stills. This octet was composed of: 4:05 A.M. (digital alarm clock), 4:05 A.M. (Harrison Ford's hand holding a match to the face of his wristwatch), 11:39 A.M. (hand holding a black wristwatch in front of what appears to be a desert safari vista), 11:39 A.M. (golden watch discarded by Dennis Hopper in "Easy Rider" lying sideways on a gravel road), 1:00 A.M. (close-up of a wall clock), 1:00 A.M. (close-up of a man pushing back the sleeve of his jacket to read his wristwatch), 4:30 P.M. (round, wooden wall clock with dangling chimes), and 4:30 P.M. (public clock affixed to an old, stone tower).

At 4:15 A.M., an image from "The Wizard of Oz" appeared on-screen. With her long, green face, the Wicked Witch of the West reminded Ghost of Alexej Jawlensky's painting *Schokko with a Red Hat*, which hangs in the Columbus Art Museum. As she turns over an hourglass filled with red sand, that wicked old hag cackles something about how when the sand runs out, Dorothy will lose her rent-controlled artist's sublet, or something to that effect. Just before the hourglass runs dry, the Tin Man smashes through the door with his axe (yikes, that's going to come out of her security deposit!) and saves day.

It was then, with the smash of the axe, that Ghost realized that he was deliriously tired. Before the imagery continued its forward surge, he quickly emu-walked out of the installation and into the morning, the motionless, neck-pillowed, DeadHead remaining behind.

Hurrying to where his car was parked, Ghost passed an eerily cinematic scene. Parked atop the sidewalk sat a solitary police car, lights ablaze. The flashing REDblueREDblue lights illuminated the block in every direction. As he watched, a short, stocky female police officer handcuffed a tall, intoxicated adolescent male. *Off to the stocks, mate!*

The streets were deserted as Carlos Spencer-Bayard drove through Columbus' CBD on route to his apartment. As he crossed over interstate 670, the radio began playing Peter Gabriel's *In Your Eyes*. Was there a more iconic song in the history of cinema? In his mind, John Cusack held his large 80s boom-box overhead. For all four years of college, a black-and-white glossy 8 x 10 photograph of this scene hung on Ghost's wall. Would that scene ever appear in *The Clock*? He wouldn't be surprised. After all, in the four hours he had just watched, John Cusack appeared more than any other actor. (Robin Williams was a close second, followed by Tom Cruise.) After watching four hours of continuous moving images, Ghost was startled by how forcefully a single lovesong on the radio seared an image into his consciousness. And speaking of songs, Ghost reminded himself to Google the name of that rap song he had heard earlier about thrift store shopping, since it was a surprisingly catchy earworm.

10:59 A.M. to 2:05 P.M

Exactly one week had passed since Carlos Spencer-Bayard's last exposure to *The Clock*; during that time, he began compiling a wishlist of things that he would like to see appear in the video. Some items on this list were obvious; for example, "The Big Lebowski" and "Pulp Fiction," but which movie would appear first, how many times would each appear, and would the clip of "Pulp Fiction" include Samuel L. Jackson shouting the word "MOTHERFUCKER!!!"? In Ghost's opinion, there are few cinematic moments more joyful than hearing Samuel L. Jackson angrily enunciate the word "MOTHERFUCKER!!!" Jackson had already made an appearance in *The Clock*; just before 5:00 P.M., he appeared in the rain accosting Ben Affleck on a streetcorner in New York City. Although he was clearly agitated, he never uttered his famous oedipal curse. *C'mon,* Ghost kept thinking, *now is the perfect time... You're talking to Ben Affleck!*

Other items on his wishlist were more personal. Would New Zealand make an appearance? "The Lord of the Rings" trilogy might, but he doubted it. He suspected that the entire genre of science-fiction was a clockless cosmos, an intergalactic Las Vegas. After all, why would anyone need to wear a wristwatch in Hobbiton or on Dantooine?

What about an image of someone drinking absinthe? *The Clock*'s obvious Francophilia led Ghost to believe that the Green Torment might make an appearance. What about Shakespeare or Nietzsche? From Zalewski's article, Ghost knew that *The Clock* included a scene from a "Hamlet," but would there be anything else? And how long would it be until he saw something that could be described as *Nietzschean*? And exactly what might that something be?

As the week continued, his wishlist grew...

What about beloved movies from his childhood, like "The NeverEnding Story," "The Naked Gun," or "3 Amigos"? He had already seen one-third of said *amigos* (Steven Martin), would he see the other two? (Chevy Chase, likely; Martin Short, doubtful) And what about "Police Academy," "Ferris Bueller's Day Off," or "3 Men and a Baby"? He had seen exactly zero-thirds of those goofy *amigos*. Would the great Steve Gutenberg make an appearance?

Or what about the Holy Trinity of Southeastern Ohio Hometown Heroes? Ghost had already spied Clark Gable, but what about Dean Martin or Cambridge's own William Boyd? Dean-o was a safe bet, but Boyd was a stretch. Would the actor best known for portraying Hopalong Cassidy hop into *The Clock*? *Fat chance*, Ghost thought. In fact, if Hopalong Cassidy did make an appearance in *The Clock*, Ghost silently vowed to hop down Cambridge's Wheeling Avenue in the buff!

Which Rock would appear in *The Clock* first: the movie starring Sean Connery and Nic Cage, the wrestler-turned-actor, or Rock Hudson? And if the answer was Rock Hudson, would Ghost recognize him? Dwayne "The Rock" Johnson kept rudely elbowing his way into Ghost's consciousness while researching *The Clock*; whenever he read how many hours a reviewer had spent watching *The Clock*, Ghost kept hearing The Rock shout, "IT DOESN'T MATTER HOW MANY HOURS YOU'VE SPENT WATCHING *THE CLOCK*!!!!"

Carlos Spencer-Bayard's third journey to *The Clock* began under an auspicious sign; when he started his car, the first song that burst from his radio was a live version of Sonic Youth's "Incinerate". From his research, Ghost was aware that Marclay first rose to prominence as an experimental sound artist/turntablist. As a sound artist, Marclay orbited the same musical solar system as Sonic Youth. In fact, Marclay, Thurston Moore, and Lee Ranaldo once shared the stage at a music festival in Canada. Their performance was recorded and later released as a CD. Just before the trio began playing, an inebriated audience member yelled, "Fuck Shit Up!" at them and the phrase, perfectly capturing the moment, became the album's title.

Does the soundtrack for *The Clock* "Fuck Shit Up"? Not exactly. While Sonic Youth is a good musical analogy for Marclay's early work, a better comparison for *The Clock* might be

Sigur Rós' nonsensical album "Með suð í eyrum við spilum en-dalaust." According to Zalewski, as Marclay rushed to finish *The Clock* ahead of its opening at White Cube, "the sound collage became ten times as intricate as the visual collage." During this time, Marclay travelled to Williamsburg, Brooklyn to work with the sound designer Quentin Chiappetta. The importance of their work together, according to Chiappetta, was to make it "so that you didn't notice clips were ending, so that you were continually pulled along." The same proleptic pull is apparent within "Með suð í eyrum við spilum endalaust," which Ghost considered to be a very beautiful album even though he couldn't understand a single word of it.

Ghost arrived at the Wexner Center fifteen minutes before the gallery was scheduled to open at 11:00 A.M. It was Super Bowl Sunday, and he was expecting a small crowd. After mill-ing around outside the installation with one other ClockHead, he ducked under the security gates as soon as they began to lift and darted into *The Clock* to catch the hour change.

"The train leaves at eleven. We've missed it!" Harry Potter wails to his redheaded friend Ron. Ghost hadn't watched a single Harry Potter movie, but he had seen Daniel Radcliffe's willy on the Great White Way. In 2008, at the end of *Equus*, at the ripe old age of nineteen years, he bounced around the stage coura-geously in the buff.

"I can't appear at eleven o'clock in the morning in an eve-ning dress!" a petulant Sophia Loren says to a perturbed Marlon Brando. Looking as granite as ever, Brando is sailing around a hotel suite in a blue bathrobe, which is much fancier than the blue bathrobe Ghost wore most mornings.

At 11:24 A.M., a troupe of tardy actors stops a train that is pulling out of the station by bellowing: "STOP... THAT... TRAIN!" Good luck trying that at the Hoyt-Schermerhorn stop in downtown Brooklyn.

A few minutes later, Ghost was surprised by a black-and-white cameo from The Man in Black. In the clip, Cash menacingly holds a gun towards a frightened female. Speaking in a thick southern drawl, the singer utters a line that would not have been out of place in one of his songs: "Ain't no alternative, you've got forty seconds to live." The imagery surges forward. A few moments later, the menacing Man in Black returns: "looks like your time's run out, lady."

Of course, viewers never see the resolution of this scene – is it too outlandish to assume that he shot her down just to watch her die? – because viewers never see the resolution of *any* scene in *The Clock*. As the imagery barrels down the track like the Wabash Cannonball, viewers are forced to do one of two things: actively resolve the scene in their imagination or forget it entirely. Using Johnny Cash's cameo as a starting point, *The Clock* cannonballs into Cameron Diaz laughing in "The Brothers McMullen," Peter Sellers being goofy in one of the "Pink Panther" movies, Big Ben (*bien sûr*), and Mark Ruffalo pleading, "There's no time. It's 11:30. She's going to be dead in half an hour!" Before the viewer has the opportunity to wonder if this quote is a sly reference to Johnny Cash's scene, a burst of annoying whistling announces the appearance of "The Breakfast Club".

In *The Clock*, clips connect to one another like scenes spied through the windows of a moving train. This realization reminded Ghost of the Townes van Zandt lyric: *Time: she's a fast old train. She's here then she's gone, and she won't come again.* As the imagery rumbles past, viewers are left visually grasping at snippets. Any viewers in search of narrative continuality – and Ghost suspected this is what Richard Brody was really in search of when he panned the piece – are destined to be as frustrated as Michael Douglas in "Falling Down" being told that *McDonald's* stopped serving breakfast at 11:30 A.M. It was now 11:33 A.M. Ghost almost missed this scene because of a trip to the bathroom. His bladder still full, Ghost returned to the installation, feeling mildly irritated, just in time to watch Douglas, with a crazed look in his eye and his buzzcut bristling with anger, lift his duffle bag from off the floor and plunk it down on the counter with a loud, menacing *THUD!* And to think: had the bathroom not been "Closed for Cleaning," Ghost would've missed this moment. (Of course, you never see Douglas' rage actually boil over: you only see the teasing build-up.)

Along with Big Ben's midnight explosion, the other scene in *The Clock* that almost every review mentioned was the noontide gunslinging streetfighting montage from "High Noon". But in Ghost's opinion, this montage was totally upstaged fourteen minutes before noon by the appearance of Christopher Walken in a military uniform. Ghost recognized the movie instantly: "Pulp Fiction".

"Five long years, he wore this watch up his ass," Walken explains, holding up the round face of a wristwatch in front of the round face of a pudgy child, who is supposed to be a young Bruce Willis. "Then he died of dysentery. He gave me the watch. I hid this uncomfortable hunk of metal up my ass two years..."

There were eight other people in the installation; everyone laughed, including Ghost.

Spoiler Alert: "High Noon" doesn't actually appear at high noon: Ghost first identified the movie at 12:08 P.M. To ring in noontide, Quasimodo swings joyously on the church bells of Notre Dame. A few minutes later, a disinterested blonde lights up a cigarette in a college lecture hall. *What university allowed students to smoke during lectures?* Ghost wondered. *Must be a Film Studies class.*

Two minutes after this clip, Laurence Olivier appears wearing tights and a tight frown; in his hand, he holds poor Yorick's skull. *Hello, Hamlet*! At the end of his speech, a bell tolls off in the distance.

At 12:31 P.M., a black-and-white man shows a woman a clock. "This is the clock?" she asks skeptically. "What's so special about it?"

"Don't you see," the man replies excitedly. "It's over three hundred years old! It's still ticking. It's withheld the test of time!" This exchange reminded Ghost of how, in the Lambert Family Lecture, Marclay said that *The Clock* will feel different as it ages.

12:34 P.M.... *BONJOUR GÉRARD*! While it's only on-screen for a flash, the face is unmistakable: *SMACK!* goes the bottom. In the clip, the sensual Frenchman is wearing a priest's collar.

If Gérard Depardieu has a face like a smacked bottom, does Tom Cruise have a face like a scrubbed toilet? This was not meant to be an insult: Cruise's face always looks so clean that it mirrors polished porcelain. What sparked this thought was a sequence that began with James Bond cutting through a rope with his wristwatch above a tank full of sharks, transformed into an image of a woman furiously scrubbing a toilet, which transformed into a close-up of Tom Cruise.

A moment later, a telephone rings. A chubby, bald comedian answers. Ghost recognized this comedian's face, but he couldn't remember his name. In the clip, it's obvious that he has overslept.

"I'll be there: 1400 hours," the sleepy comedian says hastily into the receiver.

"Speak English!" Danny Devito yells in response.

"Two o'clock," the comedian sputters out. "Two-thirty at the latest."

"OK, move your fat ass!" Devito slams down the receiver and mutters: "What a fruitcake!"

As the afternoon stretched on, the installation filled up with fruitcakes. *Shouldn't everybody be getting ready to watch the bloody Super Bowl?* Ghost wondered. Directly in front of Ghost sat an elderly couple. Every few seconds, the wife would lean over and whisper an actor or actress' name into her husband's ear. Ghost didn't recognize a single one of these names.

The Scrubbed Toilet appeared again. This time, he's talking to a man seated next to him on an airplane. "You keep staring at that watch like your life depended on it," the man says playfully.

An hour earlier, a young (maybe) Dustin Hoffman was seen riding an old bicycle along the bumpy shoreline of a slowmoving river. Strapped to the back of the bicycle was a thin square of wood with a tiny, round clock affixed to it. Just after 1:20 P.M., Hoffman places this piece of wood into the river and watches it float away from the shoreline. Amidst *The Clock*'s steady stream of visual imagery, such a strange, poetic gesture struck Carlos Spencer-Bayard as particularly poignant. *The Clock* is a visual river, in which viewers are allowed to momentarily drift away from the shores of reality. The flux of *The Clock*'s visual imagery transforms film into Heraclitean fire; and like the philosopher's famous fragment, you can never step into the same segment of *The Clock* twice. For example, Ghost could return to *The Clock* at exactly 1:09 P.M. and watch the clip of three people seated at an outdoor café table drinking what appears to be absinthe, but the experience would be different. The day would be different, his location within the installation would most likely be different, and his attention span would be different. It's possible that the clip would float past completely unnoticed, like so many others.

"What good is a watch without you?" a black-and-white soldier in a plinth helmet asks a woman, whose face is partially obscured by a glamorous black veil. Earlier, Ghost watched the same soldier spying on the woman as she purchased the watch. Because of his uniform, steely glare, and stealthy demeanor,

Ghost assumed the guy was her parole officer, not her boyfriend.

As 2:00 P.M. neared, Carlos Spencer-Bayard experienced a strange sensation: he was bored. To amuse himself, he crafted a hypnotic mantra and repeated it over and over again in his head:

Tom Cruise, Sean Penn, Johnny Depp, Big Ben…
Tom Cruise, Sean Penn, Johnny Depp, Big Ben…
Tom Cruise, Sean Penn, Johnny Depp, Big Ben…

Ghost once read in the *New Yorker* that there's a database somewhere that keeps track of every reference ever made in a college essay. (God, whose job was it to read all those college essays? He would rather work for the NSA reading personal emails: at least those had some juicy bits!) Ghost assumed that sometime in the not-so-distant future an ambitious Films Studies graduate student would record every appearance of every actor in *The Clock*. Such meaningless metadata would then be used to settle the raging debate over who was the most famous actor of our era. Ghost's guess: unfortunately not Steven Guttenburg.

Tom Cruise, Sean Penn, Johnny Depp, Big Ben…
Tom Cruise, Sean Penn, Johnny Depp, Big Ben…
Tom Cruise, Sean Penn, Johnny Depp, Big Ben…

"It's five to two," John Cleese announces authoritatively from the backseat of a parked car.

"I'm hungry!" the woman seated in the passenger seat shouts in response.

"We're all hungry," Cleese retorts in his proper English accent. "But we can't eat now, because we're in the middle of a field!"

While never a fan of "Monty Python," Ghost thought John Cleese was hilarious. He was one of those comedians who could make anything laugh-out-loud funny just by his mannerisms and manner of speaking.

"Margarita?" a sassy older woman asks while seated in a brown leather recliner.

"Mother, it's two o'clock in the afternoon!"

On that note, feeling gleefully free, Ghost once again sundered the film's embrace and quickly fled the installation. On his way across the Wexner Center Plaza, Ghost pondered a disheartening question: was *The Clock* boring? Only Pinocchio would say no. While watching the video, there were moments when the boredom reached near intolerable levels. Pondering such depths of boredom reminded Ghost of how David Foster Wallace's final novel was intended to be an investigation into boredom, but the topic became so unbearable that the author killed himself. This was not a pleasant thought. He was not even halfway through his quest to watch all twenty-four hours of *The Clock*, should he be this bored?

Nearing High Street, Ghost contemplated walking again to *Buckeye Donuts* for a quick cup of coffee, even making a pilgrimage of it. After all, it was two o'clock in the afternoon. At this time of day, coffee was essential to combat the dreaded afternoon lag. Two o'clock in the afternoon should be the start of the siesta; if he were either Rafael Nadal or Pablo Picasso, he would be asleep right now.

As he crossed High Street, *satori* struck. Of course *The Clock* was boring at two o'clock in the afternoon, the day itself is boring at two o'clock in the afternoon. *The Clock* was experiencing the same afternoon lag that he was. *The Clock*'s world was his world: their rhythms were perfectly in sync. After years of museumgoing, Carlos Spencer-Bayard had never experienced such a strange realization. It was as if he were watching a work of art shed its skein of simulacra like a middle-aged Meryl Streep shedding her bathrobe in front of Alec Baldwin's greedy stare in the movie "It's Complicated".

6:15 P.M. to 7:58 P.M.

Ghost had not always been Ghost. For years, his nickname had simply been the logical shortening of his first name from 'Carlos' to just *Los*. This was what his basketball and rugby teammates called him. But as he changed, so too did his nickname. First, he stopped playing sports; then he stopped watching sports on television; and then he stopped watching television altogether. As his bingedrinking declined, he began wanting to write more, socializing less. And when he did socialize, he would often materialize in groups without warning and disappear vaporously. Even when he was physically somewhere, his mind was elsewhere. As he spent more time alone, a casual vacancy began appearing in his interactions with other people. Absence became his defining feature: things he *didn't* do, places he *didn't* go. As his friends began noticing this change, *Los* slowly transformed into *Ghost*. But Ghost never thought of himself as a Ghost: he thought of himself as a cloud of smoke. This description he had magpied from an Elliott Smith lyric:

> *There's nothing here that you'll miss;*
> *I can guarantee you this is a cloud of smoke*
> *Trying to occupy space. What a fucking joke. What a fucking joke.*

The idea of a cloud of smoke urgently trying to occupy space was the best explanation Ghost had as to why he spent so many hours alone, writing. The absence/presence divide featured as prominently within his work as it did within his thoughts. How could anyone be certain of his *presence?* The self was a constructed entity, and language was little better: an authority no less than Montaigne once declared that there was nothing to assure him that all thought was not haunted by the ghost of unreason. So without relying on the fantasy of self or the chicanery of language, how could Ghost prove that he was a *presence?* Or to state this dilemma differently: if he were asked, like a character in his novel is asked, to prove that he "did not not exist," what would he say? Technology is no help, as our virtual identities, so carefully constructed and curated with constant status updates, frolicsome photos, suave selfies, and witty tweets, speak more of our *absence* than our *presence.*

His answer: writing. The act of writing, like the act of listening to music, was something that filled Ghost with an assured *presence.* His Writing Self was no longer vaporous; it was rocksolid, and this permanence was unshakeable. And if and when his words whispered into another person's life, he became a *presence* for them too. It was only when he stopped writing, and people stop reading what he wrote, that – *puff!* – he vaporized again.

Like writing, the act of viewing art was something that presented Ghost with a solid sensation of *presence.* It was comforting to know that art would always be there; or rather, always be *here.* Part of the rest of the world, it would also always be a part of his world.

After a rushed dinner, Carlos Spencer-Bayard arrived at the Wexner Center early, which resulted in him experiencing his first overlap. For fifteen minutes, he re-watched a familiar loop of imagery. Overlaps in *The Clock* are strange. *I've already seen this*! your right brain screams, while your left brain is busy collecting a wonderful visual menagerie of overlooked, ignored, or forgotten details from the passing images. Ghost knew that the overlap was over when an unmistakable face appeared on-screen, and *SMACK!* went the bottom.

Had Ghost stayed five minutes longer on opening night, his quest to see Gérard Depardieu would've been over before it began. At 6:39 P.M., Gérard appears tying a long, black tie while wearing a dark blue dress-shirt. Fashionably-speaking, this is not a winning combination, but with a face like that, is anyone looking at your clothing?[20]

A few minutes later, Ghost snickered while jotting down the question: "Juno, did you, by any chance, barf in my urn?"

This particular segment of *The Clock* included a mélange of recognizable actors in different roles. For example, at 6:43 P.M., Keanu Reeves appears next to Laurence Fishburne in "The Matrix". Twenty minutes later, a young Keanu shouts to himself: "Ted, don't forget to wind your watch, *dude*!"

At 6:49 P.M., Kevin Spacey appears staring into a bathroom mirror, spraying shaving cream into his palm. Ghost knew from Zalewski's *New Yorker* profile that Marclay himself, using a can of Noxzema, provided the audio for this scene. For some strange reason, this factoid made an otherwise boring scene seem exhilarating.

Just before 7:00 P.M., a young, drunk Tom Cruise stumbles into an opening at an art gallery. A female friend introduces him to the sculptor whose work is being exhibited. The work is pretty hideous: it looks like the kind of sculpture made by high school metalwork teachers. But even those sculptures are nowhere near as hideous as the artist's multicolored, striped tie. (Because that's the kind of clothing artists wear at their openings, right?) The two men begin casually insulting each other, obviously competing for the woman's affection. While gazing at one of the sculptures, Cruise muses, "but what I don't understand is how do you get the cockroaches to stay still for so long?" Whoa, move over, Clement Greenberg! For this insult, the Scrubbed Toilet takes a punch. (Because that's what happens at gallery openings, right?)

Moments later, Jim Carrey races into an empty, well-lit

---

20 If it feels like this is unjust to Gérard Depardieu's physical appearance, take a look at the photograph of him atop a scooter that appears in the February 25, 2013 *New Yorker*. He looks *minable*!

space where Morgan Freeman is waiting. "What time is it?" Carrey frantically asks.

"You're right on time," Freeman answers in his familiar, grandfatherly tone. "Seven o'clock."

This clip cannonballs into a close-up of a clean-shaven, creepy Kevin Spacey from the movie "Seven".

"What time is it?" Spacey asks, psychopathically.

"Why?" Morgan Freeman responds curtly.

"I'd like to know."

"It's 7:01."

"It's close," Spacey intones ominously.

What's close? Of course, the viewer will never know. For Ghost, the answer could be that he was close to seeing his first glimpse of Jack Bauer, who, for a brief second, appears exploring a deserted road with a flashlight.

Flashlights are extremely uncommon in *The Clock*, for whoever looks at a clock with a flashlight? On the other hand, candles are omnipresent. It's easy to forget how essential candles once were; in addition to being the world's primary source of illumination for millennia, burning candles also functioned as poignant visual symbols for the passage of time. Today, the burning candle has been replaced by the burning fag. (Hey, that terminology is okay: Marclay's European!) In Zalewski's profile, Marclay himself discussed this visual shift: "The burning cigarette is the twentieth-century symbol of time. As a memento mori, we used to show a candle, but a cigarette is so much more modern. Yet it's the same thing – you see time burning."

An image of a single burning candle set against a pitch-black background reminded Ghost of how in the very same gallery space, fifteen years earlier, he had attended an exhibition of Gerhard Richter's work. This exhibition marked his first visit to the Wexner Center. The most memorable paintings from that exhibition were a series of burning candles. A reproduction of one of these candles graced the cover of Sonic Youth's 1988 album "Daydream Nation".

On-screen, a woman answers the door holding a large, fluffy cat to her chest.

"7:30 sharp," the man on the other side of the door announces cheerfully. "I hope you like your men prompt!"

And I hope you like your women covered in cat hair! Ghost thought.

There must have been an evening event going on at the Wexner Center as a great influx of people suddenly flooded the installation and filled every available seat.

Here's something that Carlos Spencer-Bayard suspected not many people knew about him: as a child, he was mesmerized by John Travolta. Earlier that evening, while eating dinner in his apartment, Ghost had referenced the dinner table scene from "Saturday Night Fever". This scene had always been one of his favorite moments in the movie.[21] Just before 7:40 P.M., this scene appears in *The Clock*, but the imagery surges forward before Travolta could blurt out his famous request that his father not hit his hair.

Soon after this clip, Ghost realized that his parking meter was about to expire. By his calculations, his time was due to run out at exactly 7:42 P.M. For an instant, Ghost contemplated rushing out of *The Clock* to feed his meter, but instead, he chose to stay. The Wexner Center was scheduled to close at 8:00 P.M., and what were the chances that he'd be ticketed in the next twenty minutes? He counted down the minutes until his parking meter

---

21 His other favorites include Travolta coming out of the bathroom, in his skivvies, playfully shouting "Attica! Attica!" and his monologue about how everybody has to "dump on" somebody.

expired through watching *The Clock*. This was a strange sensation: Ghost had never before experienced a work of art that so actively partnered with the temporal anxiety of its viewers to avoid potential parking tickets. Just as his meter ran out, an image of Las Vegas appeared on-screen.

Had Ghost left the installation to tend to his parking meter, he would've missed what is the funniest scene in *The Clock*. The act of synchronizing watches appears in *The Clock* almost as frequently as Big Ben. This endeavor is often portrayed as being utterly ridiculous. Getting two watches to run in perfect synchronicity is nearly impossible, and furthermore, what's the point? What's a few seconds here or there? (Try telling *that* to the parking violations bureau!)

At 7:45 P.M., in what Ghost assumed was a scene from one of the "Pink Panther" movies, Peter Sellers and another man attempt to synchronize their watches. The duo humorously can't get in sync, and the proceedings are made even more hilarious by Sellers' silly accent and the fact that he is wearing a Band-Aid crookedly across his forehead.

At 7:58 P.M., Ghost was unceremoniously ousted by security from the Wexner Center. When he reached his car, he was happy to discover that his gamble had paid off. No ticket.

7:44 **P.M.** to 9:35 **P.M.**

In a vain attempt to recapture some of the sleep lost the night before, Carlos Spencer-Bayard was lying in bed thinking about beds. His was nothing extraordinary: a common queen that sat squarely on the floor atop a set of box springs. It had been purchased, years ago, from a department store in Zanesville's Colony Square Mall whose name always reminded Ghost of an elderly drunkard: Elder-Beerman's. While his bed may not have been extraordinary, it was extraordinarily well-travelled. By his count, it had been wrapped in plastic and packed into the back of a U-Haul no less than four times: from New Concord, Ohio to Boston's North End, from Boston's North End to Brooklyn's Park Slope, from Brooklyn's Park Slope to Portland, Maine's West End, and finally, from Portland's West End to Columbus' German Village.

Of late, Ghost found that he was sleeping in his bed less and less. Between his wife's penchant for sprawling across the entire mattress and his desire not to wake the "Noisy Oyster" who was sleeping soundly beside him, Ghost had assumed the habit of sleeping on the couch in the living room. He did this so frequently that he often referred to this couch as his "second best bed."

The ghost bed.

Will's will.

His mind was galloping again…

The first draft of Shakespeare's will made itemized bequests to his children, relatives, and cronies in both Stratford and London, but it failed to mention his wife. Sometime later, a single sentence was squeezed between the original lines: "Item, I gyve unto my wife my second best bed with the furniture." His "second best bed?" Where was his, to quote James Joyce, "bestabed"? The logical justification for this addition was that Shakespeare's wife was entitled to their bestabed as a widow's dower via common law, thus it was unnecessary to itemize it in a will. But by this logic, why was she not entitled to "bothabeds"? Why mention one and not the other?

Ghost had a theory. Yes, it was an outlandish theory, but it was no more outlandish than Joyce's theory that Sweet Anne was making the "beast with two backs" with all three of Shakespeare's brothers. (And come to think of it, exactly how many backs would that beast have? Three? Four? *SIX?!*)[22]

As the greatest cuckoldphobe in the history of western literature, Shakespeare obviously felt that his "bestabed" belonged to
him and him alone. The thought of his wife lying next to another
man in his bed after his death must have driven him horn-mad.
Yes, she was sixty-one years old when he died, but what did that
matter? Was that nothing? If so...

> *Why then the world, and all that's in't, is nothing,*
> *The covering sky is nothing, Bohemia nothing,*
> *My wife is nothing, nor nothing have these nothings,*
> *If this be nothing*

If this be nothing, Shakespeare be nothing. His obsession with cuckoldry was the darkengine that drove his thoughts.
Thoughts of death would have only intensified his obsession.

So here was Ghost's theory: as any Shakespearean scholar
can attest, whenever an ellipsis appears within a play, it is always
intentional. Gertrude and Claudius' relationship has no fore-
grounding; Iago has no parents; Lady Macbeth, no name. The
omission of Shakespeare's "bestabed" from his will was intentional. It didn't appear in his will because it didn't appear in his
house: he was no longer in possession of it. He had sent it to the
Globe Theater as a gift. After it burned down in 1613, during a
performance of *Henry VIII*, the Globe would've needed new props,
and beds were expensive. Thus, the harried addition to Shakespeare's will was a binding legal reminder that this gift was not to
be revoked: the bed was *not* to return to New Place. Will's widow

----

22 To be fair to Anne, this probably didn't happen. By the time Shakespeare appeared
in London in 1592, Anne was thirty-seven and the ages of his brothers were Gilbert
(twenty-six), Richard (eighteen), and Edmund (twelve). At that stage in her life, could
a thirty-seven-year-old woman be sleeping with a twenty-six year old, an eighteen
year old, *AND* a twelve year old? Probably not.

would have to make do with their "second best bed," just as she had been forced to make do with borrowing forty shillings from her father's shepherd to pay off a debt while her husband was living lavishly in lascivious London.

The thought of playgoers watching Othello murder the faultless Desdemona in Shakespeare's own bed was *unsettling*. But what aspect of Shakespeare's final years wasn't *unsettling*? His early on-set curmudgeoness, his demotion to part-time, the ending to *The Tempest* (which Ghost liked to refer to as "Good News for People That Love Bad News"), his early retirement? All of these things were *unsettling*. And perhaps the most *unsettling* thing of all was that the greatest writer the world had ever known gave up writing entirely. The rest was silence. Nothing is known of the final three years of Shakespeare's life. Were these years yet another intentional ellipsis?

Ghost believed that Shakespeare spent the final three years of his life composing his final stage exit. Was it so outlandish to think that this exit included the donation of his "bestabed" to the Globe? And was it too outlandish to think that he invited Ben Jonson and Michael Drayton out to Stratford-Upon-Avon to celebrate his fifty-second birthday... *with intent?*

Ghost glanced over at his alarm clock: twenty to eight. He didn't want to be late.

Worried about missing the 8:00 P.M. hour change, Ghost arrived at the Wexner Center early, which created another overlap. The first scene he recognized was Peter Sellers and his crooked Band-Aid synchronizing his watch.

Just before 8:00 P.M., an image of the World Trade Center appears on-screen. This imagery surprised Ghost as he hadn't seen those towers in years.

"My watch says eight o'clock. If you're not here by ten, THE DEAL'S OFF!" a man in a black-and-white film shouts into a telephone.

"Time: 8:03," Vincent Price announces flatly into a tape recorder. "Sharp stinging sensation."

The actor, who Ghost most readily associated with Michael Jackson's *Thriller* video, was wearing a lab coat and seated in a laboratory. Because of this, Ghost assumed Price was recording the results of some kind of ghoulish experiment that he has just performed on himself. Or he was stoned. This possibility reminded Ghost of Walter Benjamin writing *On Hashish*.

At 8:10 P.M., Ghost caught his first glimpse of the movie "Back to the Future". Because of its ever-present clocktower, he assumed the movie would feature prominently throughout the next few hours.

"Definite blurring of vision at 8:11," Vincent Price announces groggily.

One minute later, more blurring of vision occurs as the Scrubbed Toilet fills up a row of colorful shot glasses atop a bar. Ghost assumed that this scene must be from the movie "Cocktail"; many years ago, he had watched this movie, but he was too young to remember much of it.

After a montage of theater curtains opening, a gaggle of small children entered the installation. All of the children were wielding penlights, like little Jack Bauers. As thin streams of light danced around the dark room, the children searched for empty seats; but unoccupied seats were hard to find, as the installation was the most crowded Ghost had ever seen it. The majority of the children ended up standing directly behind where he was sitting. (He was seated in his preferred spot: furthest column from the entrance, back row, rightmost seat.) Behind him, Ghost could hear the children speaking French to their "papas." (*Who knew that there were so many French speaking children in Columbus?*) In a normal movie theater, a troupe of chattering children would elicit an angry hissing chorus of *ssshhhh*. But here, there is not a single *ssshhhh* directed towards the petite frogs. Why would they? With *The Clock*, it doesn't matter if you miss some of the dialogue, nor does it matter if your attention is diverted elsewhere. (Or perhaps no one knew the proper French translation for the word *ssshhhh*.)

What does it feel like to watch *The Clock* without knowing English? By Ghost's calculations, the video's dialogue is 75% English, 15% French, 5% Spanish, and 5% something else. Is fluency in English a necessity for enjoying the experience, or is the video as enjoyable for non-English speakers? (While he doesn't speak "Hopelandic," Ghost still enjoyed listening to Sigur Rós.) And what was it like to experience *The Clock* in a foreign country, like Daniel Zalewski did in Japan? Would it feel different?[23] Would the strangeness of being in a foreign country effect the reception of the work's visual imagery? Since he had already made the comparison to a passing train, why not compare the experience of watching *The Clock* to navigating a crowded train station? (After all, no one can deny that *The Clock* is very train-centric.) Was experiencing *The Clock* in a non-English speaking country as confusing as trying to buy (um, he could do this...) *un billet à Cluis de la Gare d'Austerlitz*?

Ghost feared that a non-English speaker would miss the humor in the scene of an adolescent girl, sporting an atrocious 80's haircut and tight pastel jeans, pacing the sidewalk, while two girlfriends stood behind her, sharing a bag of Skittles. After two or three paces, the girl turns and shouts to her friends in a thick Jersey accent: "Where the *FOOCKING HELL* is Mike

---

23 During the Lambert Family Lecture, Christian Marclay mentioned how Japanese viewers refuse to sit on the sofas, choosing inside to stand around them. To Ghost, this sounded like an extreme example of not wanting to touch the art.

Brennan!" When it's decided that Mike is not showing up, one of the Skittlesmunchers suggests that they go see "Saturday Night Fever" at the local Cineplex.

At 8:35 P.M., a black-and-white family appears seated around the dinner table. This family consists of a young married couple and what Ghost assumed was her elderly father.

"Take your preoccupation with the clock," the wife says matter-of-factly.

"That makes me *crazy*?" the father responds.

"Well," the wife continues. "You have to admit that you spend a lot of time with it, sometimes half the night."

Ghost considered himself lucky that his wife hadn't broached the same subject to him… yet.

While jotting down this exchange, the thought occurred to Ghost that Christian Marclay plays with the word "clock" much like Shakespeare played with the word "globe."

At 8:56 P.M., a young man stands outside the façade of a classic '50s diner. He's dressed for a date. She's late. He nervously looks down at his watch and whines, "Aw, where is she, Hoppy?"

Shoeless Ma'a![24] The boy is wearing a Hopalong Cassidy wristwatch! Cambridge's favorite son **DOES** make an appearance in *The Clock*! Carlos Spencer-Bayard felt extremely guilty for doubting the omnipresent power of his hometown movie star. (Sorry, Hoppy.)

Hopalong Cassidy's unexpected cameo is the highpoint of what is an otherwise boring stretch in *The Clock*. This surprised Ghost. He thought the evening hours would be more exciting. Instead, during these hours, the video is filled with a barrage of

---

24 This phrase is a replacement for *Holy Shit*! It comes from the 2010 Tri-Nations when the New Zealand All Blacks defeated South Africa in Soweto thanks to some late-match heroics by a one-shoed Ma'a Nonu.

banal actors: John Wayne looking paunchy, Kevin Costner looking tired, Jimmy Stewart looking grandfatherly, Clint Eastwood
looking stern, Matlock looking like Matlock...

Four minutes before his parking meter expired, Ghost
slipped out of the installation. His exit was not easy; because of
the random assortment of body parts strewn across the floor, he
was forced to hopalong carefully.

Since it was still early on a Saturday night and he knew his
wife and littlelion were already asleep, Ghost decided not to return immediately to his apartment. Instead, he redirected himself
to *Rafael's Silver Cloud Lounge*. Situated on the corner of Mohawk
and Livingston, directly across the street from the city's famed
"Your Friend, Shadow Jesus" church, *Rafael's Silver Cloud Lounge*
was the closest thing Columbus had to an authentic New York
City darkwood, polished brass bar.

Before learning that his wife was pregnant, Ghost had only
frequented the bar sporadically: news of the pregnancy ramped
up his attendance considerably. The exact day that he had learned
of his impending fatherhood was April 23: Shakespeare's Birthdeathday. As a Bardolater, such timing was as ominous as the fire-
drake that Shakespeare himself saw every year on his birthday.[25]

Neither Ghost nor his wife harbored any illusions about
what the pregnancy would entail; as they say in New Zealand
rugby, they both knew that they were in for some "hard yards."
In preparation of these "hard yards," Ghost quit his job tutoring
learning disabled students at Muskingum University and devoted himself full-time to pampering his pregnant wife. In addition
to being her chauffeur, he cooked, grocery shopped, cleaned, and
when strict bed-rest was bestowed, as they both knew it would
be, Ghost took over every detail, both minor and major, of man-

....
25 April 23rd is the climax of what is known today as the Lyrids meteor shower.

servanting. In his spare time, he wrotewrotewrote. Even though he never considered himself a novelist, *satori* struck while reading *Candide, or Optimism*; Voltaire's characters were practically pleading to be plucked from their pages, stripped of their French *qualitiés*, clad in American apparel, and placed in a contemporary retelling. Like *Candide*, Ghost's novel was not a typical narrative: the story was full of deaths and unexplained resurrections, creative secondbirths, lengthy dream sequences, outrageous acts of miseducation, and all those "portmantypos." One afternoon, a curt textbox appeared on-screen announcing that Spell Check had exceeded its capacity and would no longer underline misspellings; at first, Ghost was unconcerned by this development, but then he quickly began fretting over every hte and and *(sic)*. His novel also magpied sections from *The Brothers Karamazov*, *Ulysses*, *Moby-Dick*, and *A Confederacy of Dunces*. And perhaps most bizarrely, Ghost insisted on "sketching from life," stuffing his narrative with references to real people (Paul Auster, Marina Ambromovic, Moses Malone), real places (the New Orleans Museum of Art, the Rothko Chapel, *The Old Absinthe House*), and real events (Kermit Ruffins' weekly gigs at *Vaughn's*, Wagner's *Ring Cycle* at Lincoln Center, the Iraq War). He also inserted cameos from both himself and his wife into the narrative, and when they finally decided on a name for their son, he added that too.

Upon finishing the novel, Ghost began querying literary agents. Every morning, he received a fresh bouquet of rejectionflowers. Such rejection came as no surprise; in fact, it was so unsurprising that he parodied it in the novel itself. In a scene that occurs during intermission of *Das Rheingold*, after an initial burst of interest, the novel's protagonist is forced to endure numerous looks of "literaryagentagony" as his life story is rejected for publication by an agent because it is devoid of "wizardy, vampire abstinence, Swedish techonobuggery, shady sadomasochism, or murderous futuristic teenage forestry." But oddly enough, Ghost found these months of nearconstant rejection thrilling; after years of *Billy Budd*-ing everything he wrote, it finally felt like he was rising from the depths of hobbywriting to the not-so-lofty lows of stock rejection letters.

Another thrilling aspect of the process was learning just how much *sitzfleisch* he could endure: it turned out that he was something of a *sitzfleisch* samurai. He routinely wrote all morning and proofread all afternoon. When it became obvious that he was going to need even more time, he began frequenting *Rafael's Silver Cloud Lounge* after his wife went to bed. Each night, he would bring his "writer's kit": two 4 x 6 pieces of lined notebook paper, two ballpoint pens, and a healthy thirst. On his walk through German Village, Ghost would compose his thoughts so he could sit down, order a drink, and immediately get to work. When both pieces of notebook paper were filled, front and back, he would retire for the evening. Other than the servers, he rarely spoke to anyone. The more frequent his visits became, the more the servers began to recognize him, and the more they went out of their way not to bother him. They simply entered his bar tab into the computer under the name "Steinbeck" and let him work.

The only downside to *Rafael's Silver Cloud Lounge* was its popularity. Columbus was not a drinker's town: it was a drunk's town. Such drunks went to bars in large packs, consumed large quantities of food and drink, and stayed for a loooong time. Such behavior gobbled up available seating. Carlos Spencer-Bayard had a name for such obnoxious drunkards: C-bags. *Rafael's Silver Cloud Lounge* was not as C-bag centric as *Brothers Drake*, but it still tended to attract a high volume, especially on the weekends. Because of such ever-present C-baggery, there was always the chance that Ghost would be denied a seat at *Rafael's Silver Cloud Lounge*, and this was exactly what happened when he stopped into the bar on his way home from the Wexner Center. Since he couldn't secure a seat, Ghost was forced into hovering awkwardly in-between the photobooth and the handicapped bathroom, his drink in one hand and his notepad in the other. Ghost was neither pleased nor surprised; after all, it was a Saturday night. The awkward hovering was only tolerable because he hadn't intended to stay long: according to his own viewing calendar, he was scheduled to be back at the Wexner Center early the next morning.

7:43 A.M. to 10:09 A.M.

When Carlos Spencer-Bayard returned to the Wexner Center the next morning, the installation was filled with a ragged bunch of allnight stragglers. Because his preferred seat was occupied by an overstuffed dufflebag (*was that necessary?*), he was forced to sit in the middle row, middle column. *The Clock* itself is filled with images of couches, all of which appear to be more comfortable than the white Ikea couches that accompany the video everywhere it goes. If the installation was a game of tic-tac-toe, Ghost was sitting where every game began. Having sat in this seat before, he knew how uncomfortable it was. The problem with the middle couch was that watching *The Clock* for an extended period of time meant having to stretch your legs sporadically, and there wasn't enough leg-room to do this in the middle row. It was like sitting on an airplane. But this morning, Ghost was surprised to discover that the couches had been moved slightly: the front row was now far enough away that he was able to comfortably stretch out his legs. Sure, this might seem like an insignificant detail, but that's what, according to Marclay, experiencing *The Clock* is all about.

"It's 7:45 in the morning," a man announces in a hospital room. "We haven't had this much action since the Elks Club fire!"

Three minutes later, a balding Gene Hackman gets up from

a couch and walks over to a cluttered desk. Absentmindedly, he begins thumbing through a pile of mail. This color clip leaps into a black-and-white image of an envelope addressed to "Miss Molly Bloom."

Shoeless Ma'a! Ghost thought. *Bold hand*!

(Technically: *Bold (incorrect) hand*, as the envelope should have been addressed to "Mrs. *Marion* Bloom.")

Although the image only lasts an instant, for an avowed Joycean like himself, the inclusion of *Ulysses* in *The Clock* is thrilling. It was as if Marclay slipped the image into the video just for Ghost. And what made it feel even more special was the fact that the scene is completely clockless, and as such Marclay hadn't needed to include it, but he did. And why was that, if not just for Ghost?

The bigger question was what was *The Clock*'s relationship to *Ulysses*? Within his profile, Zalewski mentions the book, noting: "Marclay began thinking of the hours as chapters in a novel. This seemed fitting: in building a monument to the drama of a single day, he was following the lead of *Mrs. Dalloway* and *Ulysses*." And the Wexner Center's brochure also mentions *Ulysses*, saying: "and since [Marclay] aims to shape the sensation of a day passing, the precedent of Joyce's *Ulysses* likewise hovers nearby, fabricating a day in words rather than images (for *The Clock*, every day is Bloomsday)."

If every day could be Bloomsday, Carlos Spencer-Bayard would be in nerd-heaven. After reading *Ulysses*, in one gigantic summertime gulp, Ghost read *The Complete Annotated Guide to Ulysses*, Richard Ellman's *Ulysses on the Liffey*, and *yes I said yes I will Yes.: A Celebration of James Joyce, Ulysses, and 100 Years of Bloomsday*. He claimed Bloomsday as his favorite holiday, and meticulously crafted yearly celebrations. The reason why he loved Bloomsday so much was because it celebrated the idea of literature as a way of life, as opposed to simply being an accoutrement to life.

Does *Ulysses* "hover nearby" *The Clock*? Is the novel's structure a proper precedent for Marclay's masterpiece? These are difficult questions to answer. Perhaps from the creator's perspective, *The Clock* and *Ulysses* are similar, but what about from the viewer's perspective? From his experience with both, Ghost thought that *The Clock*'s literary precedents lay elsewhere; for him, the experience of watching *The Clock* was more akin to reading a giant novel by Thomas Pynchon. Reading one of Pynchon's panoramas meant abandoning the desire to understand what's going on, as the books are too vast to be understood. Thus reading, say, *Gravity's Rainbow* is a struggle against the struggle for comprehension; page after page, the reader feels his mind gasping for the air of understanding. During these moments, it is essential to remember the advice of Harold Bloom: "every good reader properly *desires* to drown." Pynchon's books are meant to be enjoyed, not understood. Why are Pirate Prentice's Banana Breakfasts so damn important in *Gravity's Rainbow*? (Who knows?) In *Against the Day*, why does Merle Rideout think: "if the U.S. was a person, and it *sat down*, Columbus, Ohio would instantly be plunged into darkness?" (Does it really matter?) Why is Tyrone Slothrop wearing that German Expressionist pig costume in *Gravity's Rainbow*, and what exactly is the relationship between his erections and German V-2 rocket strikes? (Good luck figuring that out!) When reading a Thomas Pynchon novel, it is best not to get bogged down in such details: just keep surging through the narrative like a runaway V-2 rocket.[26]

Another literary precursor to *The Clock*, in Ghost's opinion,

---

26 For anyone in search of advice regarding Thomas Pynchon: read *Mason & Dixon* first. It is both the best and the easiest of Pynchon's 'Big 3' to read. While rewarding, *Gravity's Rainbow* is a difficult read, and *Against the Day* is patchy.

was Italo Calvino's *If on a winter's night a traveler*, as the fragmentary, nonsensical nature of Calvino's narrative mirrors *The Clock*'s visual anarchy. In both works, beautiful scenes unfold only to be abandoned with a cruel, gleeful severity. For example, when Woody Allen fears that he's going to be late for the bank robbery because his girlfriend has gotten in the shower before him, Ghost realized that he would never know if Allen made it to the robbery on time. Hell, he wouldn't even know if he got in the shower or not. When a scene ends in *The Clock*, it's usually gone forever.

As he watched a black-and-white man carefully warm a bottle of milk on a stovetop, *satori* struck. There *was* a connection between *The Clock* and *Ulysses*: met him pike hoses.

[O rocks! Tell us in plain words.]

"Metempsychosis. It's Greek: from the Greek. It means the transmigration of souls."

Allowing *The Clock*'s torrent of visual imagery to stimulate a steady stream of thoughts is akin to inhabiting Leopold Bloom's consciousness. *Ulysses* is stuffed with Bloom's beautifully banal thoughts. For example, observing a flock of pigeons circling the Irish house of parliament, "Poldy" contemplates what it must feel like for pigeons to defecate from midair ("I pick the fellow in black. Here goes. Here's good luck. Must be thrilling from the air"); while contemplating digestion, Poldy wonders if the classical female goddess sculptures in the National Museum and Library have anatomically correct bums ("Never looked. I'll look today. Keeper won't see. Bend down let something drop see if she")[27]; and even something as humdrum as the weather stimulates a poetic outburst ("Heatwave. Won't last. Always passing, the stream of life, which in the stream of life we trace is dearer

---

27 Seeking out a nude sculpture and giving its bum a sneak-peek is always an essential part of Ghost's annual Bloomsday celebrations.

than them all"). And these are just three examples in manymillion.

If experienced properly, watching *The Clock* is an act of metempsychosis, as it allows the viewer to inhabit Poldy's expansive, "divinely commonplace" consciousness. Continuing to discuss his namesake in *The Western Canon*, Harold Bloom explains: "what is not commonplace about Poldy is the wealth of his consciousness, his capacity to transmute his feelings and sensations into images." *The Clock* reverses this phenomenon: it begins with images and allows its viewers to transmute them into feelings and sensations.

Of course, isn't this what all moving images do? What's so different about *The Clock*? Think of it this way: if *The Clock* allows viewers to inhabit Leopold Bloom's consciousness, whose consciousness do viewers inhabit when they watch normal moving images? With their crass non-stop preoccupation with commerce and sexuality, is it not the consciousness of the "worst man in Dublin": Blazes Boylan?

Would there be any more scenes from *Ulysses* stealthily embedded within *The Clock*? Perhaps *The Clock*'s shadow narrative parallels *Ulysses*' plot structure, just as the book itself parallels *The Odyssey*. Identifying such a shadow narrative would be difficult, as the novel charts the passage of a day, not the passage of time. No one in *Ulysses* eats and sleeps by a clock, especially Molly. But there are some select moments in the book that are specifically linked to time: Dignam's funeral occurs at 11:00 A.M., Molly and Blazes' "rehearsal" is scheduled for 4:00 P.M., and Poldy ends up at the National Maternity Hospital at 10:00 P.M. Would any of these moments steal their way into *The Clock*?

"You mean everybody around here eats and sleeps by a clock?" Johnny Cash asks incredulously while seated in the passenger seat of a parked car. When he hears the driver's affirmative answer, the Man in Black appears to be shocked. "What a life!" he says sarcastically.

"Gibson! Don't you have an eight o'clock?" a voice screams at a young John Cusack, who is asleep in a cluttered dorm room.

"What time is it?" Cusack replies groggily.

"Nine to 8:00."

"SHIT!"

In a flash, Cusack is out of bed and vaulting over an Ezy Chair on his way out the door. Before leaving the room, he pauses to spray deodorant under his arms and swish mouthwash around in his mouth.

Two minutes later, Woody Allen jumps out of bed and heads for the bathroom.

"Aww, don't tell me you're gonna be in the shower now!" Woody wines.

"Virgil, why do you always do this to me?" an irritated female voice responds from the bathroom.

"I'm gonna be late for the robbery."

"Well, they can always start without you."

"No, they can't. I'm the ringleader!"

The 8:00 A.M. hour change is boring, but things perk up five minutes later when a skanky-looking woman appears in a sun-soaked diner seated at a booth across from Kevin Spacey. She is wearing nail polish, a windbraker, and lipstick of all slightly different shades of purple. He was wearing thick glasses and a godawful wig. He's drinking coffee; in front of her, sits a bottle of Miller Genuine Draft.[28]

"So what do ya think?" the woman asks. "Do you think you wanna marry me?"

Before Spacey can answer, the woman continues speaking.

"What time is it?"

....
28 According to Ghost's wife, this scene is from "The Shipping News".

Spacey meekly holds out his arm so his female companion can read his wristwatch.

"8:05," she announces. "I think I'm going to fuck you by 10:00."

Who wouldn't want to marry someone like *THAT*? But should such forward behavior come as a surprise from a woman who's drinking a MGD for breakfast? Of course, she's not the only one enjoying a liquid breakfast; two minutes later, a young Nic Cage sits at a deserted diner counter, looking despondent. In front of him is a gigantic martini with two large olives harpooned by a toothpick.

At 8:16 A.M., the bloodsplattered duo of Samuel L. Jackson and John Travolta appear in Quentin Tarantino's kitchen. All three men are awkwardly holding coffee mugs. Over Tarantino's right shoulder hangs a wall clock.

"Mmm…" Samuel L. Jackson says after taking a long sip from his mug. "Goddamn Jimmie, this is some serious gourmet shit!"

Of course, Jimmy is not impressed by Jules' flattery. He's worried that his wife will return home and discover the corpse in their garage.

"You gotta make some *phone calls*?" Tarantino says in an angry whine. "You gotta call some *people*? Well, then do it! And then get the *FUCK OUT OF MY HOUSE*!"

"Hey, that's Kool and the Gang," Jackson responds. "You know, we don't wanna fuck your shit up."

That last line reminded Ghost of Christian Marclay's performance with Thurston Moore and Lee Ranaldo. The scene also reminded Ghost of how he had once struck up a conversation with Tarantino at a bar in Carroll Gardens. All he remembered from that conversation was how the director's favorite lyric from Bob Dylan's *Time Out of Mind* album, which had just been released, was the moment in "Highlands" when the waitress accuses the song's narrator of not reading women authors.

>*You're way wrong,* Dylan croons as only Dylan can.
>*Which ones have you read then?*
>*I've read Erica Jong.*

Six minutes later, John Candy lovingly snuggles Steve Martin in bed. Ghost recognized the clip instantly: it is the most memorable scene from "Planes, Trains, and Automobiles". As Ghost watched with a smile, Candy tenderly kisses Martin on the ear, which wakes him up.

"Why did you just kiss me on the ear?" Martin asks alarmed.

"Why are you holding my hand?" Candy replies.

"Where's your other hand?"

"Between two pillows…"

At 8:31 A.M., Ghost recognized a quick clip from the movie "Precious". Why is this worth mentioning? By his estimation, "Precious" is the most recent movie to be included in *The Clock*.

"Phileas Fogg is the most punctual man alive," a stuffy Englishman declares to a group of stuffy Englishmen at 8:45 A.M. The group is standing in front of a large grandfather clock in an austere booklined study. Ghost had seen these men so often, and had heard them talk so much about Phileas Fogg, that he had deduced the scene was from "Around the World in Eighty Days".

Soon thereafter, *SMACK!* went the bottom.

It was 9:00 A.M. Gérard wakes up next to Anne McDowell. He's overslept, and it's obvious that he's late for something important. Hurrying around McDowell's bedroom in a frantic, disheveled state, he looks even more like Aled de Malmanche than normal. While Gérard's bedhead is impressive, it was not nearly as impressive as Hugh Grant's, which Ghost considered the most memorable of the morning's many bedheads.

At 9:04 A.M., a polite butler serves a prairie oyster to a man lying in bed. According to the butler, the man was on "quite the bender" the night before. Ghost was glad the same thing could not be said about him. Watching *The Clock* with a hang-over would have been *excruciating*. The morning hours are such a constant cacophony of alarm clocks that he feared a hungover viewer's head might explode.

Up until this point, Ghost hadn't had a single complaint with *The Clock*, but that all changed at 9:16 A.M. The scene be-gins with an image of a man asleep on his side; as the camera slowly pans down his body, it becomes obvious that he's sleep-ing fully-clothed. Just beyond the foot of the bed, a TV is on. As the camera lingers on the screen, Ghost realized what he was watching was *real* news footage of the World Trade Center tow-ers billowing smoke. This harsh intrusion of reality shocked and repulsed him.

As an artist who was living in New York City at the time, shouldn't Marclay have known better than to include such a grue-somely inappropriate image in *The Clock*? Had he been living in England or Switzerland at the time, this decision might have been somewhat forgivable. French philosopher Jean Baudrillard was not totally inaccurate when he claimed that 9/11 never hap-pened: he just said it wrong. But what do you expect? Baudril-lard's French and 9/11 was a very American event. What Baudril-lard should've said was that there were *two* 9/11s: the *real* event that affected *real* people, and the televised event, whose visual format was no different than, say, the scene of the White House exploding in "Independence Day," or a rerun of "Will & Grace". Or to phrase it slightly differently: there was the event that hap-pened to *us* (people living in New York City at the time), and there was the event that other people watched on TV.

Soon after 9/11, art critic Peter Plagens pledged to never

review an exhibition that incorporated 9/11 imagery. The reason he did this was because some things are just too monumental – not to mention monumentally painful – to be transformed into mere art. (At the time, Plagens was living in Tribeca.) And he was right. This appalling intrusion of reality made *The Clock* appear trite and pointless. Ghost watched the remaining hour with a kind of insouciant malaise: what did he care about "Back to the Future," "Die Hard with a Vengeance," or that stupid Sophia Coppola movie about Marie Antoinette? A sour bitterness lingering on his visual palate, as he dutifully waited for the hour change.

"Shit, it's ten," Natalie Portman says nervously while standing in an open doorway. "I have to be there at ten!"

"I know a shortcut," her male friend answers. Motivated by the urgency of the moment, he extracts a white cane and begins rapidly clicking his way down a cobblestone street.

Do blind people know good shortcuts? Ghost wondered, rising from his seat. He had never thought about this before.

1:37 P.M. to 6:00 P.M.

'*Swounds.* It had happened so unexpectedly, so unbelievably that Carlos Spencer-Bayard was reluctant to tell the story for fear of being called a liar, or worse: a Jonah Lehrer. The story began with an article in *Poets & Writers* on Gerard Manley Hopkins that Ghost had stumbled upon while having lunch at *Northstar Café*. A few pages past this article, Ghost discovered a section devoted to the "new generation of small presses that is changing the way we think about books." Since his quest for publication was nearing a frustratingly fruitless conclusion, he jotted down the information for every publisher mentioned in the article. Slowly, he began the process anew: more submissions, more rejectionflowers. Finally, one publisher remained. Had this publisher said no, it was *Billy*

Budd, The Handsome Sailor time; but he hadn't said no, he said **YES**. After a brief email exchange, Ghost opened his email to discover an official offer for publication; to celebrate, he swooped his son out of his bassinet and together they danced around the apartment to Vybz Kartel's "Summertime".

The promise of becoming a published novelist realigned Ghost's creative center of gravity. He had recently been accepted into two PhD programs in New Zealand: Victoria University in Wellington and The University of Auckland. His proposals focused on the study of "Imagereality" within visual culture, which he defined loosely as the confluence of photography, philosophy, and technology. His experience with *The Clock* was a major facet of his proposal, and he had initially envisioned his darkroom notes as PhD research; but now, perhaps these notes could be put to better use. Yet first, he had to complete his quest.

Twelve days had passed since Ghost last experienced *The Clock*. Up until this point, he hadn't paid a single dollar for admission; instead, he had successfully scheduled his viewings around the Wexner Center's free hours.[29] His goal was to spend less money viewing *The Clock* in its entirety at the Wexner Center than he would have paid for a single day at MoMA.[30]

Looking ahead, Ghost decided that trying to watch the rest of *The Clock*'s afternoon hours during one of the Wexner Center's free days would be unwise, as these days always drew a crowd, and his fear was that he would encounter a line on the final day of the exhibition. Such a line could be disastrous. So far, he hadn't spent a single second waiting in line.

....

29 In addition to being free of charge during allnighters, the Wexner Center was free Thursday evenings after 4:00 P.M. and the first Sunday of every month; Sundays were ideal for viewing *The Clock* because all of the city's parking meters were turned off, and thus he didn't have to worry about exceeding the two hour limit.

30 Admission at the Wexner Center is $8 for adults; at MoMA, it's $25.

Having paid his eight dollars, Ghost entered the installation on a quiet Saturday afternoon, and immediately ran smack into somebody's back. *Crap*, he thought. *I'm out of practice!*[31]

Having arrived early (again), Ghost experienced another lengthy overlap. Re-watching sections of *The Clock* means interacting differently with its imagery. During overlaps, Ghost often found himself less concerned with the specifics of each scene — recognizing actors, guessing the movie, etc. — and more focused on locating timepieces, which can be a challenge. He also focused more on the transitions between scenes. Although they're easy to miss, such transitions are the single most important aspect of *The Clock*. For example, after John Cleese announces, "we can't eat now because we're in the middle of a field," the next clip is of a lush playing field that reminded Ghost of the lawn of some fancy East Coast boarding school. In the scene, a group of teenagers are playing football. An actor, who from a distance resembles a young Scrubbed Toilet, drops back to throw a pass. But here's the rub: Cleese is English and the teenagers are playing *American* football. Here's another example of Marclay's transition trickery: at 1:40 P.M., a young Joseph Gordon-Levitt stands in a crowded public square, holding a small wire-rimmed notebook. (It's the same kind of notebook that, for years, Carlos Spencer-Bayard used to carry with him to museums.) Gordon-Levitt opens the notebook and glances down at one of its pages: the next scene is a close-up of a piece of notebook paper written in Chinese. Could such transitions be accused of being "gimmicky... mediocre, even trivial"? Richard Brody thought so. Ghost would disagree. At 2:44 P.M., a framed poster of Picasso's *Don Quixote* appears on the wall above a man asleep on a loveseat. For years, the exact same post-

....
31 Glancing over his shoulder as he wrote, Ghost's wife just muttered: "forty-nine pages of total dorkdom!"

er hung on the walls of Ghost's various apartments around New York City. From his experience working in an art gallery, Ghost knew that prints were difficult to sell because they exhibit only a small amount of the artist's hand: posters, of course, exhibit none. Thus each medium is valued accordingly. Each transition in *The Clock* exhibits a trace of Marclay's hand. These transitions are so skillful that they often appear seamless, and the sheer volume of them is staggering. Marclay's hand is everywhere in *The Clock*: it selected everything, positioned everything, and stitched everything together with sight and sound. As Geoff Dyer points out in his *Time* magazine blurb, Marclay's idea is "audacious in its simplicity." Anyone with access to lithography tools can make a print, but not every printmaker is Picasso; anyone with the right technology can make a video montage, but not every video montage is *The Clock*.

Daniel Zalewski didn't compare *The Clock* to a lithograph, he compared it to a tapestry, saying: "others could collect the thread, but Marclay would weave the tapestry." Ghost wasn't convinced that this comparison was adequate, as tapestries are antiquated and ostentatious. To him, *The Clock* is more like the ultra-mundane art of quilting. As any dedicated quilter can attest, if you want to gauge the quality of a quilt, the proof is in the stitching; or as Marclay himself put it, "art is all in the details." When asked to describe how *The Clock* was created, Marclay sounded very much like a quilter, admitting that the process was "more labor-intensive than ambitious."

Of course, there was something else, something more personal. If anyone with a video store membership and a laptop could make *The Clock*, couldn't anyone with a notepad and access to the video record his thoughts? Sitting in the dark, Ghost often thought about a potential doppelwätcher, watching *The Clock* in some exotic locale like Yokohama, Los Angeles, or Tel

Aviv. In his darkest hours, he envisioned this person as being not only a better writer (*doppelwätcher*? What a silly word!) and more knowledgeable about punctuation (what exactly is a splice comma?), but more ambitious and better connected within the publishing world. Of course, HIS *ClockHead* would be published before Ghost's. Of course, HIS *ClockHead* would garner more acclaim. Of course, HE would be invited on a worldwide lecture tour, which, of course, would include a stop in Wellington, New Zealand, where he would not only meet Geoffrey Batchen, but also have a pint at the Centurian Tavern with Ghost's kiwi mates, Paul, Matthew, and Kenny. Ghost's *ClockHead* would become a stuffed owl sitting on his shelf between his Master's Thesis (*Slavery & the Single Perspective: Nietzsche's Perspectivism, Propaganda, & the Photographic Plague*), his absinthe memoir (*True Confessions of a Southeastern Ohio Absintheur*), and his Noël Coward-inspired one-act play (*Mr. Heath Ledger is Dead: A Comedy*). In other words, Ghost would be left playing the role of Fox Talbot to his doppelwätcher's Daguerre.

But why should any of this matter? Everyone watches *The Clock* differently. There was no guarantee that Ghost's doppelwätcher would laugh at 2:09 P.M., when a menacing English soccer hooligan stands on a train platform and shouts, "Where the FOOK are these CUNTS!" And at 2:13 P.M., perhaps Ghost's doppelwätcher won't even notice John C. Reilly dressed in the garb of a Western sheriff, describing a man as being "as dead as Good Friday."

If his doppelwätcher was Australian, which was possible since *The Clock* had been shown at the Sydney Museum of Contemporary Art, he would instantly recognize – and most likely groan loudly at the sight of – Mick "Crocodile" Dundee. Seeing Aussie Mick reminded Ghost of how Australian art critic Robert Hughes had once bemoaned the fact that many Americans still consider "Crocodile Dundee" to be a work of social realism. It also reminded him of how the first installment of "Crocodile Dundee" was one of the few movies Ghost had ever watched in the old Cambridge movie theater, which closed before he reached a proper moviegoing age.

After grabbing his friend Wally's wrist and turning it over to look at his watch, Paul Hogan stares searchingly at the sun.

"It's 2:20. We'd better get going," he says tersely to his ladyfriend.

After he walks away, the woman glances at her watch in amazement: her back was turned when Mick consulted Wally's watch.

"It's exactly 2:20!" she says to Wally. "How did he do that?"

"That's why he's the best bushman in the territory," Wally answers with mock seriousness.

One of the movies Ghost was not surprised to see during this segment of *The Clock* was "3:10 to Yuma". Although he had never watched this movie, it was easy to spot because of Christian Bale and Russell Crowe's fabulous facial hair: Ghost suspected that no beard in the Old West ever looked *that* good.

At 3:00 P.M., a woman with a high-pitched voice welcomes Woody Allen into her apartment. It's obvious that they've never met before; there seems to be a strange sexual underbelly to their interaction, but maybe that's because there always seems to be a strange sexual underbelly to any interaction involving Woody Allen. Their conversation begins awkwardly. After Allen admits that his friends think that he has a great sense of humor, the woman squeals, "MINE TOO!" For a moment, the awkwardness subsides.

"You're going to LOVE this," the woman says, leading Allen into her living room to show him a wall clock depicting two pigs having sex.

"Isn't that a PISSER!" she squeals. "And take a look at this," she says procuring a pocketwatch whose hands depict a bishop having sex with a woman.

The awkwardness returns.

"Wow," Allen says fumbling for the right words. "That's really... disgusting."

This scene ends at exactly 3:10 P.M. and Ghost expected that the next clip would be from "3:10 to Yuma," but instead, a long, dopey clip of the Beatles appears.

Just as he begins writing "Where's 3:10 to..." a beautiful beard appears.

"Where's the 3:10 to Yuma," beautifully bearded Christian Bale demands, pistol in hand.

"Running late, I supposed," answers a frightened railroad clerk.

"How late?"

"Beats me. It gets here when it gets here."

"Goddamn trains," beautifully bearded Russell Crowe growls. "You never can rely on them."

Five minutes later, James Bond punches a woman in the face. (Spoiler Alert: it's really a man!) 007 appears frequently in *The Clock*. Having never watched an entire James Bond movie, Ghost never knew which particular movie was which, but the frivolousness, friskiness, and Britishness was always unmistakable. Every appearance reminded Ghost of his favorite James Bond anecdote, which was from an old Saturday Night Live skit. In the skit, Bond, as played by Chris Parnell, suavely goes to his doctor for a routine check-up and learns that he has over a hundred STDs, three of which only appear in sharks. A good SNL parody can contaminate any movie and/or political campaign.

After watching Mary Poppins take to the sky, Ghost left the installation to feed his parking meter. The maneuver worked like clockwork: he arrived at his car two minutes before his meter was due to expire, deposited enough quarters to get him through another forty-five minutes, and returned to his seat, all in under ten minutes. Upon returning to the installation, Ghost observed a prophetic message written underneath a round, outdoor time-piece: "Do not squander time. It is the stuff life is made of."

At 3:57 P.M., a man sits pensively below a version of Ro-din's *Le Penseur*. Seeing this sculpture reminded Ghost of how art appears infrequently in *The Clock*. In addition to Picasso's *Don Quixote*, Ghost recalled seeing the artist's outdoor Chicago sculpture and an Alex Katz painting, but not much else. The seated man rises and walks out of the frame. The next clip is a close-up of Julie Andrews. Ghost recognized this clip instantly: it is his Plymouth Rock. He was now re-watching the very first section of *The Clock* that he ever experienced.

After twenty minutes, Ghost took a break. He didn't have to be back in the installation until 5:04 P.M. Feeling slightly truant, he breezed into the Wexner Center's Heirloom Café for an espresso. The café was nearly empty. Occupying a small ta-ble over-looking Maya Lin's *Groundswell*, Ghost could still faintly hear *The Clock*'s soundtrack. From a distance, this soundtrack was a low, monstrous grumbling that sounded like Smaug with an empty stomach; the longer he stayed away, the longer it felt like *The Clock* was beckoning him to return.

Casually flipping through his notepad while swirling the tiny dark tempest of his espresso in a circular motion around its tiny whiteporcelain cup, Ghost was having trouble keeping his mind focused. A single thought kept rudely elbowing its way into his consciousness: hair. His was still there. Surveying the scalps of his friends, Ghost considered himself lucky. Some of his college roommates had started talking openly about Rogaine immediately after graduation. Ghost had a theory that all men, especially those of Lithuanian heritage, primarily fell into two hair categories: Arvydas Sabonis (confidently full) and Žydrunas Ilgauskas (hopelessly bald). Both he and his father were Sabonises, this led him to believe that his littlelion would be too; but that morning, after a family walk around German Village, Ghost pulled off his son's beanie cap and *whoosh*... Ghost knew that his son would eventually lose his baby hair, but he thought this would be a gradual process: he never expected a single *whoosh* of a beanie cap would whisk it all away. The sudden *whooshing* away of his son's hair made Ghost feel like a mischievous magician pulling a tablecloth out from underneath an unsuspecting tablesetting.

Staring down at his suddenly bald again littlelion, Ghost was consumed by fear. Would his son have to endure life as an Ilgauskas? The fear of bestowing negative traits – or conversely the failure to bestow positive traits – was one of the most unpleasant aspects of parenthood. This fear reminded Ghost of an old *New Yorker* cartoon depicting a father and son walking along a beach at sunset. Both men are wearing khaki shorts and have giant Kim Kardashian-sized asses. The caption reads: "Thanks for almost everything, Dad."

Upon closer inspection, Ghost was happy to discover that his littlelion wasn't completely bald: there was a tiny swathe of hair encircling the bottom of his head. Because of its size and location, this swathe reminded Ghost of a monk or an old Jewish shopkeeper who sold cheese on the Lower East Side. Upon closercloser inspection, Ghost realized that his littlelion also bore an eerie resemblance to Jackson Pollock, as depicted in the Hans Namuth photograph that was framed near their front door. His bald baby boy: the miniature monk, the old Jewish shopkeeper, little Jack the Dripper.

Just after 5:00 P.M., the final shootout from "The Good,

The Bad, and The Ugly" is interspersed with scenes of James Bond fighting a duel, whose steps are counted off by a midget wearing a tuxedo. If it can be said that James Bond is the romantic embodiment of what it means to be a British male, can the same thing be said about American men and Clint Eastwood? Do all American blokes secretly yearn to be a tight-lipped, unshaven, cigarchomping vigilante, who fights for the good against the bad, while wearing the ugly? And where exactly *did* Clint Eastwood's character get that godawful shawl? A rummage sale in Norman, Oklahoma? A Flea Market in Rancho del Ugly? Did an octogenarian leave it in his hooch after a one-night fling? That shawl looks so scratchy that Ghost doubted even the Dude from "The Big Lebowski" would wear it.

"The cheaper the crook, the gaudier the patter," Humphrey Bogart scolds a young gangster at 5:19 P.M. *The cheaper the shawl, the gaudier the pattern*, Ghost thought, still thinking about "The Good, The Bad, and The Ugly", as a clip from yet another Nic Cage movie appeared on-screen. Why does Nic Cage appear so frequently in *The Clock*? Is it because his movies tend to be so bad that they are *always* available in every video store anywhere on earth?

> **Young, pimply video store clerk:** That guy who rents all the Nic Cage movies was in again, boss. This time he rented *National Treasure*!

> **Old, grumpy video store owner:** He must be an artist or something.

"What time is it?" a woman asks petulantly.

"When you asked me a minute ago, it was 5:42," a man responds angrily. "It's now 5:43. When you ask me a minute from now, it'll be 5:44!"

At precisely 6:00 P.M., a door opens and a familiar man bursts into a familiar song.

"I feel a surge of deep satisfaction..."

[*Hey, me too*, Ghost thought.]

"I run my home precisely on schedule..."

[*The same thing can be said about me and parking meters*... well, not *exactly* the same thing; because the man is British, he chews up the first half of the word "shed'ule." Ghost distinctly remembered people in New Zealand doing the same thing.]

"Consistency is the life I lead."

9:04 P.M. to 11:33 P.M.

Being early once again, Carlos Spencer-Bayard made his detour to *Buckeye Donuts* for an 8oz coffee before proceeding to the Wexner Center. Next to the cash register, he spied a stack of coasters advertising *The Clock*. This struck him as strange. How many inebriated undergrads had spent a single minute watching *The Clock*?

As he strolled down High Street, coffee-in-hand, Ghost detected an unmistakable buzz in the air. It was Saturday night, and this meant that *The Clock* would be crowded. But even when crowded, Ghost seldom had trouble finding a seat. The reason for this was that the installation's couches accommodate three people, and no one in the Midwest does anything in odd numbers: everything is accomplished as a couple. Thus, every pack of Midwesterners is divisible by two. So even if every one of *The Clock's* couches were occupied, there would be a smattering of single seats available, barring dufflebags and/or feet.

"For a charming, intelligent girl," a handsome black-and-white man says to an attractive woman at 9:38 P.M. "You seem to surround yourself with a remarkable selection of dopes."

Yeah, me too, Ghost thought to himself. The reason why

Ghost considered his fellow clockwatchers dopes was not because they insisted on travelling everywhere in even numbers, but rather because of their collective insistence on awkwardly snickering at *everything*. Ghost was not particularly opposed to collective awkward snickering, he just found it annoying when it was in response to things that blatantly weren't funny. Of course, this rule did not apply to his littlelion, who was such a snickeroo that he had acquired the nickname "Chucklebutt." In addition to peak-a-boo, his son chucklebutted at fake burps, silly looks, and funny voices, such as Ghost's spot-on Robert Goulet impersonation. He also chucklebutted whenever Ghost sang along with nonsensical Jamaican reggae songs like Yellowman's *Zungguzungguguzungguzeng* or Eek-A-Mouse's *Wa-Do-Dem*. But more than anything, Chucklebutt loved to laugh at the sight of his father doing push-ups. A single set of fifteen would send him into such fits of giggles that Ghost often feared that he would burst his constraints and joyously tumble from his bouncy chair. Who needed Zumba or P90x when you had the Parental Push-up Plan?

With *The Clock*, the collective awkward snickering was motivated by common video trickery; for example, someone in a black-and-white movie glances down at their wristwatch and the video jumps to a color image of a gaudy 80's Swatch watch. [*SnickerSnickerSnicker*] Or a black-and-white Basil Rathbone, as Sherlock Holmes, picks up a telephone and dramatically says "Hello" and the imagery jumps to a color clip of a woman angrily slamming down her telephone receiver. [*SnickerSnickerSnicker*] Such visual trickery appears constantly in *The Clock*. By Ghost's estimation, ten such scenes must appear per hour. How many do you have to watch before such scenes cease to be snickerworthy? But such a question is pointless: whenever large groups of Midwesterners assemble, no one snickers alone.

Visual trickery involving phone conversations is *The Clock*'s

Ur-Hamlet. In 1995, Marclay created a seven-minute thirty-second video montage of phone conversations. The film, which is simply titled *Telephones*, is so silly and nonsensical that it would've made Tristan Tzara giggle. After watching so much of *The Clock*, not to mention having already viewed *Telephones*, it is obvious that Marclay gets a rush of Duchampian joy every time he splices clips of silly phone conversations together.

"What's the use of having a war, if you don't learn from it," a general in black-and-white says at 9:55 P.M. While he was not sure exactly what movie this quote was from, Ghost was sure that it was one Dick Cheney never watched.

"It's ten o'clock," a nurse says tenderly to a man playing a piano in an empty room. "Lights out, Lieutenant." *Thank you, nurse!* Ghost thought. The Lieutenant's song was made up of atrocious lyrics about time falling like drops of rain on the window. Marvin Hamlisch, he ain't!

Four minutes later, the clocktower from "Back to the Future" is struck by lightning. Interspersed with shots of Marty McFly and Doc Brown are scenes of a young Tom Hanks not being able to sleep because of the loud barking of a nearby dog. Ghost recognized this scene as being from "Turner & Hooch". This movie, along with "The Dream Team" starring Michael Keaton and Doc Brown, were the final two movies he had ever watched in Cambridge's old downtown movie theater.

At 10:10 P.M., a confident teenager sits in the passenger seat of a moving car, showing off his new Casio watch to the driver, who is also a teenager. The watch is gigantic: it looks like a beltbuckle. The watchwearer is explaining how the watch can store up to twenty phone numbers, and how tonight, he's planning on filling up all twenty. He ends his monologue by bragging, "I live my life like a French movie."

"Time's up, asshole," a bloodied LL Cool J says menacingly

in the next clip. *The Clock* includes very few rappers. The only other rapper Ghost can remember seeing is the artist formally known as Mos Def (now Yasiin Bey), who appears seated in the backseat of a taxi at 8:11 A.M. The one rapper that Ghost expected to see more of in *The Clock* was Will Smith, but he hardly makes an appearance.

"What are you reading," a man asks from the top bunk of a military bed.

"*Love's Captive*," the man on the bottom bunk answers dispassionately.

"Is it about sex?"

"No, it's about 10:30."

This exchange illustrates two things that are noticeably absent in *The Clock*: sex and books. Midwesterner's rejoice: *The Clock* is safely devoid of sex. People talk about it; for example, at 10:46 P.M., a man leaves a message on a woman's answering machine – she's in bed, listening – that begins, "Hey, it's me. Your designated Fuck Boy," and James Bond is always getting interrupted before or after doing it – why do we never see James Bond actually having sex? Is it because he can only last 0:07? – but seldom does any actual sex occur during *The Clock*. Ghost suspected that this was because people seldom look at a clock while having sex, Sting excluded.[32]

While contemplating *The Clock*'s lack of sex, Ghost rose from his seat, figuring that he might as well go to the bathroom now and not risk missing the hour change. Lost in thought, he was not paying much attention to how crowded the installation was. He exited the darkness, rounded the corner, and instantly a

---

32 Do Sting sex jokes ever get old? Ghost hoped not. Here was his favorite from – who else? – Dennis Leary: "Sting says he can have sex for eight hours. Eight hours! Just imagine the friction: you could fry bacon in that bed!"

quote from Hellboy popped into his head: "something's wrong."

There was a line! He had been cast out!

Lines were such an infamous part of *The Clock* whenever it was exhibited in New York City that the *New Yorker* devoted a "Talk of the Town" piece to interviewing clockwaiters at Lincoln Center. According to rumor, the average wait-time in New York City was forty-five minutes. Although it had been years since Ghost last lived in New York, he was not so far removed from its cultural landscape to know that attempting to view *The Clock* there, especially in the winter, would be a competitive, bladder-threatening nightmare. But this was not the case in Columbus; he had already watched over twenty hours of *The Clock* and hadn't yet spent a single second stuck in line.

But this changed at 10:52 P.M. Of course, his first response was to panic. *Fuck it*, Ghost thought. *I'll just go to Rafael's Silver Cloud Lounge!* But then he noticed that it was almost eleven o'clock; surely, people would leave the installation after the hour change. Plus, he only had half an hour left to complete his scheduled allotment.

Sure enough, a mass exodus occurred immediately after 11:00 P.M. Two minutes later, Ghost reentered the installation, just in time to see an image of a Komodo Dragon. (Those things terrified him!)

At 11:05 P.M., a black-and-white man lies in bed smoking a cigar to the sounds of "Danny Boy". How many images are there in *The Clock* of people smoking? Ghost guessed the answer was in the thousands. Watching *The Clock* is a visual reminder of how accustomed we've all become to the smoking ban. (*Thank you, Ralph Nader!*) Seeing images of people smoking in restaurants, bars, or at work just seems weird now; not to mention, seeing people smoking in bed, classrooms, courtrooms, even hospital waiting rooms.

Five minutes later, Ghost finally recognized the interior of a bar, but he couldn't remember its name; it was in the East Village, across the street from the southeast corner of Tompkins Square Park. He recognized the joint from its corner entry and huge, horseshoeshaped bar. Having spent the majority of his adult life in bars around the globe, Ghost would've been disappointed had he not been able to recognize a single one in *The Clock*. In this particular scene, Mickey Rourke picks up an envelope from a woman seated at the bar and they banter about the possibility of her losing her job.

At 11:20 P.M., as Ghost is quickly scribbling down the quote "little people swallow time like hamburger," three men appear seated at a card-table playing poker. In front of each man is a glass of absinthe, which is recognizable by its unmistakable green hue. By Ghost's count, this is the third appearance of absinthe in *The Clock*. Almost two hours earlier, he noticed a green glass in front of a solitary man seated at a kitchen table. Looking bored and lonely, the man is watching petals fall from a colorful bouquet of red and yellow tulips.

As Ghost neared the end of his scheduled time allotment, a question ghosted through his consciousness: why hadn't he seen Harvey Keitel yet? After all, he had seen Jean-Claude Van Damme, Shia Laboef, and Gary Busey. Where was "The Wolf"? Although he was not a huge Harvey Keitel fan, Ghost enjoyed recounting the story of how the actor once sprawled out on the carpet next to him at MoMA to watch a psychedelic video by Pipilotti Rist. While living in New York, he had encountered many celebrities, but this was the only encounter that involved lying on the floor at a museum.

At 11:30 P.M., a black-and-white woman looks up from a table strewn with puzzle pieces. Although she's wearing a glamorous evening gown, she looks bored. Ghost didn't blame her:

who gets dressed up just to put a puzzle together?

"Charlie, what time is it?"

With this quote, Carlos Spencer-Bayard knew that he had successfully watched all of *The Clock* from noon to midnight. With only the A.M. hours left, Ghost was getting close to completing his quest.

9:50 A.M. to 11:10 A.M.

Carlos Spencer-Bayard hated milk. 1%, 2%, 3%, Half 'n Half, Whole, Skim, Organic, Soy, Almond, Pecan: it didn't matter. He hated all varieties and percentages equally. He particularly hated those tiny cartridges of non-dairy creamer that so stubbornly refused refrigeration. Even the sight of someone else drinking a glass of milk or pouring creamer into their coffee made him squeamish. And this squeamishness was so intense that it extended to any creamy white food-like substance: mayonnaise, cottage cheese, cream cheese. Even vanilla ice cream was too suspiciously jizz-like for his liking. If something looked like it came out of the human body, Ghost was in no great hurry to put it back in.

As someone who prided himself on being tolerant, Ghost was thankful that he could not be classified as lactose intolerant. To him, that phrase sounded so callous that it reminded him of redneck fathers who wouldn't allow their daughters to date black guys. Another reason why Ghost was happy being lactose tolerant was because it allowed him to eat cheese, and he was a notorious cheese-eater. He loved all variety of cheeses: smoked Gouda, Irish cheddar, Havarti, Gorgonzola, Brie. He even occasionally enjoyed a ghastly piece of stinky cheese. His current favorite cheese was the soft white texture and beautiful darkpurple rind of Drunken Goat. In his lighter moments, he even went so far as to *envy* the existence of such creatures. Goats that were allowed to drink all day? This sounded like an ideal way to be reincarnated.

Being lactose squeamish, the real question was why didn't Ghost find the act of breast feeding more repulsive? After all, breast milk didn't just *look* like bodily fluid, it *was* bodily fluid; and yet breast milk didn't bother him at all. He even found the complex process of cleaning the various breast feeding instruments meditational. Standing at his kitchen sink, slowly working his way through a sudsy plastic tub full of tiny bottles, nipples, spill guards, bottle tops, flanges, breast pumps, and those delicate whiteplastic triangles that reminded him of the pope's funnylooking hat, Ghost bounced a strange Latin word around his brain like a basketball: *honorificabilitudinitatibus*.

Honorificabilitudinitatibus: (n) the state of being able to achieve honors.

Ghost wasn't sure if the word was the longest in the Latin language. It might be. He could Google it, but not right now. In Shakespeare's day, the word was thought to be the longest word known to man, and it appears humorously in *Love's Labour's Lost*.

Extracting a tiny brush from the tub of milky sudsy water and gently inserting it into the bulbous curvature of an upsidedown nipple, Ghost pronounced the syllables out loud: *honorif-ic-abilitud-init-a-tibus*.

Ghost never expected to become a published author. To him, the phrase possessed more grandeur than the mere initials PhD. When he was eight-years-old, he decided that he no longer wanted to play in the NBA; instead, he wanted to be a published author. And ever since that day, the desire to hold a book of his in his hands burned passionately inside him. He thought about it during his sleepless nights. He thought about it in every English class he had ever underachieved in. He thought about it every time he read a book or attended a reading. And he thought about it every time he visited a bookstore.

[bouncebouncebounce…]

Ghost repeated the syllables softly to himself: *Honorif-ic-abilitud-init-a-tibus.*

Using a damp papertowel, Ghost traced the rim of a spill guard before looping the little riveted hoop around one of the topmost poles on the drying rack.

In 1569, Shakespeare's father applied to the College of Arms for a coat of arms. Being American, Ghost had no idea what a coat of arms was or why it was important. He assumed it was some kind of status symbol, like a new sports car, a visible tattoo, or a big badass belt buckle. The application languished. Seven years later, facing financial ruin, John Shakespeare withdrew from public life. The situation was so dire that he stayed away from church services for fear of being arrested as a debtor.

In 1596, five years before his death, John Shakespeare's claim was renewed. The logical assumption was that this renewal was instigated by John's son, "Shakespeare ye player," who, at the time, was a successful actor and playwright in London. This time, the application was successful.

When Ghost Googled an image of Shakespeare's coat of arms, he was shocked at how beautiful it was. With its striking yellow and black motif, it reminded him of Taranaki's rugby insignia. Stretching diagonally across a yellow crest is a black stripe on which sat a yellow spear. A second spear is held by a screaming eagle perched atop a steel helmet, beaver down. Underneath the imagery, a banner declares: *Non sanz droict* (Not without right). In his play *Every Man Out of his Humour*, Shakespeare's "seriocomic" rival, Ben Jonson, ridiculed this motto, and the coat's yellow color, with the pronouncement: "Not without Mustard." Later, Shakespeare repaid the jest by modeling Malvolio on his choleric rival.

But Jonson's jest was not the most demeaning thing ever written on the subject of Shakespeare's coat of arms. "His name is dear to him," James Joyce wrote in *Ulysses*, "as dear as the coat and crest he toadied for, on a bend sable a spear or steeled argent, honorificabilitudinitatibus, dearer than his glory of greatest shakescene in the country."

Toady: (v) to obsequiously flatter.

Was Shakespeare a sycophant? Only a blockhead would say no. He fawned over his aristocratic friends, in particular the Earl of Southampton and Lord Pembroke. But in regards to his coat of arms, wasn't he acting as an agent for his aging father? Was this toadying, or simply being a good son?

Out of the milkypool, Ghost extracted a flange. *What a strange word*, he thought to himself as he rinsed the curious kazoo-shaped object under a clear stream of cleanwater.

Being a chronological Bardolater, Ghost's particular interest was transposing events from Shakespeare's life onto the dates of his plays. Once a theory had passed the chronology test, it had to be tested against the ultimate examination: *Hamlet*. While he was renewing his father's claim with the College of Arms, Shakespeare wrote *Romeo and Juliet*, *A Midsummer Night's Dream*, and *The Merchant of Venice* in rapid succession. All three plays revolve around characters who "deny thy father and refuse thy name." And as for *Hamlet*, the play's subtitle could be *Deny thy father*.

Shakespeare himself must have made a similar denial. He was the firstborn male, the family heir. And yet, he never learned any of his father's many trades: he was not a glover, a whittawer, or a wool dealer. He exhibited more interest in the flowers of the field than the field of local politics. And, perhaps most damning of all, he denied his father's God. John Shakespeare was a suspected Catholic: his son worshipped no deity but Eros.

Stephen, the Dubliner, subtlest heresiarch of all the punchdrunks was right, the corpse of John Shakespeare does not walk the night. From hour to hour it rots. Like Hamlet, Shakespeare denied his real father in favor of a ghostfather. Somewhere, somehow someone must have introduced young Will to the art of playing. This someone – yes, it could've even been a clown – must have borne the youngster on his back a thousand times and kissed his lips he knew not how oft. This forgotten player was Shakespeare's truefather; and when this truepenny died, nothing could expel the winter's flaw. The globe grew cold. The only warmth left in Shakespeare's life radiated from a single undying unquenchable all-consuming fire: *honorificabilitudinitatibus*. Shakespeare toadied for no man, but himself: the coat of arms belonged to him and him alone.

Non sanz droict

The plastic tub empty, Ghost rinsed his hands and used a tea towel to wipe the excess water off the counter: cleaning the breast milk accoutrements always made a swampy mess. Once the counter was dry, he glanced at the clock above the stove: he had to leave soon.

A few minutes later, Ghost eased his Chrysler Sebring into a parking spot along 15th Street. The car had once belonged to his mother, and while he had been driving it for almost two years, Ghost never felt comfortable parallel parking it. The sightlines were too severe. Thankfully, the parking spaces along 15th Street were easy to nose into.

Having slept poorly, his intake of caffeine was already high; and thus, he decided that a *Buckeye Donuts* detour was unnecessary.

"Time for coffee!" a secretary yells from her desk after looking at her watch at 9:55 A.M.

Three minutes later, a young Robert de Niro appears in a tiny, sparse apartment. In his hand, he is holding a small notebook. As he furtively moves around the apartment, he attempts to add up some allotment of time in his notebook. He's struggling. The clip ends with him slowly counting down the seconds, as he leaves the apartment and walks onto the street.

Ghost commiserated with young Bob: adding up all the hours he'd spent clockwatching wasn't easy. So far, he had watched twenty-one hours and forty-four minutes of the video, but this number contained a plethora of holes and overlaps; for example, he had three major holes, totaling one hour and thirteen minutes. This number was offset by six overlaps, totaling one hour and forty-seven minutes. But were such calculations a good indicator of how much time he had spent watching *The Clock*? Wouldn't it be better to just count backwards from twenty-four? By this method, he only had four hours and eighteen minutes left to watch. Such stubborn calculations reminded Ghost that time was as stern and unforgiving as Robert de Niro's mug.

Just after the clip of Natalie Portman and her blind, short-cut-savvy friend, a black-and-white German general appears standing at a train station. After a pause, he shouts into a phone receiver: "I'm tired of your inefficiency, Dietrich!" (And Ghost thought he was being pedantic about time!)

At 10:05 A.M., Sarah Jessica Parker marries (maybe) Mr. Big in what Ghost assumes is supposed to be City Hall in downtown Manhattan. Ghost's brother loved "Sex in the City," but he didn't know a single thing about the show – he didn't know Mr. Big from Mr. Pink – but the same thing couldn't be said about getting married at City Hall in downtown Manhattan. Ghost knew from experience that such a setting was nowhere near as romantically picturesque as "Sex in the City" made it appear. His marriage consisted of mountains of paperwork, a hungover witness, a hallway full of Chinese people, and a Justice of the Peace who was such a butch lesbian that she sported the same haircut as Michael Douglas in "Falling Down". When their ceremony was complete, this Justice shouted "NEXT!" like a barber behind schedule.

"Don't tell me you can cook," a black-and-white man says to a woman, who is standing in front of a gas stove. Both characters look glamorous and vaguely familiar. It took him a moment, but Ghost realized that this was the same man who, at 9:38 P.M., chastised the same woman for surrounding herself with a collection of dopes.

"This is very good cognac," an older woman says seductively to a younger man.

"It's 10:15!" the young man answers in amazement.

"Perfect," the cougar purrs.

Something tells me, she can't cook, Ghost thought to himself.

Three minutes later, a voice yells, "Pilgrim, give us a hand!" An ungainly young soldier runs inside what is left of a building that has been bombed. A moment later, he and two other soldiers carry a grandfather clock into the street. The sound of an airplane engine is heard overhead. The other two soldiers scatter, leaving the ungainly youth struggling to hold the gigantic grandfather clock all by himself.

Because of the name "Pilgrim," the trio's army uniforms, and the war-torn imagery, Ghost recognized the scene as being from Kurt Vonnegut's "Slaughterhouse Five". With the appearance of what was, for years, his favorite novel, Ghost began thinking again about the role of books in *The Clock*. It was slim pickings. On the whole, cameos of books were like Michael Keaton sightings: very infrequent. But why should this come as a surprise? In the eternal struggle of how to spend leisure hours, aren't books and moving images sworn enemies? Books and movies hate each other like MI6 hates SPECTRE. "We may divide the whole struggle of the human race into two chapters," James A. Garfield said shortly after becoming President. "First, the fight to get leisure; and then the second fight of civilization – what shall we do with our leisure when we get it?" How often are people seen

reading in movies? (B*oooo*ring!) And furthermore, what does reading have to do with the measurement of time? Isn't that precisely
why people pick up a book, to forget about time? Thus it's no
surprise that *The Clock* is extremely insouciant towards books.[33]

A visual example of *The Clock*'s insouciance towards books
appears at 10:23 A.M., when Judd Nelson is seen angrily tearing
pages out of a book and throwing them across the room. When
Emilio Estavez – who's wearing a hideous pastel muscle-shirt –
points out how disrespectful he's being, Nelson rudely responds,
"O yeah, Mo Lay really pumps my nads!"

"It's Molière," Molly Ringwold corrects.

"He's one of my favorites," Philip Michael Hall chimes in.

C'mon, Ghost thought, *even legendary super-nerds don't read
Molière in High School*!

While conspicuously devoid of books, *The Clock* does include many scenes of authors at work, or rather, not at work; for
example, at 10:26 A.M., Johnny Depp appears seated in front of
a typewriter. He's wearing the official garb of authorial insomnia:
a bathrobe. His hair is frazzled and there are large bags under his
eyes. Whatever he's working on, it's obviously not going well.
Ghost felt a gleeful sensation at the thought of such a handsome
actor spending hours in a make-up chair getting made to look
like a frustrated writer.

At 10:36 A.M., a black-and-white image of a man running
towards the water on a deserted beach segues into Anna Paquin
dancing on a blacksand beach, while twirling long strands of seaweed. By Ghost's estimation, this is the first appearance of New

---

33 When people do appear reading in *The Clock,* they're inevitably doing so in bed; for
example, Nic Cage reads *The Orchid Theft* at 3:33 A.M., John C. Reilly reads a book by
Montel Williams at 8:43 P.M., a woman reads *The Sensuous Woman* at 4:16 A.M., and
an Irish boy reads a book on falconry at 6:57 P.M. (That must be a real pageturner!)

Zealand in *The Clock*. As every JAFA[34] knows, the beach scenes in
"The Piano" were filmed at Karekare, which is one of Auckland's
unforgettable West Coast beaches. Just before the scene jumps to
Charles Bronson —why is he so prominent in *The Clock*? — there's
a quick close-up of a brooding face underneath a black broad-
brimmed hat.

Kia ora, Harvey Keitel!

At 10:44 A.M., two scenes of caskets being loaded into
funeral carriages caused a quote from *Ulysses* to rattle through
Ghost's consciousness: "He's a bloody ruffian I say, to take away
poor little Willy Dignam." Shouting this line in a crowded pub
was another highlight of Ghost's annual Bloomsday celebrations.

Just before 11:00 A.M., Ghost felt a joyful sensation of
warmheartedness as he watched a choreographed clip of nurses
with newborn babies in their arms pirouetting down the hallway
of a maternity ward.

"The train leaves at eleven," Harry Potter wails to his friend
redheaded Ron. "We've missed it!"

On his way home, Ghost took a quick detour to the Columbus Museum of Art. Left on Broad. Sunday morning traffic. Easy.
Travelling east. The original National Road.

As its name suggests, Broad Street was once Columbus'
Champs-Élysées. Mississippian in its width – eight lanes! – the
street's shores are lined with old, ambitious architecture: church-
es, mansions, social clubs, etc. But the grand boulevard is ghostly now. Franklinton, Olde Towne East, Bronzeville: no one cares
about these places anymore. Over time, Columbus' axis realigned.

34 JAFA is a semi-derogatory term for urban Aucklanders that Ghost always considered
akin to 'Yuppie.' The letters stand for "Just Another Fucking Aucklander." The universal identifier for a JAFA is a love of fancy espresso drinks. Kiwis also associate the
acronym with the name of a common chocolate candy. During his time in Auckland,
Ghost wholeheartedly embraced his JAFA-ness.

All the action was north: the Short North, Campus, Clintonville, and finally: the suburbs.

Ghost shuddered as he took a left on Cleveland Avenue and entered the Columbus College of Art & Design. Suburbia scared him: all those identical houses, all those identical people, all those identical lives. It was creepy. New Albany might as well be Amityville.

Beware: Artist Crossings, Ghost thought as he turned right and passed underneath CCAD's gigantic A^r_T arch. Easing into the museum's halfempty parking lot, Ghost relived his long history with the Columbus Museum of Art. In college, he and his brother used to make frequent trips into Columbus on lazy Friday afternoons. Back then, his favorite thing to do was to lie underneath Mel Chin's *Spirit*. For being so unforgettably gargantuan, the installation was surprisingly simple: a wooden barrel squeezed between the ceiling and a thick rope that stretched tightly across the narrow room. Staring up at the underbelly of the bulging barrel, Ghost learned an early museumgoing lesson: never underestimate the joy of being able to view a work of art while lying on the floor. After college, the Columbus Museum of Art was the site of his first date with his future wife. Before entering the museum, they walked down Broad Street in search of lunch; options were meager, and they ended up in the original location for the *Wendy's* fastfood chain. His wife ordered a salad. This was the first and last salad he had ever seen her order anywhere in their many years together. Later that afternoon, in what Ghost often thought of as his own *yes I said yes I will Yes* moment, the two artlovers reclined in front of the museum underneath Henry Moore's *Three Piece Reclining Figure*. And there was more: as newlyweds, days before departing for New Zealand, the museum had been the site of their going-away party. A large group of family members from both sides of the family met in the museum's parking lot, pausing for a group picture on the back steps, before venturing inside to view an exhibition of Duane Hanson's sculptures. Ghost still snickered remembering how his Grandmother-in-law had loudly whispered, "why are we standing over these *PEOPLE*? We're being *RUDE!*" as the group hovered around a sculpture of the artist and an obese elderly woman seated at a cluttered plastic table.

After parking near the museum's rear entrance, Ghost hurried up those same back steps and entered the museum. *No need for a map*, he thought as he galloped across the entrance atrium and up the concrete staircase that led to the second floor. The Columbus Museum of Art is a boutique-sized museum. Even with a travelling exhibition, it is difficult to spend more than an hour in the place. But because of his long history with the institution, it appears labyrinthine in Ghost's memory. Every corner, every corridor is haunted by the ghost of paintings past. *An overstuffed Schnabel used to hang there*, Ghost thought glancing to his left as he ascended the main staircase. *Crockery*. And directly in front of him, he noticed how Kehinde Wiley's huge Hip-Hop reimagining of *The Portrait of Andries Stilte II* had been removed. *All the Dutch Standard Bearers in the crowd say, "HO!"* The small room at the top of the staircase that used to be *Spirit*'s lair was now being used to showcase the museum's upcoming expansion plans. Did this mean that *Spirit* might rise again? Ghost hoped so, as he would welcome the opportunity to recline under the piece as an adult.

Turning left, Ghost entered the museum's rectangular interior. At the heart of the museum sat the sunlit courtyard where Ghost had first encountered Deborah Butterfield's work. As he passed the courtyard, he glanced inside: *yup, still there*, he thought as he observed the sculpture standing quietly in a corner, its dull horse eyes staring dispassionately at a clunky Dale Chihuly chandelier. As a former art preparitor, Ghost harbored an intense dislike of glass art. Yes, it could be pretty, but from an art historical perspective, it was utterly pointless. And from an art preparitor's perspective, glass art was perilous.

The room at the far end of the coldmarble corridor was normally home to the museum's Cubist collection. For a small, middle-of-nowhere museum, the Columbus Museum of Art possessed a surprisingly world-class collection of Cubism; and this wasn't just Ghost's opinion, an expert no less esteemed than Gertrude Stein had once declared: "in the Columbus Museum of Art I came into a room and it was a pleasant one. It was all Cubist and good Picassos and Juan Gris and others but really good ones. There had never been anything like that either in choice or quality or like that in any other museum." *Holy Picasso*! Gertrude Stein had said *THAT* about the Columbus Museum of Art?

But this afternoon, the museum's Cubist collection, along with the entire West Wing, had been replaced by an exhibition devoted to one of *The Clock*'s ghostfathers: Mark Rothko. At first, this ghostfathering might appear bizarre: Ghost himself would've never connected the two artists had Rothko not been mentioned near the end of Zalewski's profile. In the article, while attending a party at Whitechapel Gallery, Marclay noticed a framed memo that accompanied a small exhibition of Rothko's work. The memo stated: "Walls should be made considerably off-white with umber and warmed by a little red. If the walls are too white, they are always fighting against the pictures, which turn greenish..." Observing this memo, Marclay claimed to feel "vindicated" in his stubborn insistence that *The Clock* never be shown in "suboptimal conditions."

Ghost breezed into the exhibition and instantly grimaced. Like most Abstract Expressionist solo exhibitions, the show began with canvas after canvas of not abstraction, but abCRAPtion. Of the group, only de Kooning began his career with an ounce of natural talent; every other Abstract Expressionist began as a "burly bricklayer," to borrow Harold Bloom's description of Ben Jonson. The first two rooms of the show were full of bricks. There really wasn't much Ghost could say about it, it was just bad art; in fact, he could easily envision his old painting professor, George Bogdanovitch, kindly bestowing C- after C- on Rothko's early work. But like the rest of his burly bricklaying buddies, Rothko got better. There was no *Eureka* moment, no juicy art historical story: it was just *hard work*. That was Abstract Expressionism's greatest lesson: *hard work* yields good art. Sure, talent helps, but it's not essential. Lay enough bricks and you can make something beautiful. Day-after-day, brick-after-brick, Rothko went to his studio and over time, beauty found him. There was a definite parallel to Marclay's meticulous methodology.

Almost exactly halfway through the exhibition, the brick-tide started to turn. One of Ghost's old college roommates lived in Houston, Texas, and he once asked Ghost to explain the Rothko Chapel. Being the only art historian in his circle of friends, Ghost often fielded such questions. His friends wanted to know (read: demanded) what difficult art meant and why it was important. As an art historian, he was supposed to be able to unlock the mystery and explain the magic. Such interactions tended to stick in his memory. He still remembered being dragged into the Cy Twombly room at the Philadelphia Museum of Art by his wife, who demanded an explanation. His answer: "beats me, Sweet-pea. I have no idea why Twombly's work hangs in museums, as opposed to local garage sales." (It should be mentioned that his wife did not find this answer sufficiently satisfactory.) In response to his friend's question about the Rothko Chapel, Ghost's answer went like this: there are two kinds of art: art you love and art you'd love to live with. Rothko's work was a good example of "love to live with" art. Ghost could easily envision an artlover staring at a Rothko canvas day-after-day without ever getting tired of it. Rothko's canvases were like soothing music: some songs grow tiresome after a listen or two, while others reward repeat listening.

As he passed between rooms, Ghost realized that *The Clock* could also be categorized as "love to live with" art. After all, in a way, aren't we all *already* living with it? What Marclay did was colonize the screen. Up until *The Clock*, the screen was a bland wasteland of mediocrity, a simple surface for transmitting information, like those gaudy billboards that plague highway travel (TACO BELL'S BEEFY CRUNCH TACOS ARE NOW ONLY 99 CENTS!). *The Clock* proved that the screen could be a provenance of beauty. If human beings are going to be required to spend the rest of their lives staring into the abyss of a glowing screen, why shouldn't they experience something beautiful?

Standing in front of two lovely small Rothko paintings that hung near the end of the exhibition, Ghost perceived an even more subtle connection between the artist and *The Clock*. Like Marclay, Rothko was preoccupied with the experience of viewing his work – who warmed their walls with umber? Those kinds of kooky demands from artists drive art preparitors crazy – but Rothko's preoccupation with the experience of viewing his work was what resulted in the creation of the Rothko Chapel. It wouldn't be outlandish to envision a Marclay Chapel popping up in some exotic global art destination. Why not? The preoccupation with experiencing their art explains why each artist was so particular about their work's installation: the details define the experience, the rest is just imagery.

8:23 P.M. to 9:30 P.M.

Brainfogfag: Carlos Spencer-Bayard knew the feeling well. Sluggish synapses. Knackered neurotransmitters. Even the smallest, most inconsequential decision felt like pushing a thought-boulder up the steep slopes of Mount Taranaki. In *Ulysses*, the portmanteau *brainfogfag* appears at the end of a stream of thought as Leopold Bloom enters Nighttown. Two hours later, Poldy is still awake, conversing with his chandelier-assaulting, soldier-insulting friend Stephen at Dublin's version of *Buckeye Donuts*. Their conversation is clunky, but this clunkiness was intentional: Joyce insisted that the section was "meant to represent the intercourse and mental state of two fagged out men."

After the daily demands of parenting (i.e. liontaming), Ghost often felt fagged out. This feeling was not so much physical as mental: his mind was exhausted, his creativity spent. Before the birth of his son, Ghost had attempted to anticipate what parenthood would be like. The physical exhaustion was easy to see coming − it was like an angry elephant charging directly towards him − but the mental exhaustion had been a sneak attack. The thought process involved in parenting was nothing like the normal non-parental thought process. To say that this difference was "night and day" would be incorrect: it was hunter-gatherer and Google. Being a parent means constantly thinking in three dimensions: past, present, and future. In regards to the present, a good parent resembles an orchestra conductor: Ghost fancied himself a more frazzled, less frizzy version of Gustavo Dudamel. Every morning, he ascended the parental podium and commenced flapping his arms like an aggressive sparrow, in an attempt to coax, control, and counterbalance the daily crescendos and diminuendos. Less *fortissimo*! More *tranquillo*! *Scherzoso, staccato... VIVAMENTE*!

While orchestrating the present, a good parent also has to

be simultaneously remembering the past and anticipating the future. For example: the timing of his littlelion's morning nap effected the timing of his breakfast; when and how much he ate for breakfast effected when and how much he could be expected to eat for his mid-morning snack, which effected the timing of his afternoon nap, and so on. Orchestrating, remembering, and anticipating was the three-dimensional rhythmic thump of parenthood.

During particularly stressful moments, Ghost almost thought that he could feel his synapses stree*e*tching, as his cerebral cortex was rented out as a fancy neurological yoga studio. He envisioned colorful plastic stretching blocks piling up in a corner and odd ropes clinging to the ceiling. Amidst the clutter, rows of neurotransmitters awkwardly sprawled across fancy yoga mats stretching their long tentacles in every direction.

Very good class, a soothing instructional voice cooed. *Now let's try Parent Pose. Lie down on your back. Throw your left arm over your head, while resting the inside of your right elbow across your eyes. Very good. Now slowly roll your face away from the nearest light source. Very good. Now hold that pose while trying to remember every member of the 1994 Phil Jackson coached Chicago Bulls ...*

Ghost was reclining on his couch, contemplating his *brainfogfag*. Was he crazy or did the circular mental motion of parenthood resemble art history? Remembering the past, orchestrating the present, while anticipating the future? Wasn't that the rhythmic thump of an art historian's heart, too? It was an interesting comparison. Like parents, art historians coddled and scolded, their attention to detail notoriously obsessive; and they worked long hours, toiling away doing what others might deem drudgery. And what exactly were they after? Was it not the joy of discovering beauty in unexpected places? As a reward for their dedication, were art historians not often asked to wear the itchy, chafing wreath of under-appreciation? Their work was under-valued, if valued at all. Seldom did people understand the importance of what they were doing or comprehend just how hard they were working. Obnoxious office jobs were like daycare: they were simply someplace to go where someone else took care of you. Minimal mental effort. Minimal *brainfogfag*. Minimal reward.

And breathe… Very good class, the soothing imaginary voice cooed again. *Now let's try Clock Pose.*

Lifting his head, Ghost glanced towards the kitchen, squinting slightly to read the red numbers emanating from the digital clock atop the stove. He had just enough time to empty the "nuclear waste" and tidy up the apartment before leaving for the Wexner Center. *How could a child who was not even crawling yet make such a mess?* Ghost thought as he swung his legs off the couch.

Brainfogfag or not, Ghost felt a tinge of unprecedentedness: he knew that he was close to completing his quest. Resolutely holding his breath, Ghost stepped on the base of the diaper bin, causing its silver lid to spring open. Even without taking a breath, he couldn't avoid the stench: it was like he could *feel* it. How did a handful of dirty diapers smell so bad? Attempting to refocus his mind on something other than the pootrid aroma that was engulfing his apartment, Ghost contemplated the ambitious clockwatching schedule that he had devised the night before. Being the exhibition's final weekend, the next twenty-four hours were crucial. To say good-bye to *The Clock*, he was planning to watch three installments in their correct chronological sequence: evening, morning, and afternoon. It would be difficult, but Ghost felt confident. The only segment that he couldn't miss was the four hour stretch that began at (*Ouch!*) 4:00 A.M.

For his evening installment, Ghost arrived at the Wexner Center just as Nighttown was beginning to crescendo. As he slowly drove along East 15th Street, he passed four prison-issue buses waiting to whisk students away to bingeheaven. Congregating outside one of the large fraternity houses that flanked the street, he noticed a group of frat bros wearing togas. The scene reminded Ghost of the start to the Indianapolis 500: *date rapists… start your hormones!*

The Wexner Center appeared to be set-up for an all-nite art binge. A large BBQ tent had been assembled on the plaza in front of the museum and parked nearby was a Mikey's Late Night Slice food truck. Pizza in Columbus could be summed up in two words: gooey & gross. The philosophy appeared to be that the only reason anyone would ever want to eat a slice of pizza was inebriation, and if you're inebriated, are you really going to care what your food feels and tastes like?

As the next twenty-four hours were *The Clock*'s last, Ghost was very curious to observe the installation's attendance. In New York City, one of two things always happened on an exhibition's final day: procrastinators panicked and swarmed or there was a collective shrug that translated into 'Oh, that show's still around?'

Although the installation was crowded when Ghost arrived, there was no line, and he was able to easily slide into his preferred seat. Since he was re-watching the entire segment, Ghost's primary interest was inspecting the stitching.

At 8:36 P.M., a man and woman in black-and-white discuss where to go for dinner. She suggests that they stay in. "I'm a sensational cook," she says heading for the kitchen. "But I'm afraid that I haven't any sensational food," the man shouts after her. The next clip is of a familiar blurry-eyed, bathrobe-wearing Johnny Depp. *Ah*, Ghost thought, *I remember him: the tortured writer.* Trance-like, Depp extracts a TV dinner from his freezer. Turning around stiffly, he shoves the dinner, box and all, into a microwave oven and pushes *START*. So much for sensational food! This clip cannonballs into a close-up of a hand pushing a VHS tape into a VCR. (Remember those?)

"What time is it?" Chris Tucker asks Ice Cube as they stand on a sparse front porch.

"8:50," Ice Cube answers with his unmistakable aggressiveness.

"I'm just gonna go in the house and chill," Tucker replies.

"O, now you're getting *SCARED*!"

Nine minutes later, a little girl in a fancy dress sits at an elaborate dinner table.

"What time is it, Daddykins?" she asks the obese man seated next to her.

"One minute 'til nine," Daddykins answers verbosely.

At 9:07 P.M., Ghost recognized yet another clip from "The X-Files". As the imagery surged into a scene of Charles Bronson (again?) wearing a red bathrobe and smoking a pipe in an impressive mancave, Ghost wondered why "The X-Files" appears so frequently in *The Clock*, especially in comparison to "24". By his calculations, "24" only appears three times in *The Clock*, and all three of these appearances are fleeting. On the other hand, whenever Agents Scully and Mulder appear on-screen, they drone on for an eternity. Ghost suspected that this decision might have been politically motivated, as Marclay was working on *The Clock* during the height – and heightened security – of the Bush/Cheney administration. Politically speaking, "The X-Files" is neutral, while "24" leaves a distinctly Republican aftertaste in a viewer's mouth, like a dirty gun had just been stuck in there during an "enhanced" interrogation. The majority of Ghost's Obama Zombie friends expressed mild shock upon discovering his infatuation with "24". How could he watch a show that endorsed torture? The answer to this question was that he wholeheartedly supported torture… on television. How else could anyone be expected to stop a homicid-

al Serbian madman like Victor Dr*aaaaaaa*zon, especially seeing
how Jack had already killed Victor Dr*aaaaaaa*zon, but he didn't
really die, and now he's back with a personal vendetta against
Jack, his family, and the President of the United States, using
classified information that he's getting, unbeknownst to Jack,
from one of Jack's ex-girlfriends, who somehow managed to learn
Serbian in the month and a half since Jack dumped her!

4:00 A.M. to 8:12 A.M.

The nightwatchman was awake thinkingthinkingthinking.

According to Harold Bloom, the single most useful sentence ever uttered in regards to Shakespeare belonged to Thomas Carlyle: "If called to define Shakespeare's faculty, I should say
superiority of Intellect, and think I had included all under that."
Shakespeare was not just a great writer, he was a great thinker.
Consider, the Dane. Hamlet's most famous soliloquy, "To be or
not to be," is not a discourse on being v. not being (i.e., death),
it is actually a discourse on thinking. Anticipating Descartes by
some thirty years, Hamlet defines being as thinking. The opposite of thinking is action. Ruled by rage or jealousy or passion,
any animal can act. Action is unthought; and thus, "To be or not
to be" juxtaposes the life of the mind v. the ways of the flesh. To
Hamlet, flesh is folly. Throughout the play, the squeamish prince
exhibits an intense revulsion towards the flesh, beginning with
the opening lines of his first soliloquy:

> *O that this too too sullied flesh would melt,*
> *Thaw and resolve itself into a dew...*

As the play progresses, Hamlet accuses poor Polonius of
being a "fishmonger," torments Ophelia for womankind's use of
cosmetics, fixates on his mother's "dexterity" within "incestuous
sheets," shocks his pal Guildenstern by insisting that "the King

is a thing," and mockingly manhandles Yorick's rotting skull. In each instance, his "gorge rises" as his thoughts become fleshified. To Hamlet, thoughts live in a cloistered nunnery, while flesh lives in the moister, uncloistered kind.

Next to him in the nightdarkness, Carlos Spencer-Bayard's son emitted a loud snort and noisily rolled over in his crib. As usual, his wife was sprawled across the bed, forcing him onto a sliver of mattress so small that it reminded him of that famous contested patch of Poland. All around him hung a perfect geometric cube of blackness.

Within the span of fourteen consecutive months, Shakespeare writes *King Lear*, *Macbeth*, and *Antony and Cleopatra*. Fourteen months. Driven hard by avarice and esteem, Shakespeare obviously has no trouble churning out wordswordswords. Writing, revising, and overseeing the production of three plays in fourteen months would have been easy for a dramatist of Shakespeare's natural professionalism. But what of the plays themselves? The cosmological emptiness that contaminates both *Lear* and *Macbeth*? The triumphal apex of perspectivism that radiates within *Antony and Cleopatra*? Macbeth's murderous imagination? Cleopatra's drag-queen theatrics? Arch-villain Edmund's Marlovian qualities v. reluctant avenger Edgar's Shakespearean qualities? Macbeth's erectile malfunction? Lady Macbeth's curious namelessness? The drunken porter's quibbles about equivocation? When did a successful overworked stage manager/actor/dramatist/business partner/moneylender/grainhoarder find the time to think up such things? The Bard was a busy man. His dayhours were consumed by the busyness of business, his nighthours by "cakes and ale." Cloaked in darkshadows, Shakespeare fawned over his aristocratic friends, bedded Burbage's bawd, drank, and whored. So when did the greatest thinker in the history of Western thought find time to do all his great thinking?

Carlos Spencer-Bayard had a theory: he suspected, like him, Shakespeare was stalked by insomnia. Of course, there is no evidence of this within the plays themselves: the word *insomnia* did not appear within the English language until after Shakespeare's death. But Shakespeare's drinking and whoring support the theory. Drinking is an easy antidote to insomnia, as it loosens the mind's destructive clutch and acts as a temporary balm against the nightly churningburning twistingturning. As for whoring, little in Shakespeare's oeuvre suggests that he was particularly interested in physical intimacy: Eros was what he was after. Perhaps, like the black prince, Shakespeare was repulsed by the flesh, but an insomniac must pass the lonely nighthours somehow. Insomnia also explains the darkening that occurs between the Forest of Arden and the prison of Elsinore. Insomnia is an arching infliction; at first, it is not a noose or even a nuisance, it resembles a riotous comedy overstuffed with an ensemble cast. (*Marlowe*! *Southampton*! *Essex*! *Kyd*! *WHORES*!) And while one's oldfellows drift off to sleep, the insomniac merrily continues the festivities. Why not? He would just be lying awake anyway. But over time, cakes and ale grow stale, as mirth is replaced by melancholy, surfeit by dearth and death. (Marlowe's murder, Southampton's betrayal, Kyd's unkind torture, Essex's ruinous rebellion, and the whores grow churlish and unwholesome.) Only insomnia remains unchanged. The play being over, the insomniac is left to close the curtain; and once this curtain is closed, all that remains is the self-devouring mind and a body consumed by the darknothingness of night.

Ghost's son let out a loud sigh and began breathing noisily through his mouth. To Ghost's ears, this noisy mouthbreathing eerily resembled gasping, deepening the darkness.

And what of the son? Ghost grimaced, this was not a topic that he particularly enjoyed contemplating. Hamnet Shakespeare died at the age of eleven in 1596. That same year, Shakespeare finished *A Midsummer Night's Dream* and began *The Merchant of Venice*. Two years later, he wrote *Much Ado About Nothing*; the year after that, *As You Like It*. Are these the works of a grieving father who lost his only son and heir? And what of the son's famous namesake? In *Shakespeare: The Invention of the Human*, Harold Bloom surmised that Shakespeare, and not Thomas Kyd, wrote the *Ur-Hamlet* anytime between 1589 and 1593.[35] If this is true, it means that Shakespeare revised the play that bore his son's name *after* his son's tragic death and failed to include a single mention of a dead son.[36] Why?

Adieu, adieu, adieu. Remember me, so says the ghostfather.

What do we remember most about Shakespeare? Is it not his horn-madness? Being so irrationally obsessed with cuckoldry, Shakespeare must have doubted that his son was really his. He must have considered the child "sullied flesh."

A little more than kin, and less than kind.

Remembering that line made Ghost shudder. In an attempt to clear his mind, he glanced over at his alarm clock: it was almost time.

Ever since the creation of his initial clockwatching schedule, Ghost knew that this segment would be the most difficult; thus he saved it until the exhibition's final day, knowing that there would not be a line. Now that he was so close to completing his quest, Ghost didn't want his final hours derailed by a wait.

Rising at 3:30 A.M., Ghost entered Ohio State's campus at a quarter 'til four. Nighttown. Being early, he instinctively stopped into *Buckeye Donuts*, where even at this hour, there were

....

35 An early version of the play was added to the repertory of what became the Lord Chamberlain's Men when Shakespeare joined them in 1594: the company never acted anything by Kyd.

36 In a subtle twist, both Laertes and Hamlet are fatherless when they perish.

a dozen or so people in line when he arrived. On his way to the Wexner Center, his 8oz coffee in hand, Ghost did something unprecedented: he jaywalked High Street. Like Karangahape Road in Auckland, High Street is usually so chocka with traffic that it's extremely dangerous to cross without using the crosswalks. (Of course, this doesn't stop people from doing it all the time.) But at this early hour, there wasn't a single car in sight. Upon reaching the Wexner Center Plaza, Ghost noticed that the BBQ pit had been de-assembled and Mikey's Late Night Slice was nowhere to be found, leaving the plaza empty and eerily quiet. Because he was moving so quickly, Ghost arrived at the Wexner Center with his coffee still scalding hot. Not wanting to miss anything, he hid his coffee cup in the coat-check room. Normally, Ghost wouldn't have done this, but seeing how his coat was the room's only occupant, he figured it was safe.

The installation was more crowded than Ghost expected. He attributed this to all the publicity surrounding the show's final weekend (read: coasters). Most of the couches were occupied by people in various states of repose: lying across the cushions, slumping down to use the back of the couch as a headrest, curling up on the armrest like a disinterested kitten, etc. To Ghost, all of these positions looked extremely uncomfortable. Ghost never tried to get comfortable while watching *The Clock*. It was impossible. The couches were there for practicality, not comfort.

Ghost secured his preferred position. Directly in front of him, a couple flopped around like two whales crammed into a fishtank trying to get comfortable; at first, Ghost felt sorry for them, then he noticed that the man had taken his shoes off. Gross.

At 4:00 A.M., James Garner announces the time from the movie "Maverick". Ghost recognized the movie, having seen it while in high school at the Zanesville Cineplex on a date with a girl who was totally out of his league. One minute later, a familiar emu struts on-screen. The sight of this strange creature walking into someone's bedroom elicits a burst of awkward laughter. Of course, this awkward laughter sets off a chain reaction. *There's nothing wrong with quietly smiling to yourself instead*, Ghost thought as the laughter subsided.

"I'm going to throw something out here," Kevin James says to Adam Sandler at 4:03 A.M. This conversation segues into a clip of a shoe being thrown out of a window. [More awkward collective laughter.]

At this early hour, *The Clock* is filled with scenes of glamorous people sleeping and/or not sleeping for a myriad of reasons; for example, Amish interruptions. At 4:30 A.M., a particularly loud alarm is heard ringing. In the next scene, a distinctly unglamorous Amish man enters a dark room, holding a lantern. At the far end of the room, Harrison Ford is sleeping.

"It's 4:30," the Amish sourpuss announces. "Time for milking."

Ten minutes later, Dane Cook unsuccessfully attempts to shoo a woman from his bed. She looks comfortable: he looks unsettled.

"I have to work tomorrow," Cook says while pacing the room.

"Everybody has to work tomorrow," the woman replies sleepily. "It's Tuesday."

"Well, I have a strict 'No Sleep Over' policy," Cook responds.

As if in response to such douchebaggery, a minute later, a woman in a black-and-white film exclaims, "a man like *THAT* doesn't deserve Civil Rights!"

The 5:00 A.M. montage contains a rapid burst of memorable quotes, which range from the polite ("Bonjour, Mr. Eisenhower: this is your five o'clock wake-up call.") to the wise-ass ("Don't you cops ever sleep?" a bathrobe-wearing Bogey asks two police officers) to the badass (Clint Eastwood walks through a barracks full of sleeping marines hollering, "drop your cocks and grab your socks!" among other aggressive unpleasantries).

From Zalewski's *New Yorker* profile, Ghost knew that 5:00 A.M. was the most difficult hour for Marclay to fill. As filler, the artist was forced to use fifteen minutes of random dream sequences. "You have to imagine that, if you've been up watching and it's 5:00 A.M., you're in a weird state of mind," Marclay explained. "I decided to play with that."

The first lengthy dream sequence begins at 5:10 A.M. and ends with a man saying soothingly to his wife, "Go back to sleep, Cleva." (*Cleva*? *What kind of name is Cleva*? Was Ghost dreaming?)

A few seconds later, Cedric the Entertainer's husky baritone announces the beginning of *The Nighthawk Hour* radio program from the movie "Talk to Me".

After an hour and fifteen minutes of nearconstant struggle, the couple in front of Ghost finally leaves the installation at 5:15 A.M. Soon after their departure, Ghost snuck into the coat-check room for a sip of coffee, which was not only safe and sound but also still quite warm. Unfortunately, it was also still bad. Sitting in a coat-check locker for over an hour to cool does little to improve scalding cheap swill.

At 5:20 A.M., Ghost recognized the ending from "As Good As It Gets". In the scene, Jack Nicholson and Helen Hunt wait for their local bakery to open. A minute later, there's a beautiful image of the sun rising over the Brooklyn Bridge.

But it's not all warm croissants and sunshine at this hour; moments later, an Asian doctor, who looks all of twenty years old, informs Jean Claude van Damme that his brother is paralyzed.

Six minutes later, a lovely, lengthy sequence of Paris waking up appears on-screen. In the soft glow of morning, large streetcleaning trucks encircle the Arc de Triumph, spraying sanitizing fluid in every direction. The streets are deserted. In front of Maxim Café, a worker quietly hoses down the sidewalk, as another sweeps up loose fag butts. *A beautiful montage of a beautiful city*, Ghost thought.

Of course, not everyone finds France enchanting. After Forrest Whitaker wakes up Robin Williams in "Good Morning Vietnam," Sarah Jessica Parker appears, talking on the phone with (maybe) Mr. Big. She's drinking a giant Cosmopolitan: he's in bed.

"What are you doing?" she asks suspiciously.

"I think it's called sleeping," he answers.

"So you're funny in France," she snaps back.

At 5:41 A.M., Orson Welles' familiar moustache and mouth floats on-screen to whisper: "Rosebud." This famous scene bowlingballs into an image of Jeff Daniels[37] flying over Los Angeles, bowling ball in hand. (Ghost suspected the dream sequence from "The Big Lebowski" would make an appearance during this hour.) The next scene is the bloodflood flowing down empty hotel hallways in "The Shining". This lengthy dream montage ends with a shot of Big Ben. In what has to be the video's longest Big Ben-less stretch, this was the first sighting of *The Clock*'s heroic protagonist all morning.

Surprisingly enough, the 6:00 A.M. montage is the most enjoyable hour change in all of *The Clock*. First, Richard Dreyfuss humorously attempts to wake up Bill Murray in "What About Bob?" by screaming in his ear and vigorously bouncing him up and down on the mattress; next, Robin Williams screams, "Good Morning, Vietnam!" This iconic shout cannonballs into a clip of Murray smashing his alarm clock to the tune of "I've got you, babe" from "Groundhog Day". A moment later, Jennifer Aniston

---

37 According to Ghost's wife, this is actually Jeff Bridges: Ghost never could keep those two actors straight.

wakes Jim Carrey by snatching the covers off him. Obviously aggrieved by this act, Carrey proceeds to pout and flail about in the bed like only Jim Carrey can. This clip segues into Julie Delpy lying in Ethan Hawke's lap underneath a large, heroic public monument. From the surrounding scenery, it's obvious that the duo is somewhere deep in the heart of old Europe. As she stares sleepily up at him, Hawke recites a poem in his best Dylan Thomas voice. The montage ends with Kirsten Dunst waking up on a football field in "The Virgin Suicides". It was at a reading in celebration of this novel's 10th anniversary that Ghost heard Jeffrey Eugenides discuss *sitzfleisch*. This reading was also the first time he heard Eugenides referred to as a "pirate facial hair aficionado."

Five minutes later, Tom Waits removes his shirt in preparation for getting into bed with a sleeping blond, causing him to wonder, why wasn't Waits on Ghost's original wishlist? After all, Ghost was currently reading a book of Waitsian interviews. At one point in the book, the ghoulish crooner is asked by his record company to interview himself. Released as the press release for *Orphans: Brawlers, Bawlers, & Bastards,* this mock interview is titled "Tom Waits on Tom Waits: True Confessions". Two of the questions from this *faux* interview struck Ghost as extremely relevant to *The Clock*:

Q: Favorite scenes in movies?

A: De Niro in the ring in "Raging Bull". Julie Christie's face in Heaven Can Wait when he [Warren Beatty] said, "Would you like to get a cup of coffee?" James Dean in "East of Eden" telling the nurse to get out when his dad has had a stroke and he's sitting by his bed. Marlene Dietrich in "Touch of Evil" saying "He was some kind of man." Scout saying "Hey, Mr. Cunningham" in the scene in "To

Kill A Mockingbird". Nic Cage falling apart in the drugstore in "Matchstick Men"... and eating a cockroach in "Vampire's Kiss". The last scene in "Chinatown".

Q: Can you describe a few other scenes from movies that have always stayed with you?

A: Rod Steiger in "The Pawnbroker" explaining to the Puerto Rican all about gold. Brando in "The Godfather" dying in the tomatoes with scary orange teeth. Lee Marvin in "Emperor of the North" riding under the boxcar, Borgnine bouncing steel off his ass. Dennis Weaver at the motel saying "I am just the night man," holding on to a small tree in "Touch of Evil". The hanging in "Ox-Bow Incident". The speech by Rutger Hauer in "Blade Runner" as he's dying. Anthony Quinn dancing on the beach in "Zorba". Nicholson in "The Witches of Eastwick" covered in feathers in the church as the ladies stick needles in the voodoo doll. When Mel Gibson's Blue Heeler gets shot with an arrow in "Road Warrior". When Rachel in "The Exorcist" says, "Could you help an old altar boy, Father?" The blind guy in the tavern in "Treasure Island". Frankenstein after he strangles the young girl by the river.

At 6:10 A.M., a shirtless, buff white man (maybe a young Harvey Kietel?) smokes a cigar on a couch while squeezed between two large black men. The coffee-table in front of them is littered with empty beer cans, overflowing ashtrays, and a half-empty bottle of Wild Turkey. *Wow, that was some morning! It's also quite the tight squeeze.* After watching this clip, Ghost noticed that next to him four people were squeezed into one of the installation's couches. This was the second time that morning he had seen this happen. Such a seating arrangement looked terribly uncomfortable, but perhaps they were doing it for warmth; for the first time in his quest, he was cold. He even contemplated going out to the coat-check to retrieve his jacket.

While shivering slightly, Ghost was envious of what appeared to be a Navajo rug worn by an attractive woman, who enters a jail cell where Dame Judi Dench is waiting. Dame Judi is also wearing a very warm-looking shawl.

"What's the time?" Dame Judi inquires.

"It's time for you to die!"

At 6:30 A.M., a red sports car accelerates recklessly through a crowded train station in an attempt to catch a departing train. (Good luck doing *that* at Hoyt-Schermerhorn!) After making an aesthetic, tiresquealing, halfspinning stop on the platform, Michael Caine jumps out of the car and leaps onto the moving train. *Wow*, Ghost thought. *Who knew that Michael Caine was such a badass! And who has to move that car now?*

Five minutes later, an Asian manservant enters a room balancing a cup of coffee on a silver tray. In the corner of the room sleeps (another maybe) Steve McQueen. The servant wakes sleeping Steve with the question: "Coffee, sailor man?" This clip reminded Ghost that there was still a few sips left of his coat-check coffee.

On the whole, the waking hours of *The Clock* are very serene, as there are many images of people in various stages of repose: single women sleeping soundly, single men sleeping unsoundly, couples waking up together, and women waking up with (egads!) Woody Allen.

"I haven't slept that well in years. Is it noon?" Allen asks his bedmate, who might be a young Barbara Streisand.

"It's 7:00!" she replies.

As the waking hours transform into the working hours, there are numerous scenes of people in various stages of preparing for work: getting dressed, brushing their teeth, realizing they're late and rushing out the door, etc. No arrival at work is more dramatic than when, at 7:10 A.M., a bruised Marlin Brando leads a group of longshoremen onto the job in "On the Waterfront".

At 7:15 A.M., an image of a man asleep underneath a framed James Ensor poster bleeds into an image of a man, who looks like a French version of Elvis, playing chess with a clerkish friend at a stylish French café. Was this a mistake? Ghost knew for a fact that the same duo is seen playing chess at 4:00 P.M. Even the most obsessive chess fanatics can't play for nine straight hours, right? The reason why Ghost remembered the original scene was because the interior of the café reminded him of a French restaurant he used to frequent in Park Slope.

At this point, the countdown began: Ghost wondered exactly what image would complete the loop. Images cascaded past his eyes, as his clockquest neared its conclusion: electric razors, Clint Eastwood in prison, Basil Rathbone as Sherlock Holmes, Mel Gibson asleep gun-in-hand, Johnny Cash, Big Ben (twice), the pocket watch from "The Good, The Bad, & The Ugly," Robin Williams as a creepy blonde, Nina Myers from "24" checking her watch (don't trust her, Jack!), Seth Rogan's naked ass…

"I'm naked. Did we have sex?" he asks an attractive blonde[38], who is shooing him out of her bed.

"Yes," she answers.

"Nice!"

Carlos Spencer-Bayard completed *The Clock*'s eternal circle at 7:45 A.M. It was actually not an image that signaled this com-

....
38   According to Ghost's wife, this attractive blonde is Katherine Heigl.

pletion, but the sound of a familiar funky bassline layered over the cascading orchestral crescendos of Richard Strauss' *Thus Spake Zarathustra*. From that point on, everything Ghost watched was the visual eternal reoccurrence of the same.

As "funky *Zarathustra*" plays, a middle-aged man exits a Brooklyn Brownstone and begins walking down a street strewn with debris. The scene reminded Ghost of his years spent living on Grand Street in Williamsburg, Brooklyn.

Feeling euphoric, Ghost remained in the installation until 8:12 A.M. The last scene he watched was of the Man in Black seated in a parked car.

"What a life!"

2:24 P.M. to 4:30 P.M.

This was it: the final hours of *The Clock*. Carlos Spencer-Bayard was expecting a large crowd. It was the first Sunday of the month, which meant free admission; also, at 2:00 P.M., Maya Lin was scheduled to deliver a lecture in the Mershon Auditorium in celebration of the twentieth anniversary of her sculpture *Groundswell*. To mark the occasion, the work had been completely restored. (Good, it needed a celebrity makeover!) Since he was already planning on being at the Wexner Center to say goodbye to *The Clock*, Ghost figured he might as well attend the lecture.

After a particularly Rockwell Kent winter, Columbus was experiencing its first gorgeous spring afternoon. As he cruised the campus in search of a parking spot, Ghost observed hordes of hungover, halfnaked undergrads frolicking with Frisbees and beanbags in front of crumbling campus houses. Having to circle the block twice before he found a parking spot behind the Newport Music Hall – it was the farthest away he had ever parked for *The Clock* – Ghost was late for Lin's lecture. (Him? *LATE*!)

Ghost contemplated foregoing the lecture entirely, but decided that he should at least stop in for a few minutes. He especially wanted to see how crowded the auditorium was; sure enough, it was packed. Were all of these people interested in Earth Art? Ghost highly doubted it. He suspected most people were there to cheer for Maya Lin, who was the local art community's equivalent to a star quarterback. As an undergrad at Ohio State, Lin had won the competition for the Vietnam Veteran's Memorial in Washington D.C. After this victory, her career exploded as an artist/landscape architect/groundskeeper/greenskeeper... okay, Ghost was not really sure how to describe Maya Lin's career: he suspected simply being Maya Lin was her full-time job.

After much difficulty due to darkness, Ghost found a seat on the isle at the very far end of the auditorium. What he found most interesting from Lin's lecture was her background; like Atul Gawande, she was from Athens, Ohio. According to the *New York Times*, Athens, Ohio is the second poorest city in the entire country.[39] Ghost found this factoid unbelievable, and he repeated it often. Lin's father, Henry, was a ceramicist, who became dean of the arts department at Ohio University. What Ghost also found intriguing were the images of Lin's most recent earthsculpture, which she claimed was located "just outside of Auckland, New Zealand" at a facility that resembled the Storm King Center in Mountainville, New York. Being familiar with Auckland, Ghost knew for a fact that there wasn't much "just outside" the city. Because of its proximity to water, Auckland doesn't sprawl; and because of its volcanic geography, there isn't much flat land around the region: everything either slopes up towards a volcano or down to the water. And after spending two years within Auckland's artworld, why was Ghost unfamiliar with an outdoor sculpture

---

39 The poorest place in the country is the Ultra-Orthodox Jewish village of Kiryas Joel, New York.

facility that resembles Storm King?[40]

Ghost found the rest of Lin's lecture disinteresting. So much of what she does unfortunately reminded him of golf course design. Of course, there's nothing wrong with golf course design: it just ain't art. Because of his growing disinterest, Ghost snuck out of Lin's lecture after only fifteen minutes. His fear was that once the lecture was over, the crowds would groundswell into *The Clock*. Such a surge could potentially derail any hope of catching the segment between 4:00 P.M. and 4:30 P.M., which was Ghost's favorite segment of the entire video.

Ghost entered the installation just as Robert Redford walks into an old New York City diner and sits at the counter. The installation was crowded, but there was no line. Unable to procure his preferred seat, Ghost was forced to share a couch in the middle row with a snickerer: seated directly behind him were two more snickerers. If he was going to make it to 4:00 P.M., he would have to hold his spot for over an hour and a half.

At 3:00 P.M., Ghost recorded more particulars from the scene involving Woody Allen and the "disgusting" sexwatch. The woman is attractive, but her clothes are atrocious: she is wearing a pink sweater with lightblue Hawaiianshirt spandex, which are pulled up too high. She is also tall, towering over the diminutive Allen.

"Hi. I'm Lenny," Allen begins.

"You must be my 3:00 appointment. Come in," the woman answers.

(*Appointment? Huh?*)

First, the awkward banter, then the commonality: their senses of humor. Next, the wallclock whose pendulum depicts

---

40 The sculpture turns out to be located on Gibbs Farm, which is about an hour north of Auckland on Kaipara Harbour. The facility is only open to public viewing by appointment.

copulating pigs.

"Isn't that a pisser!" the woman squeals with glee.

Finally: the pocketwatch.

(*Where was she concealing it? Spandex doesn't have pockets.*)

"As the main spring goes back and forth," she explains, "the bishop keeps fucking her in the ass!"

"Wow. That's really... *disgusting.*"

Although it had been over a month since he first watched this segment, Ghost was surprised by how much of the imagery he remembered. Some scenes were so familiar that he could complete them in his mind: James Bond confronts a "woman" in mourning... *here comes the punch*; Nic Cage scrutinizes a $100 bill... *here comes the water bottle*; a man holds up at a pocketwatch at a café table... *here comes a close-up of Kevin Spacey*; ragingbull Robert De Niro calls for his steak... *here comes a nasty domestic dispute.* Not wanting to watch this ugly scene again, Ghost closed his eyes. When he opened them, something strange happened: he stopped recognizing imagery. At 3:26 P.M., he recognized a foxy, blind woman standing in her kitchen. Ghost knew that this woman told time by placing the palms of her hands on the face of her kitchen clock. In this earlier scene, the woman enters her apartment while three men, in hiding, wait for her; because she is so attractive and blind and the trio of intruders so swarthy and nefarious, this is one of the most suspenseful sequences in the entire video. But Ghost didn't remember the scene of her, in her kitchen, offering a cup of coffee to a male friend; and he certainly didn't remember seeing Jack and Meg White seated together in a dark bar. While he instantly recognized the movie as "Coffee and Cigarettes," he didn't remember ever seeing this particular scene in *The Clock* before, and he knew he would've remembered seeing it, as the White Stripes were his all-time favorite band. And why didn't he remember hearing the song from "The Who's Tommy"

at 3:28 P.M.? After all, this was one of the first Broadway musicals he ever saw. He might be the only music fan alive who owned
the original cast recording from the Broadway show *before* owning
the actual The Who album. And why didn't he remember the
miniature train-set that appears in an attic at 3:34 P.M.? Surely, seeing this would've reminded him of his uncle's old train-
set that was assembled in the attic of his grandparents' house in
Rocky River, Ohio. By his quick calculations, Ghost was missing
twenty minutes of recognizable imagery. This was too long for a
bathroom break and too short for a trip to *Buckeye Donuts*. How
did this happen? Had he made a mistake on his timetable? He
was utterly befuddled.[41]

At 3:45 P.M., Ghost recognized a clip from Spike Lee's "He
Got Game". In the scene, Ray Allen aka Jesus Shuttleworth –
what a cringeworthy name! – is offered a platinum and diamond
wristwatch by a rather swarthy fellow. The scene ends with Allen
casually flipping a basketball over his head as he walks out the
gymnasium door... *SWISH*!

Yeah, right! Ghost thought. *Not even George Gervin makes that
shot*. Ghost had a pet-peeve about basketball movies that were totally unbelievable, for example: "The Basketball Diaries". Scraw-
ny sissyboy Leonardo DiCaprio and 5'8" Mark Wahlberg are two
of the best basketball players in New York City? *Yeah right*.

Spike Lee's silly scene finger-rolls into Tom Hanks announcing that he only has seventy-five minutes left. *Left before
what*? For Ghost, this announcement was strangely prophetic, as
he was planning on sundering the embrace in exactly seventy-five
minutes.

One minute later, Maya Lin's lecture ends and there is a

41 Mystery solved: according to his notepad, Ghost left the installation to feed his parking meter at 3:25 P.M. and returned at 3:34 P.M. Sometimes pedantry pays.

sudden surge of clockwatchers. A pleasant-smelling, overweight man sits down next to Ghost. He is panting heavily as if he had just walked up numerous flights of stairs. Or maybe Ghost just thought this because on-screen Ethan Hawke, Julie Depry, and her cat Che were walking up numerous flights of stairs to her apartment.

Ghost was getting close to 4:00 P.M. To make the time go quicker, he attempted to watch long segments of *The Clock* with his eyes closed. In Zalewski's profile, both Marclay and Scott Martin, the White Cube technician who accompanies the work to every installation, suggest trying this. It's not easy: Ghost found that his eyes were constantly drawn back to the imagery. Popping his eyes open, Ghost caught a glimpse of French Elvis and his clerkish friend playing chess. *Still playing, mes amis?*

Ghost closed his eyes again. Trying to relax his mind, Ghost wondered how long it would be before he returned to the Wexner Center and whose work would be exhibited?[42]

"Four o'fucking clock? FUCK ME! No man, that's bad!"

Seth Rogan's profanity signaled the beginning of Ghost's favorite segment.

At 4:12 P.M., the attractive blind woman reappears. As she is about to enter her apartment, the three swarthy intruders scatter and hide themselves. One man hides behind the door; the ringleader, who is wearing an odd pair of oval sunglasses, hides beneath the stairs; the third member of the group, who appears to be holding a harpoon, hides behind a doorframe at the bottom of the stairs.

"Sam, are you here?" the blind woman asks as she enters the apartment.

....
42 One month later, he attended the opening for a solo exhibition by the artist Paul Sietsema. The show was no *The Clock*.

After pausing a moment in silence, the woman answers herself in a *faux* man's voice, "No, Susie. I'm not here."

The blind woman descends the stairs and enters her kitchen. Walking over to the sink, she places the palms of her hands softly on the face of her kitchen clock. As she does this, there's a close-up of her face: her features look angelic in the soft glow. The suspense is heightened by the fact that, because she's blind, the intruders are in essence hiding in plain sight. What are their intentions? Wouldn't a blind person smell them? They're sweating like pigs, especially the guy with the harpoon. And where exactly did that guy get a harpoon? As the trio watches in silence, Susie goes over to her desk and begins making a phone call using a rotary phone. Just like with her kitchen clock, she deciphers the numbers on her phone by gently placing the palm of her hand over the dial.

And just like that: the scene is gone.

At 4:17 P.M., a man sits on a bed in an empty room, staring out of a small window at the ocean. Why is this scene in *The Clock*? There is no visible clock and no logical connection to its surrounding scenes. These omissions add to the image's intrigue. While watching the serene scene, Carlos Spencer-Bayard decided that this was his favorite moment in the entire twenty-four hour loop.

He also decided that the funniest moment in *The Clock* occurs three minutes later. (Midwesterners be warned: this scene involves sex.) In the scene, a couple achieves simultaneous orgasm. As the man climaxes, he begins making a slew of silly sounds and faces. The installation bursts into laughter. This time, because the scene is actually funny, the laughter doesn't irritate Ghost.

After a quick glimpse of Bruce Willis in "Pulp Fiction" descending a flight of stairs, samurai-sword-in-hand, Ghost started planning exactly how he would exit the installation for the final time. Just before 4:30 P.M., a lengthy sequence begins involving a blonde French schoolboy, who is seated at his desk near a window. Outside the window hangs a large clock. The boy is fidgety: the clock's hands are moving agonizingly slow. He's obviously counting down the seconds until the school day is over, so he can rush home to... *what do French schoolboys rush home to do?* Ghost highly doubted it was to watch *Yo! MTV Raps* like he used to.

The second hand continued its agonizingly slow, circular clicking.

Tick. Tick. Tick...

Finally, the second hand hits 4:30 P.M. The boy lurches out of his chair and stands awkwardly beside his desk. But there's a problem: the bell hasn't rung yet. The teacher angrily yells at the boy to sit down, or at least that's what Ghost assumed she was saying: he didn't know for sure since she was speaking French. The boy ignores his teacher and continues to awkwardly stand next to his desk.

Finally, the bell rings.

He's free.

As he leaves, I leave, Carlos Spencer-Bayard thought as he rose from his couch and navigated his way towards the exit.[43]

Carlos Spencer-Bayard on Carlos Spencer-Bayard: True Confessions

Q: Favorite scenes in movies?

A: John Travolta and Uma Thurman in "Pulp Fiction" dancing to Chuck Berry's "You Never Can Tell." Harrison Ford saying to Carrie Fischer: "You like me because I'm a scoundrel. There aren't enough scoun-

---

43 Glancing over his shoulder, Ghost's wife just shouted: "Dorkelujah! You're done!"

drels in your life" in "The Empire Strikes Back". Joe Pantoliano yelling, "LENNY!" in "Memento" and Guy Pierce correcting him: "It's Leonard." Roberto Benigni humorously marching off to his death while his son watches in "Life is Beautiful". Laurence Fishburne in "The Matrix" telling Keanu Reeves, "You are not a slave." Chow Yun-Fat's death speech in "Crouching Tiger Hidden Dragon". Jeff Bridges telling the Malibu sheriff that Jackie Treehorne "treats objects like women, man" and then getting hit in the face with the sheriff's overbrimming coffee mug in "The Big Lebowski". The "motor boat" conversation on the stairs in "Wedding Crashers" between Vince Vaughn and Owen Wilson.

Q: Can you describe a few other scenes from movies that have always stayed with you?

A: Kim Jong-il mispronouncing the word "inevitably" in "Team America: World Police". Philip Seymour Hoffman preaching while enjoying a bowel movement in "Cold Mountain". Ed Harris trying to keep his bicycle steady with a basket-full of beer bottles in "Pollock". Holly Hunter playing the piano on the black sands of Karekare while Anna Paquin dances around her twirling seaweed. Jonah Hill trying on pants that are "too tight... *way too tight*" in "Superbad". Al Pacino yelling "Attica! Attica" in "Dog Day Afternoon". The scene in "Ferris Beuller's Day Off" where Cameron kicks his father's fancy sports car out of the garage and it falls into a ravine.

Q: Favorite scenes from *The Clock*?

A: The old man sitting on the bed, staring out the window at the sea (4:17 P.M.). The boy meticulously drawing a clock on his wrist with a charcoal pencil and holding it up to his ear when he's finished (11:10 A.M.). The clip of a man standing on a dock, a scythe resting on his shoulder, ominously ringing a bell at 10:34 A.M. The image of a prison guard adjusting a noose against the nightsky with a clocktower illuminated in the distance (8:59 P.M.). Seeing a brilliant sunrise through the balcony door of an Eastern Bloc apartment building at 7:59 A.M. Peter Sellers synchronizing his watch (7:45 P.M.), the funny, French sex scene (4:20 P.M.), and the blind woman and the three burglars (4:15 P.M.). The clock that floats away in the river atop a square piece of wood (1:22 P.M.). The scene of a group of Islamic men kneeling down to pray in a mosque at 12:41 P.M.

Q: Can you describe a few other scenes from *The Clock* that have stayed with you?

A: Francis McDermott saying, "I've known my share of naughty boys who like to oversleep" at 10:06 A.M. The Sultan showing off his collection of timepieces to an Arabian bandit, who says: "you're the King of Time!" (4:45 P.M.). Hugh Grant and a ladyfriend running down Mulberry Street in Manhattan at 1:34 P.M.; she stops running, overcome with laughter, and begs Hugh to stop doing his funny run. "My funny run?" Hugh replies obviously hurt.

"That's just how I run." The carefully stacked column of matchsticks that appears at 4:06 P.M. The
scene of two naked people smoking a bong in bed
(10:30 A.M.). Watching a man, with a wild look
in his eye, sit down in a black-and-white landscape
that looks like the remnants of a library that has just
been bombed; as paper and books blow everywhere,
the man says in an unhinged voice, "Time. Time.
Time. There's Time enough at last!" (12:20 P.M.)

Conclusion

He was still there, breathing in the armpit air. It had been a
long time since Carlos Spencer-Bayard's littlelion last slept on his
"Poppa pillow." That morning, almost by accident, Ghost rested
the drowsy infant on his chest as he reclined on the couch to read
On the Genealogy of Morals. As he began pageturning, he felt the
boy's breathing slow as he crept stealthily towards the soft oblivi-
on of sleep. Amidst the steadily slowingslowing breathing, Ghost
felt the tiny creature angle his body into his armpit, resting his
forehead against the crook of his shoulder. *Why would anyone
want to sleep like that?* In his mind, Ghost envisioned his littlelion
dreaming pleasantsmelling dreams of fragrant fields covered in
the woodspice flowers of Maine's moosewild wilderness. Sure, his
deodorant smelled good, but why would anyone want to drift off
to dreamland using clouds of it as a pillow? Ghost always mistook
the name of his deodorant – *Tom's of Maine* – for Tom O'Maine,
which reminded him of Tom O'Bedlam. *Poor Tom's a-smelling good
and he's a-cold.*

Surrounded by the silence of a sluggish Saturday morning,
Ghost was enjoying his bookish escape. Since the birth of his son,
Ghost had set himself the goal of reading all of Nietzsche's ma-

ture work in their correct chronological order.

The long winter was almost over. Outside his oddshaped windows, spring was just beginning. Carlos Spencer-Bayard's littlelion had been asleep on his chest for over an hour.

"Man would rather will *nothingness* than *not* will."

With that sentence, Ghost completed Nietzsche's masterwork. Not wanting to wake his sleeping son, Ghost gently placed the book on the floor beneath the couch. With nothing else within arm's reach, Ghost closed his eyes and contemplated *The Clock*. As he did so, he could feel the tiny tremors of his son's babyheart beating on top of him. He imagined life as a vast, labyrinthine museum. Exhibited on the walls of this imaginary museum was imagery from every work of Imagereality ever watched, *The Clock* included. The Antiquities Wing was devoted to old black-and-white films; the Modern and Contemporary Galleries housed recent movies and television shows; "24" was installed in the new American Wing; the Asian Wing was full of foreign films. Within this imaginary Museum of Imagereality, the sheer volume of imagery was overwhelming: movies, television, YouTube videos, Facebook memes, advertisements, etc. Imagereality is everywhere; it is to the 21st Century what the invention of photography was to the 19th. Being a viewer means constantly curating contemplative, ethereal exhibitions; for example, Pacino/De Niro was akin to MoMA's Picasso/Matisse, while watching MTV was similar to attending the New Museum's triennial *Younger Than Jesus*. Year after year, you wander room-to-room, aimlessly. Whatever catches your eye is permanently etched into your memory, and thus becomes part of who you are. Visual memories are the fabric from which we all stitch together the quilt of self. *The Clock* was now part of who he was.

There's a word for such museological musings: *metemuseumpsychosis*.

[O rocks! Tell us in plain words.]

"It's Greek: from the Greek. It means the transmigration of museum and soul."

And still a single, profound question haunted Ghost's experience with *The Clock*: why bother? Why had he repeatedly climbed out of a warm bed into a cold world at blue o'clock in the morning? Why had he bothered braving an ill-tempered winter, not to mention an ill-tempered infant, simply to experience a work of art?

A loud sigh echoed from his armpit, as Ghost felt a sudden surge of babyheart beats. Whenever he thought of his son's heart, Ghost was reminded of those tiny bottles that liquor stores stocked next to their cash registers. Small but powerful, each bottle was a perfect, tiny replica of a larger self; and just like these larger selves, each bottle was filled with *fullness*.

Before becoming a father, Ghost could've easily anticipated what being a father was like: the exhaustion, the daily diaperdrudgery, the noise and joys, the snuggles and struggles. But what he could've never envisioned was the *fullness* of the experience: the highs were so stratospheric, the lows so oceanic that no deepsea diver would dare plumb their dark depths. The ancient Gnostics had a word for such fullness: *pleroma*.

Parenthood is *pleroma*. Is it fun? Ay, there's the rub. The title of Jennifer Senior's recent book on parenting, *All Joy and No Fun*, is a succinct summarization of, to quote the book's subtitle, "the paradox of modern parenthood." But couldn't that title be reversed for a book on everything that wasn't parenting? Wouldn't *All Fun and No Joy* be the perfect title for a book on, say, "the paradox of modern bingedrinking?" In the mad rush to embrace the current collective cultural obsession with Fun, was it possible that joy had been trampled over and forgotten? For years, Ghost worshipped Fun. During those years, he had mistakenly bought into the misbelief that parenthood was a burden. He now believed the exact opposite; in his opinion, teenage pregnancy was more valuable than a college diploma. Parenthood taught him a valuable lesson: anything you can do halfdrunk isn't worth doing at all. With one scissorsnip of an umbilical cord, gone were all the squandered hours of so-called Fun; and once they were gone, Ghost realized that none of these Fun worshipping activities compared to the simple joy of watching a babyboy stretch out his tiny babybody across your chest for an afternoon nap, or the expectation of a joyous bouquet of openmouthed smiles when he awoke.

So why did so many of Carlos Spencer-Bayard's friends devalue parenthood? A quote ghosted through his consciousness.

"Man would rather will *nothingness* than *not* will."

Ghost often thought of the Midwest as a vast, everlasting emptiness. Being a Midwesterner meant inventing clever new ways to combat this terrifying emptiness: overeating, bingedrinking, worrying, complaining, feelgood religions, football – those bloody games go on *forever*! Rugby matches are played in real time and only last ninety minutes – exercise, sports practice, Go Bikes, cornhole, prattling (what Lucretius called, "snoring while awake"), and the two biggest emptiness eradicators: television and work. In *Les Miserables*, Victor Hugo mused, "subtract 'time is money' and what's left of England?" Couldn't a similar question be posed about the Midwest? Subtract "life is work" and what's left of the Midwest? Cornfields? Cows? *Colonoscopies?*

So why did Carlos Spencer-Bayard seemingly waste so much time watching *The Clock*? (Not to mention all the time spent writing, editing, and organizing this manuscript.) Shouldn't he have just accepted the Urban Arts Space's bizarre job offer and watched *The Clock* for an hour or so on some random Sunday? Instead, he turned down the Urban Arts Space and spent almost thirty-two hours clockwatching.

"Take your preoccupation with the clock."

"That makes me *crazy*?"

His armpit quivered slightly. Burying his face deeper into the darkness, his sleeping littlelion emitted a low murmur of satisfaction. Glancing towards the little creature curiously perched atop his chest, Ghost scrutinized the curvature of his head. Had he ever looked at the back of anyone's head so intently before? Just beneath the boy's Jackson Pollock patch of hair, Ghost observed the tiny indention where spine meets skull. In anatomy class, did students learn the name for this indention? When Hamlet was rudely manhandling poor Yorick's yab, the tips of his dirty fingers must have been touching this exact spot.

The defining aspect of *pleroma*, as far as Ghost could tell, is change. As a parent, Ghost attempted to adhere to a daily schedule, but he knew that every day was destined to be different, and weeks were as different from each other as the currency of foreign countries. The same thing could not be said for his list of emptiness eradicators: everything on that list exhibited high levels of *changelessness*. If emptiness is perceived as neverchanging, whatever is employed to eradicate this emptiness also has to be changeless. Years ago, Søren Kierkegaard pointed out that God's *changelessness* was, for many people, his most comforting characteristic. *It must change* is life's law. Watching television doesn't change us. Worrying doesn't change us. Work doesn't change us. Only *pleroma* changes us. Carlos Spencer-Bayard learned this from reading the "Great Shapesphere." Shakespeare is peerless *pleroma*: his work can sustain a wealth of contemplation. Ruminate on Sir Toby Belch and Sir Andrew Aguecheeck and do they not begin to resemble today's inebriated college students? Scrutinize the "sham puritan" Malvolio and is he not the precursor to today's pious fools who preach the nullification of nudity and mischief?

Listen to Polonius: do we not encounter such snorers every day? Or contemplate Marc Antony's cry, "I am dying, Egypt, dying": is this not the call of the common dust that is waiting just on the edge of the darkness to engulf us all?

As Shakespeare must have known, the ancient hermetists believed that when primordial man fell, he did so into a cosmos of *sleep*. To read Shakespeare is to be awake. But being awake means being aware that there is only one true form of *changelessness*, i.e. that "undiscover'd country from whose bourn no traveler returns." Shakespeare's dying art taught us the art of dying. And nowhere is this more apparent than in his final production: *The Tragedy of William Shakespeare, Prince of Players*. This tragedy begins with the playwright's demotion to part-time status at the young age of forty-seven. As a part-timer, Shakespeare wrote substantial parts of, at least, three plays in collaboration with John Fletcher: *Henry VIII*, the lost *Cardenio*, and *The Two Noble Kinsmen*. So why did the directors of the Globe Theater demote Shakespeare? Ghost suspected it was because of his early on-set curmudgeoness. After Cleopatra's self-slaughter, Shakespeare gave up writing for his audience. Even though his plays remained wildly popular, he stopped caring what anyone thought about them. The audience wanted a comedy, they got *The Tempest*: they wanted drama, they got *The Winter's Tale*. Upon reading the rough draft for *The Tempest*, Ghost envisioned the conversation between the Bard and the board of directors of the Globe Theater went something like this:

> **Board of directors:** [tactfully] You know, Will, Bermuda isn't really located in the Mediterranean between Italy and Tunis.

> **Shakespeare:** No tongue! All eyes! Be silent.

> **Board of directors:** [awkwardly] Will, old chap,

remember how, in your last performance review, we talked about trying to have a more positive attitude?

Shakespeare: For this, be sure, tonight thou shalt have cramps!

Board of directors: [with forced diplomacy] Look, Will, we've decided to cut down your hours to part-time and make you share an office with John Fletcher.

Shakespeare: Thou poisonous slave!

Board of directors: [suggestively] Or, you know, you could just retire...

The final three years of Shakespeare's life were empty: he wrote nothing. Lying in his bestabed next to his unfaithful wife, surrounded by the sullied flesh of his notchildren, the nightmadness finally overtook him. He was without faith, family, or friend. He loved everyone and no one. His career over, when he looked back over his life's work he saw nothing but shadows. And worst of all, he was still *awake*.

After donating his bestabed to the Globe, Shakespeare invited Ben Jonson and Michael Drayton out to Stratford-Upon-Avon to cheer him up. The day he picked for their visit was the day *before* his birthday. Why not the day itself? Because that day Shakespeare had selected for his self-slaughter. If you like the epilogue, James Joyce advises in *Ulysses*, look long upon it. As early as *Julius Caesar*, Shakespeare exhibited a strange preoccupation with the idea of a birthdeathday.

> *This is my birth-day; as this very day*
> *Was Cassius born*

the doomed schemer tells Messala before recounting to him

the "fatal" omen he has seen that has convinced him that both defeat and death are near. And then turning away from Messala, Cassius bids farewell to his friend, the noble Brutus, with the lines:

If we do meet again, we'll smile indeed;
If not, 'tis true this parting was well made.

Is it not possible that Shakespeare himself uttered these very same lines to Jonson and Drayton as they were leaving New Place? Later that night, still halfdrunk, Shakespeare lay awake, awaiting the sun. When he saw its firstlight, he knew his own birthdeathday had finally come. Shakespeare was no stranger to poison, having written about it many times. With resolve, if not relish, he drank a dram and lowered himself silently into bed next to his sleeping wife. And with that deathdrink, Shakespeare finally slept.

[**Heavy curtain**]

Why bother?

Art is not simply the mirror of nature: art is being. To be without art is not to be. When Shakespeare lost the Globe, the globe lost Shakespeare. Art is the only reason to endure the rash indignities and rude indiscretions of life. In the Egypt of our own lives, we are all dying: beauty is our only weapon of self-defense.

A quiver.

A tremor.

A shake.

With a great groan, Ghost's littlelion lifted his head from out of his armpit.

He was awake.

About the Author

Scott Navicky is the author of *Humboldt: Or, The Power of Positive Thinking* (Chicago Center for Literature and Photography, 2014). He attended Denison University and the University of Auckland, where he was awarded an Honors Master's Degree in art history with a focus on photography theory. He currently lives in Columbus, Ohio. He does NOT work at Whole Foods.

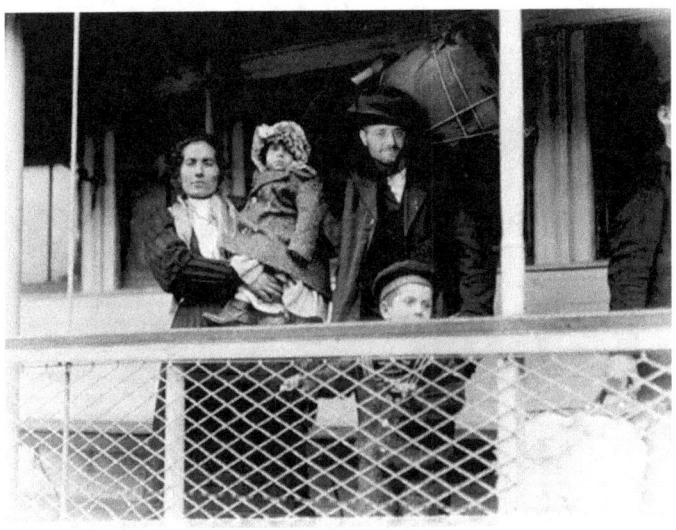

ACKNOWLEDGEMENTS

Humor essays/Photography theory/Short stories is a genre that doesn't really exist, and this explains why the working title for this project was "The Unpublishable." Getting my first novel published was difficult: I figured this one was mission impossible. And for years, it was. Years. And then one afternoon, I received an email from Charlie Franco at Montag Press that memorably began "Yes, absolutely. Without a doubt." This message was so unexpected and astonishing that I immediately had to lie down. Charlie's "Yes, absolutely" welcomed me into Montag Press' wonderful family, which includes Mara Hodges, Nicholas Morine, Zachary Amendt, and Rick Febre. And speaking of wonderful families, I have never taken for granted how loving and supportive mine has always been. We Navickys are a bookish bunch: we love books and each other fiercely. I am also very lucky to possess a talented extended creative family, which includes Hannah Stephenson, Andrew Miller, Fernando Flores, Paul Brobbel, and Joyce Sampson. This might sound strange, but [shrug] I'm a strange fellow: thank you Emperor Haile Selassie I for your wisdom and guidance. And finally, a message to my children: thank you for napping, being so sweet to your poppa, and saying such crazyfunnybeautiful things that can so easily be plopped straight into my work.

www.ingramcontent.com/pod-product-compliance
Lightning Source LLC
Chambersburg PA
CBHW071253220526
45468CB00001B/107